AIR RAGE
CRISIS IN THE SKIES

ANONYMOUS AND
ANDREW R. THOMAS

Prometheus Books

59 John Glenn Drive
Amherst, New York 14228-2197

Published 2001 by Prometheus Books

Inquiries should be addressed to
Prometheus Books
59 John Glenn Drive
Amherst, New York 14228–2197
VOICE: 716–691–0133, ext. 207
FAX: 716–564–2711
WWW.PROMETHEUSBOOKS.COM

04 03 02 01 00   5 4 3 2 1

Library of Congress Cataloging-in-Publication Data

Thomas, Andrew R.
    Air rage : crisis in the skies / Anonymous and Andrew R. Thomas.
        p. cm.
    Includes bibliographical references and index.
    ISBN 1–57392–917–4 (alk. paper)
    1. Air rage. 2. Anger. 3. Aggressiveness. I. Title: Crisis in the skies. II. Title.

HE9787.3.A4 T49 2001
363.12'4—dc21   2001019975

Printed in the United States of America on acid-free paper

For Chino, the most interesting person I know

—ANDREW R. THOMAS

For Mother and Dad

—ANONYMOUS

CONTENTS

8 CONTENTS

ACKNOWLEDGMENTS

For many months, only a few people ever imagined that a book on air rage would ever come to print. One of those was Wendy Keller. Without her unwavering support over the years for this project and many others, this book could never have been written.

Linda Regan, our editor at Prometheus, was instrumental in keeping us on track as we continued to expand the scope of the book. The adage that "there is no good writing, just good rewriting" was never so true as when we worked with Linda.

Shane Enright of the International Transport Workers' Federation in London helped tremendously in providing the global perspective crucially needed for this subject. The time he spent with us was invaluable.

The sessions with Bob Cox were some of the most important conversations we had in preparing the final draft of the manuscript. His keen interest and frankness will always be appreciated.

Thom Winninger, mentor and friend, will forever have a special place reserved for him. Anyone seeking to live a life based on character, family, and dedication to principles would be best served by looking at Thom's life.

Finally, words cannot express the gratitude to each of our families, who put up with seemingly endless hours of "book business" and supported us all the way through.

INTRODUCTION

Abnormal, aberrant, and abusive behavior on the part of thousands of airline passengers each year—known as air rage—is by far today's greatest threat to the safety and security of the flying public. More than terrorism, mechanical defects, or crowded skies, passenger misconduct has become the foremost danger to the 1.5 billion individuals who travel annually by airplane.

Recent years have seen a logarithmic increase in the number of air rage incidents worldwide. Almost every day we hear of another passenger who flipped out, rushed the cockpit, or tried to strangle a flight attendant. Ask any frequent flier and he will tell you of a time when he saw another passenger getting loud, threatening a customer service agent, or just being downright crude or obnoxious.

Still, even with the reporting of the most sensational cases, the flying public is pretty much left in the dark as to the sheer number of air rage incidents taking place. Interestingly, the media, governmental agencies, and the airlines themselves repeatedly underreport the scope and nature of the problem. Formal estimates by such entities place the annual number of air rage cases in the hundreds. Yet, investigations by the authors of government and airline industry documents place the actual number of air rage cases to be closer to ten thousand per year.

One may wonder at the disparity between actual air rage cases and those reported to the public. The reasons are complex and many.

11

It would be easy to simply blame the airlines for the problem. Today, rightly or wrongly, it seems the airlines have become the scapegoats and whipping boys for anything that is wrong with air travel. Many members of the media, passengers, government officials, and union leaders are eager to blame only the airlines for creating an environment that can lead to passengers committing air rage. Overstuffed cabins, easy access to alcohol, smaller seats, lousy food, chronic delays, and poor customer service are regularly placed squarely at the feet of the airlines. The detractors seem to say that if we could only make the airlines do x or y then air travel would be a better experience and people would not commit air rage.

Such thinking is not only uninformed, it is dangerous.

The difference between the real number of air rage cases and what the public is being told exacerbates an already volatile situation because it fails to inspire a call for solutions to the problem. Instead of dealing with air rage head-on, as was done with hijackings and drunk drivers, the solutions for controlling this problem have come half-baked, piecemeal, or never at all. What is being created is truly a crisis in the skies.

In order to fully understand the magnitude of the air rage crisis, it is critical to recognize the root causes of the problem. Then, and only then, is it possible to analyze the solutions being offered to reduce the number of air rage incidents. That is what this book is about.

Written from a journalistic perspective, this book provides inside information, incident reports, and detailed research that has never been reported before—anywhere—on air rage.

In the instances when air rage is reported in the media, alcohol or illegal drug use by air rage offenders is overwhelmingly blamed as the detonator for the explosion of the rage that follows. Unfortunately, however, there are several other root causes of air rage that are rarely, if ever, discussed. This book fully explores all the fundamental causes for the genesis and rise of air rage.

In addition to alcohol and drugs, the other causes include mental illness, the use of the commercial airlines to deport illegal immigrants, the confusion and delays caused by carry-on baggage, the broken air travel system, the economic realities of the airline business, the lack of clear and accurate reporting of air rage incidents, and the lack of consistent and stern penalties for air rage offenders. Each is explored at length here.

The appendix is designed to provide the reader access to key government documents that concern the handling of air rage incidents.

The nearly one hundred air rage incidents described in this book are taken from a wide variety of sources—including news reports, governmental investigations, airline inquiries, and interviews with passengers, flight attendants, pilots, and ground crew. The names of some of those involved have been either changed or left out. Yet these stories are all true.

It is our wish to make this book the most informative analysis of the scope and magnitude of the air rage crisis. You can let us know your thoughts or share your air rage experiences with us by contacting us at our Web site, www.AirRage.org.

1

THE PHENOMENON
OF AIR RAGE

In recent years, public expressions of discontent, despair, and detachment have seemingly become everyday occurrences in our stressed-out and overloaded lives. The explosion and expression of rage in various forms appears to be one of the new realities of twenty-first-century life. Combative, menacing, or nasty individuals can be found almost everywhere. Classrooms, offices, day care centers, airplanes, roadways, and even places of worship have become the unwitting, yet mundane, settings for the anger and frenzied whims of so many disturbed people.

All kinds of industries in every corner of the world have experienced this disconcerting trend. The aviation industry is certainly no exception. Once unthinkable in the days when people traveled in their Sunday best and sipped champagne before takeoff, aggressive, threatening, or dangerous behavior on the part of airline passengers has been chillingly and exponentially on the rise. Further, bad behavior in this industry poses a unique and more complex threat than in most other places.

Surprisingly, according to a recent Gallup Poll on air travel, the majority of commercial airline passengers say they are generally satisfied with the air travel experience. The study found passengers' biggest complaints focused primarily on the practical elements of flying, including leg room and seat width, as well as in-flight food. For most of us who fly, this comes as no surprise.[1]

Yet in the same survey, one-third of all travelers reported they occasionally become enraged at the airlines or airline employees during the process, including almost half of all passengers who fly five times a year or more (see table 1).

Table 1. How often, if ever, have you personally felt a sense of rage at the airlines or airline employees when you are flying?[2]

	All passengers	1 flight per year	2–4 flights per year	5+ flights per year
Frequently	7%	6%	7%	9%
Occasionally	27%	19%	29%	37%
Never	66%	75%	64%	54%

In an enclosed aircraft, traveling five hundred miles an hour at thirty-three thousand feet, you cannot merely turn your back on a violent, threatening, or uncomfortable situation. If you're walking down the street and see two individuals fighting on the corner, or hear a drunk getting loud, or witness somebody urinating on the sidewalk, it doesn't require too much effort to distance yourself from the situation. You can turn around and walk away. You can cross the street. Or, if inclined, you could call 911. On an airplane, you have none of these options available to you. You are stuck—with nowhere to go and no hope for the police to come and save you. The only resources at your disposal are your wits and the strangers around you. Take a look at what happened on a flight from Las Vegas to Salt Lake City.

At 9:20 P.M. on August 11, 2000, Southwest Airlines Flight 1763 took off with 121 passengers aboard. The flight was delayed a few minutes, but, according to the captain, it would make up the lost time in the air and still arrive on time.

Once the plane reached its cruising altitude and the flight attendants began serving drinks, a nineteen-year-old man, Jonathan Burton, stood up, took a drink off the tray, and returned to his seat without a word. The flight attendant politely told Burton he should have waited for someone to take his order, but he didn't seem to pay attention. A few minutes later, he was on his feet again and headed to the rear of the plane. Burton rummaged through the cabinets in the galley until he found some peanuts. He grabbed a few bags and returned to his seat.

After a few more minutes, Burton stood up and began pacing up and down the aisle. He walked all the way to the front of the plane, then all the way to the back, and then again toward the cockpit. All of a sudden, without any provocation, Burton raised his voice and kicked in the folding door to the cockpit. A panel of the door opened up and Burton put his head and shoulders through, screaming, "Somebody needs to fly this plane!"

Burton was subsequently pushed out by the pilots and left standing outside of the cockpit.

A flight attendant urged Burton to calm down while a group of passengers escorted him back to his seat. Before getting to his row, Burton was confronted by several passengers in an exit row.

Suddenly, somebody yelled that Burton was trying to open the emergency door. People jumped over seats to get away from the door. Children started crying. Meanwhile, the passengers escorting Burton forcefully grabbed him and told him to "chill out" and "settle down."

Burton seemed to get ahold of himself and sat down. It seemed that the worst had passed.

Then, as the plane began its descent into Salt Lake City, Burton exploded again without warning, jumping up, throwing punches, and spitting on those around him. Several men began fighting with Burton. He decked one of them with a clean uppercut to the jaw. Others grabbed his arms and legs, stretched him out, and pinned him on the floor. At least four guys stood or sat on his limbs, occasionally stepping on Burton or kicking him to keep the muscular young man subdued.

When the plane finally landed in Salt Lake City, police officers who boarded the plane found Burton unconscious in the aisle, with five or six people restraining him. Passengers had their feet on his head, throat, and right arm. Another held his left arm. Burton was bleeding from the mouth with a "huge knot" and "discoloration" on his forehead, as well as contusions on his chest. He was, however, breathing, the police reported.

Police placed handcuffs on Burton's motionless body as passengers warned that Burton would fight again if he came around. Paramedics tended to the bloody passengers and to Burton, but he was declared dead at the local emergency room just after midnight.[3]

Immediately after the incident, there was speculation that Burton died from a drug-induced heart attack. However, further investigation by Utah's chief medical examiner revealed the death a homicide by suffocation. Yet after a full and complete FBI investigation, U.S. Attorney Paul Warner declined to press charges against any of the passengers.

"We determined there wasn't sufficient evidence to sustain a criminal charge," said Warner.

Through his spokesperson, Warner continued: "The call was made after considering whether they could convince a jury beyond a reasonable doubt that there was criminal conduct involved in the way those passengers reacted. The U.S. Attorney doesn't believe there was [criminal conduct]."[4]

How would you have reacted had a passenger like Jonathan Burton been on your last flight? The authors consider ourselves pacifists to the infinite degree. Yet there is a part of both of us that really empathizes with those passengers. And, although it is hard to admit, there is another part of us, within our guts, that is almost glad they did what they did. We realize the young man had his whole life ahead of him. Still, when we think about the number of people he could have killed, the number of lives he could have ruined, we sometimes believe that we would have acted the same way those passengers did.

"DISRUPTIVE PASSENGER BEHAVIOR" VERSUS "INTERFERENCE WITH FLIGHT CREW" VERSUS "AIR RAGE"

For years, the aviation industry, organizations that represent airline employees, and governmental agencies have wrestled with creating standardized language to describe the wide range of behaviors exhibited by those who act out on airplanes or in airports. As a result, misbehavior on the part of airline travelers has been described using myriad terms. The most prevalent are *disruptive passenger behavior*, *interference with flight crew*, and *air rage*.

Disruptive passenger behavior is a term widely used by leading global organizations like the International Transport Workers' Federation (ITF), which represents pilots' and flight attendants' unions all over the world. The ITF defines disruptive passenger behavior as:

> Any behavior on board an aircraft which interferes with the cabin crew in the conduct of their duties, disrupts the safe operation of an aircraft, or risks the safety of occupants onboard an aircraft, excluding premeditated acts of sabotage or terrorism.[5]

Organizations like the ITF focus almost exclusively on what happens on board the aircraft. This perspective is quite understandable since they represent pilots and cabin crews. As a result, the ITF is primarily interested in knowing what prevents standard safety and security measures from being taken; in other words, those situations that are almost unique to aviation: for example, the lack of escape routes or reinforcements that crews face in flight, the legal complexity associated with acts committed on board aircraft, and the serious risks to the safety of passengers that they pose.[6]

Interference with flight crew is the term the Federal Aviation Administration (FAA) uses. As the agency that serves at the forefront of aviation jurisdiction for the U.S. government, the FAA is entrusted to enforce the Federal Airline Regulations (FARs). The laws and definitions concerning passenger misconduct on all U.S. carriers and on all flights coming to or departing from the United States are spelled out as follows :

> An individual on an aircraft in the special aircraft jurisdiction of the United States who, by assaulting or intimidating a flight crew member or flight attendant of the aircraft, interferes with the performance of the duties of the member or attendant or lessens the ability of the member or attendant to perform those duties, shall be fined under title 18, imprisoned for not more than 20 years, or both.[7]

Until quite recently, the U.S. Federal Code only placed a priority on passenger behavior directed toward flight crews while on board an aircraft. In May of 2000, the code was amended to include "any other individual on the aircraft" as well. However, within the statute, there is still no regard for behavior directed toward other nonflight personnel, i.e., gate agents, counter agents, and customer service representatives. Moreover, the statute only applies to an aircraft when the doors are closed. It has nothing to say about passenger behavior on the jetway, in the gate area, or throughout the rest of the airport. As we will explore later on, this ambiguity in the law is causing a tremendous amount of confusion for airline staff and law enforcement agencies that have to respond to air rage incidents outside of an aircraft.

Unlike the specific, very legalistic definitions offered by disruptive passenger behavior and interference with flight crew, *air rage* has become a catchall phrase for any and all aberrant behavior surrounding the air travel experience. Air rage seems to encompass a much broader scope of experiences than merely what passengers do aboard an aircraft. Air rage and the behaviors it embodies often start and end beyond the closed doors of a commercial airplane.

In fact, some of the more violent and bizarre incidents of passenger misbehavior have had their origins at the departure gate or the ticket counter.

On July 22, 1999, before boarding a plane in Newark, an irate passenger slammed the head of the Continental gate agent to the ground, breaking two bones in his neck. The passenger was traveling with his in-laws and five children to Orlando, en route to a Disney World vacation. One of the children ran through the waiting area onto the jetway. The gate agent turned to stop the child when he accidentally bumped into the passenger's wife, who was also chasing her child. The attacker allegedly grabbed the gate agent, put him in a headlock, and threw him to the ground—causing the gate agent to permanently lose half the mobility in his neck. The attacker was arrested, charged with aggravated assault, and later acquitted.[8]

There was an arrest in this case, although the local police, not the FAA, handled it, because the gate agent was a member of the ground crew rather than the flight crew. However, in far too many cases, aberrant passenger behavior is allowed to go unpunished because it falls outside the realm of the federal statute.

While waiting to check in for her flight from San Diego, a woman traveling with two small children sprayed breast milk on a customer service representative because she was told to unplug her breast pump. The electrical cord connected to the breast pump ran across a high-traffic aisle in the gate area and was causing other passengers to trip. When first asked to unplug the cord, the woman said her newborn had not eaten for three hours. Understanding the situation, the customer service agent responded calmly, asking the woman to complete her task as soon as possible. After more than thirty minutes, the customer service representative returned and asked the woman to discontinue the use of the breast pump. The woman, indignant about the request, removed the breast pump from her chest and proceeded to squirt breast milk at the customer service representative. Local police were called, but after a few minutes they decided not to press charges because no interference with flight crew had taken place.

During the boarding of a United Airlines flight from San Francisco to Reno, a man attacked and stabbed a woman he apparently did not know as the two were walking down the jetway. The man, who had flown from Seattle, knifed the woman in the back with a three-inch blade. Other passengers reportedly subdued the man until police arrived. The weapon was described as a Swiss army knife and was the kind that most likely would not be confiscated during the security check. Fortunately, the woman, who suffered multiple injuries to her back, survived. Police described the incident as "bizarre."

Although all of these incidents fall outside the very legalistic bounds of disruptive passenger behavior and interference with a flight crew, they more than qualify as instances of air rage.

WHAT IS AIR RAGE?

Like other difficult-to-define human activities, air rage may take on any number of shapes, sizes, or forms. But in the end, it is a type of behavior that is abnormal, aberrant, or abusive within the context of generally accepted social norms and values. In other words, when someone acts crazy or menacing.

Whether it is checking in your luggage, courteously answering the security questions, passing through the security checkpoint, waiting patiently in the boarding area, walking calming down the jetway, locating your seat, mindfully storing your carry-on luggage, preparing for takeoff, passing time away quietly, eating an in-flight meal peacefully, disembarking promptly from the airplane, or moving expeditiously through the arrival airport, you as a passenger are expected to do certain things in certain ways that are collectively held as decent and acceptable behavior. Anything beyond those parameters falls into the category of air rage.

Such a categorization may seem like too wide a brush with which to paint the entire airline experience. With literally 1.5 billion passengers flying every year on millions of flights all over the world, it seems intellectually dishonest to group all antisocial behavior on the part of passengers under the umbrella of air rage. Generalizations of this kind beg the question: Isn't air rage an oversimplification that dilutes the real problems surrounding bad passenger conduct? And isn't annoyance and even anger sometimes justified? Moreover, is air rage just a lot of hype and not much else?

On the surface, this would all appear to be true. Maybe air rage is merely a contrived expression to explain the reality that in any instance, a certain number of human beings will always misbehave—regardless of the situation. Maybe, at the end of the day, air rage is simply a trendy phrase invented by flight attendants, pilots, and, journalists to argue for better pay and working conditions, and, in this case, to sell more books. Yes, this all may be true.

Yet two overriding issues compel us to look deeper, to explore whether air rage is real or not.

THE PREVALENCE OF AIR RAGE

The first compelling issue before us is the prevalence of air rage incidents. Industry reports estimate that 44 percent of all adults in the United States flew on at least one commercial airline trip during the past year. That number is expected to continue rising in the foreseeable future.

As more passengers are flying on more planes every year, the incidents of air rage are increasing exponentially. The "official" numbers from the FAA on its Web site (www.faa.gov) say that 266 cases of interference with flight crew were reported from U.S. carriers in 2000. However, for a number of reasons to be detailed later in this book, the accuracy of this number is clearly in doubt

If, for a moment, we were to take a look at only FAA-related responses to incidents in the United States, we would find the number of interference with flight crew cases to be simply staggering. During the year 2000, 5,548 individuals employed by the FAA had as one of their duties the requirement to respond to probable incidents involving interference with flight crew. This number includes 1,131 full-time security professionals: air marshals and civil aviation security specialists. The other 4,417 are airway flight standards specialists. The primary responsibilities of these individuals concern aircraft maintenance as well as airline and pilot certification. However, in many areas of the country, they are the only FAA employees available. As a result, they also are given the investigative role in cases of interference with flight crew where no full-time security personnel exist.

After exhaustive examiniation of FAA and FBI case files, local police reports, airline incident and irregularity reports, interviews with cabin and cockpit crews, and communications from the flying public through our Web site, we are convinced that the actual number of interference with flight crew cases approximates ten thousand each year in the United States. This total represents more than 1.7 cases per FAA employee responsible for investigating probable instances of interference with flight crew. This is clearly a staggering disparity from the 266 incidents reported officially to the FAA by the airlines in year 2000.

Even more disconcerting, this number would not have included the fight with the gate agent, the angry woman with the breast pump, or the stabbing in the jetway. Therefore, we can assume the actual number of air rage cases to be much higher.

According to the International Air Transport Association, the global association representing the airline industry, there were some twelve thousand cases of disruptive passenger behavior worldwide in 2000, with more than ten thousand of those occurring on U.S. carriers. Says Senator Bill Frist (R) of Tennessee, "We're witnessing a growing trend in unruly and out-of-control passengers."

During the summer of 1999, the House of Representatives held the first ever hearings on in-flight violence. Legislation was introduced into the Senate to increase fines for those disruptive passengers and to make it easier to arrest in-flight offenders.

Sen. Harry Reid (D) of Nevada, a sponsor of a bill on air rage, says, "There are more than merely hundreds, I think we can say thousands, of these incidents every year. . . . It's a real serious problem."

For more than twenty years, the National Transportation Safety Board (NTSB), has been the world's foremost authority on crash investigations. The mission of the NTSB is simple: to ascertain the cause or causes of an airline crash. Beyond the dozens of scientists, forensic specialists, and FBI agents on every crash investigation team, it is also the responsibility of the NTSB to determine whether air rage was a contributing factor to the plane's demise.

Lloyd's of London, through its subsidiaries Brockbank Syndicate Management Ltd. and Aon Group Limited, have launched the first air rage insurance coverage. The policy will indemnify airlines for the cost of diverting an airplane and interrupting a flight should the pilot consider it necessary to land and eject an unruly passenger. The policy will also pay for injuries caused to the crew or other passengers by the offending person or persons and will pay an amount to compensate passengers for time, trouble, and inconvenience suffered.

Because of the scope and magnitude of the problem, air rage has gone from being an unspoken problem that the airlines would not publicly address, in part out of concern about driving away revenue, to one that they are being forced to confront. The management of airlines is now being compelled to recognize publicly what governments, passengers, civil aviation authorities, flight attendants, and pilots have known for quite a while: air rage poses one of the most serious threats to the safety and security of the flying public today.

Air rage has become so prevalent and pervasive that even celebrities are getting caught up in the mix.

On an American flight from Dallas to Miami, tennis starlet Anna Kournikova caused a commotion, forcing the pilot and police to intervene. The crew told police that Kournikova, age eighteen, refused to put her miniature Doberman pincher in its carrying case, as federal law requires. According to Major Mike Hammersmith of Miami-Dade police, Kournikova and her mother, Alia, argued at length with flight attendants about the dog during the flight. As a result, the pilot had to leave the cockpit to settle the situation. At the crew's request, police met the plane when it landed in Miami.[9]

Professional motorcycle racers Nicky Hayden and Roger Lee Hayden are under investigation from the FBI regarding their alleged misbehavior on a Northwest flight from Memphis to Owensboro, Kentucky. Ten of the commuter plane's sixteen passengers, who included the racing Haydens as well as family members and friends, were detained by Davies County sheriff's deputies after the pilot and flight attendant said the group was unruly during the trip. The pilot called for police to meet the plane when it landed because the group was purportedly throwing things at flight attendant Cindy Salsbery and calling her names, including obscenities.

The group was apparently upset about the lack of air conditioning and drinks being served, and that they had not been allowed to use the restroom, according to the report filed by Davies County Sheriff's Deputy Kent Taul. The plane was littered with items of trash when police arrived and inspected the plane's interior.[10]

When passengers get extremely out of control during a flight, the final measure is to summon the captain or the first officer to control them. That's when the rest of the passengers should get worried. It means that half the flight crew is back in the passenger compartment trying to stop a fight. And the one remaining at the controls has the commotion in the rear of the airplane on his mind. That means the pilot is probably paying a little less attention to that line of thunderstorms ahead or to surrounding air traffic in the congested, overcrowded skies. Under such circumstances, air rage can end up in a catastrophic disaster.

On an Eva Air flight from Los Angeles to Taipei, Hong Kong pop star Ronald Cheng allegedly went berserk, forcing the captain to intervene and subdue the out-of-control rock-n-roller. Captain John Erving said he was forced to act when the singer began beating up his copilot, who had gone to rescue a flight attendant from a headlock in the first-class section. Before leaving the cockpit, Captain Erving said he awakened the reserve crew and put them in control of the plane—"flying the aircraft in their underwear while he knocked out the raving, intoxicated singer with a flashlight."

Cheng had been drinking whiskey and champagne since takeoff and had spent twenty minutes smoking in the toilet. He set off the smoke alarm and emerged "completely intoxicated, very altered, and yelling for more whiskey" before dozing off in his seat for a while, said Captain Erving. About three hours into the flight, Cheng woke up, started singing, and shouted obscenities. When a flight attendant refused to serve him any more whiskey, he grabbed her and put her into a writhing headlock.

Captain Erving said the flight attendant's screams sent First Officer Meng Chao rushing to her aid from the cockpit. Minutes later, Chao was calling for help after Cheng grabbed him by the throat. Erving then summoned the resting crew before going to confront the singer. The two scuffled and Captain Erving split Cheng's head open with the flashlight.

"He was out for the count, bleeding badly. I was horrified, fearing I had really harmed him," Captain Erving said.

The pilot called for help from a doctor on board while other crew members handcuffed Cheng. The plane was diverted to Anchorage, Alaska, where Cheng was taken off the plane.[11]

There have been dozens of unsolved accidents worldwide over the last ten years that may have been contributed to in some way by air rage. The reality remains that air rage is a real threat and it must be dealt with head-on.

THE COMMONALITY OF THE
AIR RAGE PROBLEM

The second compelling issue surrounding air rage is the commonality of the problem on a global scale. Air travel has become one of the most standardized commercial activities in the world today. The driving experience, for example, varies greatly based on whether you are in a sedan, an SUV, or a pickup. The road looks much different if you are behind the wheel of a Ford or a Fiat, rather than a Ferrari. If you are driving in Japan, Australia, or Britain, you drive on the opposite side of the road than in the United States, Canada, or China. The topography and the conditions of the roads all vary immensely, depending where you are at any given moment.

Air travel is not this way at all. One of the authors, Andrew R. Thomas, has traveled to more than 150 countries on all seven continents over the past ten years. He's flown on more than eighty-five airlines in Africa, South America, Asia, the United States, and Europe. He's sat in first class, business class, international economy, and coach. And, frankly, it's all pretty much the same.

Whether you traveling to Tallahassee or Timbuktu, you can expect to fly in only one of a few models of aircraft—a Boeing 777, 767, 757, 747, 737, or 727; a McDonnell Douglas MD 80, DC10, or DC9; or an Airbus A340, A330, or A320. Whether you are in first class or coach, you will be seated in pretty much the same way—facing forward. The air quality inside the cabin will invariably seem poor. Because of the 0 percent humidity, your nose gets dried out whether you're on British Airways or Air Burkina. The food is always marginal at best, whether you're in first class or in the back of the plane. The drink selection is almost always the same: beer, juice, and canned soda, Evian, Johnnie Walker Red, and cheap table wine. Whether in Buenos Aires or Boston, delays and cancellations occur for the same reasons: mechanical failures, weather, security, or air traffic control overload. Regardless of where you are, the safety lecture prior to takeoff is given in English. In places where hardly anybody speaks English, the flight attendant will always issue instructions in both the local language and English. Even the airsick bags look the same, except for the differing airline logos on their fronts.

Because of the commonality of the product and the service, the problems confronted during the air travel experience are generally the same worldwide. And because of this reality, we are able to identify a commonality in the kinds of air rage incidents that take place. Further, we can offer informed explanations as to the reasons why.

This ability to isolate air rage and see the multifaceted problem for what it really is provides us with the opportunity to create and implement common solutions. The remainder of this book will explore the root causes of air rage and look at some actions that are being taken to confront this burgeoning crisis in the skies.

2

THE BROKEN SYSTEM

The United States has the largest civil aviation system in the world. Forty percent of all worldwide passenger air traffic occurs in the United States. The system is breathtakingly large:

- 19,000 domestic airports
- 550,000,000 passengers flying each year
- 800,000,000 passenger bags handled each year
- Millions and millions of tons of freight and mail handled each year

In 2000, approximately seven thousand air traffic controllers at 475 commercial airports supervised over 68.5 million takeoffs and landings. Air travel has become so routine, so ordinary, that we tend to forget what an extraordinary accomplishment it really is. People and cargo are carried around the world in a matter of hours, and in most cases it seems like a "piece of cake." In some ways, though, we are victims of our success. How much more growth and prosperity can the U.S. civil aviation system handle?

James Goodwin, the head of United, the world's largest airline, says the global skies are teeming with so many planes that the entire commercial aviation industry is near crisis. Goodwin adds, "The skies are crowded and getting more so every day."

Speaking at an international aviation conference in December 1999, Goodwin said that unless something is done soon, severe delays will become routine, creating backlogs with serious or even catastrophic implications.[1] Another leading aviation industry executive, Frederick Smith,

29

chairman, president, and CEO of Federal Express Corporation, warns that flight delays and cancellations will get worse unless something is done to restrict the number of flights scheduled at the nation's major airports.

Smith, a vocal proponent of aviation deregulation when he started his company in the 1970s, says, "It's amazing to me to watch people talk about this issue [of flight delays and cancellations], but nobody wants to face up to the fundamental issue" of too many flights being scheduled to take off and land with too few airports and runways to handle them.[2]

The Port Authority of New York and New Jersey recently decided to limit flights at LaGuardia Airport to address severe airline overscheduling and the resulting delays and cancellations.

David Carty, chairman and chief executive officer of American Airlines, said, "In 1999, 70 percent of all flights at LaGuardia arrived within fifteen minutes of schedule. In 2000, the percentage fell to 30 percent and is falling." He added, "Something's got to give."[3]

Carty and Smith agree that more airports and runways are needed, but that alone will not solve the problem of delays in the near term because such projects take many years to complete.[4]

As in the United States, the situation in Europe is getting close to the breaking point. Peak-time delays at European airports regularly average more than a half hour, with more than one in three of all flights delayed by more than fifteen minutes.

The overloaded air traffic control system, an antiquated hub-and-spoke system, insufficient airport capacity, more passengers flying every year, and the growth of the airline industry are making the skies above us as crowded as the highways on the ground.

THE AIR TRAFFIC CONTROL SYSTEM

In 1978, the federal government deregulated the airlines but maintained the air traffic control system. That system, designed in the 1940s, is an aging patchwork of computers and communications networks. Industry experts estimate it would cost at least $75 billion over the next five years to modernize the FAA's air traffic control system, yet Congress appropriates only about $3 billion a year for improvements.

The top 20 busiest FAA airport traffic control towers, in order, are:

Atlanta International, Georgia
Chicago/O'Hare International, Illinois
Dallas/Ft. Worth International, Texas
Los Angeles International, California
New York La Guardia, New York
Van Nuys, California
Phoenix Sky Harbor International, Arizona
Detroit, Metro Wayne County, Michigan
Las Vegas/McCarran International, Nevada
Metropolitan Oakland International, California
Miami International, Florida
Minneapolis/St. Paul International, Minnesota
Boston/Logan International, Massachusetts
Lambert/St. Louis International, Missouri
Denver International, Colorado
Long Beach/Daughtery, California
Washington Dulles International, Virginia
Philadelphia International, Pennsylvania
Covingtion/Cincinnati International, Kentucky
Houston/G. Bush Intercontinental, Texas

THE HUB-AND-SPOKE SYSTEM

The antiquated hub-and-spoke system, which was created in the 1960s, is still a way of life for most airlines. The concept is simple: fly all your passengers to one particular city and connect them on to other cities. This is primarily done to maximize revenues by increasing load factors. In other words, the more people per flight, the more cost effective. Passengers from all over the United States and the world converge into one location and connect on to their final destinations.

The top sixty airports in the United States connect more than 90 percent of all passenger traffic. Unfortunately, a problem at one airport halfway across the country affects travelers everywhere else. Delays at Chicago/O'Hare, the second busiest airport in the United States, can create havoc across the nation. In 2000, only 70.4 percent of the flights departing from O'Hare International Airport in Chicago left on schedule. Los Angeles International Airport reported that only 72.5 per cent of departing flights left on time. And at New York's LaGuardia Airport, only 44.9 percent of all flights arrived on time!

AIRPORT CAPACITY

Since 1990, only eighteen new runways have come online to ease traffic congestion at major airports across the nation. Only one new airport— Denver International—has been built in the last ten years. The lack of foresight and expansion on the part of the nation's airports is costing billions of dollars in expenses associated with delays alone. The government, airlines, and, ultimately, passengers all lose because of this lack of vision.

Opposition to new runways and airport expansions has risen in recent years. Homeowners and environmentalists, concerned about noise, pollution, and other impacts on the areas surrounding the nation's airports, have launched effective protest campaigns to bring almost completely to a stop any airport development anywhere. The inability of airports to expand has led to traffic jams, lack of adequate parking facilities, long lines at counters, crowded gate areas, poor restroom quality, and countless other inconveniences for travelers at the nation's airports.

All of these factors may have a direct impact on the passenger and the mood he or she will carry on board a flight. Lately, merely traveling through the airport has become an adventure within itself—and the passenger hasn't even left the ground.

THE RISE IN THE NUMBER OF PASSENGERS

The simple fact of more people flying then ever before certainly contributes to the broken system. The U.S. government estimates that more than 1 billion passengers will travel on U.S. airlines by the year 2007, a nearly 50 percent increase over the current numbers.

How did the nation's air system reach a breaking point? Ironically, it is a by-product of our prosperity. Who would ever imagine that this would be a national crisis? Despite complaints about price gouging of business travelers and some recent fare hikes, the cost of flying in real terms (minus inflation) has actually declined. In short, most Americans can now afford to fly. As a result, more and more people are building air travel into their lifestyles.

People now regularly work in one city while their office may be located several states away. Others dash off to weddings or social events in distant cities, just for the weekend. It's a far cry from the days when air travel was a luxury and folks would don their Sunday best for a rare flight.

All of this has created a much higher "load factor" for the airlines. Today, airlines typically fill 75 to 80 percent of their seats, compared to 50 or 60 percent just a few years ago. That creates profits but it also leaves much less room for error. On Labor Day weekend in 2000, Delta Airlines sold 408,000 of 416,000 available seats, and on June 30, United Airlines said it had experienced a load factor of 89.5 percent, a thirty-five-year record.

THE GROWTH OF THE AIRLINE INDUSTRY

In most of the 1990s, life was pretty good for the nation's airlines. But in recent years, that growth has gotten to the point of being out of control. The goal of an airline during periods of prosperity is to purchase, lease, or borrow as many aircraft as possible, in order to meet customer demand. In the short term, airlines must collect as many passengers as possible and recruit them for their frequent flier programs. Customer loyalty is everything and will carry the airlines through the difficult, slower times.

As the number of aircraft increases for each airline, airport terminal delays increase, as well air traffic control delays. How many aircraft are too many? How many flights a day do you need between two cites before the market becomes saturated? Unregulated, unrestricted growth can be a short-term benefit but may be a long-term mistake. When the passenger traffic begins to decline and a competitor offers cheaper seats, an airline is forced to alter its strategic plan. Overnight, it may be forced to chose new destinations, open cities, hire new staff, and sign contracts that may hold it bound for months or years.

In order for a typical airline to make money, it must get a least fourteen to sixteen hours per day of aircraft utilization or risk the onset of losses. Every hour that an aircraft sits on the ground is considered lost revenue. Increasing the aircraft fleet also means increasing flight crews.

Recently, while traveling aboard a major air carrier, it was readily apparent to me that not one of the three pilots on the flight deck was over thirty years of age. Young, inexperienced flight crews are dominating the airlines today. This is by no means an indication that they are unqualified to fly, but rather a new direction for the airlines. Due to age restrictions imposed by the FAA, pilots are retiring in record numbers and they are being replaced in record numbers with younger and younger flight crew.

Airlines used to be particular about who flew their multimillion dollar airplanes and generally hired pilots from the Air Force. Today, pilots are churned out by flight schools in order to meet the increased demand. Airlines have no choice except to hire whomever they can in order to fly the increased schedules. The thinking in the industry now seems to be, if you have a license you can fly with us—experience is secondary.

It is clear that customer service on the airlines is not what it used to be, primarily due to growth. Obtaining employment in the airline industry just ten to fifteen years ago was a very difficult and tedious task. Rigid standards were set for height and weight requirements, a clear complexion was a must, and several interviews later you might just be selected to be a ticket agent. Today, due to the growth and prosperity, airlines unable to find enough station help may have to settle for less than satisfactory service employees. A pleasant appearance, a caring attitude, and manners may not be so easy to come by. There doesn't appear to be company loyalty, which was so prevalent just a few years ago; now, it's only a job.

One of the attractions and most precious fringe benefits of working for an airline is the ability to travel and fly for free. Today, with increasing numbers of passengers and crowds, it's almost impossible for employees to travel nonrevenue. Rescinding this benefit creates an unfriendly environment. Moreover, it's not an easy job to stand in front of unpredictable, demanding passengers day in and day out.

The following thoughts and comments were provided from passengers flying on the airline of their choice who were asked to describe their traveling experience in one sentence.

"By the time I found a parking space in the remote lot, my flight had departed."

"An aluminum tube filled with people and all their germs."

"Delays, delays, delays."

"The seats were too small."

"The coach food was not fit for my dog."

"Stuff was stolen from my luggage."

"The service was a joke."

"The flight attendants were snippy."

"Next time, Amtrak."

"It was too hot, the air conditioning pack broke, and they flew the plane anyway."

"Someone took my original seat, so I got to sit in the middle seat for 5 hours."

"They lost my luggage and didn't seem to care."

"The last gate, why is it always the last gate?"

"A kid screamed the whole way."

"The flight crew missed their connecting flight, so they canceled mine."

"7 hours, 3 stops, and 9 bags of peanuts . . . but I saved $45.00."

"The fat guy next to me had on a tank top, need I say more?"

The point of illustrating these comments is not to blame the airlines for the current state of air travel, but rather to highlight the fact that no one entity is to blame for the current state of affairs. It is obvious by the comments that so many factors come into play, yet every entity in the air travel industry has the responsibility to clean up its own act.

✳ ✳ ✳

Air traffic control problems, the antiquated hub-and-spoke system, inadequate airports, as well as the growth of the airline industry and the numbers of passengers, are creating a snowball effect that is getting increasingly out of control. These factors are causing the system to be broken. And the manifestations of that broken system are probably most evident in the rise of mishandled baggage, flight delays, and flight cancellations.

Table 2. Mishandled-Baggage Reports
Filed by Passengers

Airline	November 2000 Reports per 1,000 passengers	November 1999 Reports per 1,000 passengers
TWA	5.61	3.97
America West	5.56	4.57
Southwest	5.54	4.13
American	5.20	4.32
United	5.11	5.33
Continental	5.07	3.04
Northwest	4.96	3.65
Delta	4.62	3.11
US Airways	4.19	4.13
Alaska Airlines	3.02	3.74

Source: Office of Aviation and Proceedings, U.S. Department of Transportation

MISHANDLED BAGGAGE

The sheer fact that there are record numbers of passengers has added to an astronomical increase in mishandled baggage. Table 2 gives the rate of mishandled-baggage reports by U.S. carriers and for the industry. These baggage statistics are filed with the Department of Transportation on a monthly basis by all U.S. airlines that have at least 1 percent of total domestic scheduled-service passenger revenues.

FLIGHT DELAYS

A flight is defined as "on time" by the Department of Transportation if it arrives and departs within fifteen minutes of the original flight schedule used by the airlines. Where the fifteen-minute threshold comes from is unclear. It seems completely arbitrary. Moreover, it can very well exacer-

Table 3. Overall Percentage of Flights Arriving on Time, November 2000

Airline	Percent of total arrivals on time
TWA	81.5
Continental	80.0
Southwest	75.1
Northwest	74.5
US Airways	74.1
American	72.3
United	69.1
America West	67.5
Delta	67.4
Alaska	66.1
Total Average	72.8

Source: Office of Aviation and Proceedings, U.S. Department of Transportation

bate the problem of flight delays because the total number is, by definition, underreported (see Table 3).

Flight delays are caused by a variety of factors, and create a snowball effect on airline and airport operations. Flights can back up a nationwide system, compounding the situation, which may take days to recover from. Primary flight delays are caused by severe weather, aircraft maintenance, runway closures, customer service issues, air traffic control system decisions, and equipment failure.

In terms of delays, Table 4 provides one of the most comprehensive analyses of the nation's busiest airports.

For anyone who has gone through chronic delays during a flight, there is no doubt that the experience can be exceptionally frustrating. In one of the more violent responses to a delayed flight, an individual opened fire with an assault rifle at the Minneapolis/St. Paul International Airport. The individual was stopped when he attempted to enter the checkpoint carrying the weapon, distraught over employment issues that were apparently complicated by a flight delay. The gunman repeatedly fired his weapon at the security checkpoint, injuring several screeners with broken glass. The

Table 4. Operations, Enplaned Passengers, and Selected Delay Rankings Using Selected Databases and Criteria

Airport	OPSNET Delays per 1,000 Operations	Rank	Total Delays	Rank	ASPM Avg. Arrival Delay (Minutes)	Rank	ASQP Flight Arrivals	Percent On Time	Inverse Rank	Enplaned Passengers (thousands)	Rank	OPSNET Total Oper	Rank
LaGuardia	155.9	1	61,120	1	21.8	1	8,838	73.1	13	10,785	18	392,047	22
Newark	81.2	2	37,132	3	14.3	5	9,686	74.7	15	14,904	12	457,182	18
Chicago	63.3	3	57,545	2	15.8	4	22,365	69.0	7	31,483	2	908,977	2
San Francisco	56.9	4	24,478	5	17.4	2	10,042	60.3	2	16,431	8	430,554	21
Boston	47.5	5	24,120	6	16.6	3	8,647	72.8	12	11,066	17	508,283	11
Philadelphia	44.5	6	21,521	7	13.4	6	9,490	73.7	14	10,346	19	483,567	14
Kennedy	38.8	7	13,930	11	12.2	9	3,386	78.5	23	10,137	20	358,951	26
Atlanta	30.9	8	28,229	4	12.0	10	19,867	72.5	11	37,224	1	913,449	1
Houston	28.1	9	13,785	12	8.9	25	10,153	81.7	28	14,735	13	490,568	12
Dallas/Ft. Worth	23.8	10	20,638	8	9.2	23	18,799	72.5	10	27,581	3	865,777	3
Phoenix	22.0	11	14,024	10	11.0	14	14,818	66.8	5	16,083	9	638,757	5
Los Angeles	21.9	12	17,141	9	12.7	8	16,003	60.0	1	24,007	4	783,684	4
Dulles	19.5	13	9,339	14	11.5	12	4,175	80.5	25	6,830	29	479,931	15
St. Louis	18.2	14	8,837	15	11.1	13	12,726	70.3	9	14,923	11	484,224	13
Detroit	17.6	15	9,780	13	8.8	26	11,570	80.8	26	16,563	7	554,580	6
Cincinnati	15.4	16	7,360	16	10.7	17	5,115	82.0	30	7,610	26	477,654	16
Minn./St. Paul	12.7	17	6,658	17	8.4	29	10,982	75.7	16	18,944	5	522,253	8
Miami	11.3	18	5,849	18	11.9	11	5,237	77.9	21	12,721	15	516,545	10
Seattle	10.4	19	4,653	19	10.3	20	7,687	66.7	4	13,062	14	445,677	20
Las Vegas	8.0	20	4,178	20	10.6	18	10,605	68.1	6	15,311	10	521,300	9
Reagan National	8.0	21	2,727	22	9.1	24	7,084	78.0	22	6,657	30	342,790	28
Balt.-Wash. Intl	6.9	22	2,181	24	10.9	16	7,632	81.7	27	8,002	25	315,348	29
Orlando	6.3	23	2,297	23	11.0	15	7,827	77.1	20	12,529	16	366,278	25
Charlotte	6.0	24	2,748	21	7.9	30	10,113	82.8	31	9,442	21	460,370	17
Pittsburgh	3.8	25	1,695	25	8.6	27	8,146	82.0	29	8,014	24	448,181	19
San Diego	2.5	26	520	28	9.9	21	5,486	65.0	3	7,248	27	207,916	31
Denver	2.2	27	1,177	26	13.4	7	10,469	69.3	8	17,435	6	528,604	7
Salt Lake City	2.0	28	720	27	9.6	22	6,067	76.2	18	8,709	22	366,933	24
Tampa	1.6	29	435	29	10.6	19	5,506	75.8	17	6,912	28	278,632	30
Memphis	0.4	30	143	30	8.5	28	4,418	78.8	24	4,524	31	386,335	23
Honolulu	0.0	31	N/A	31	N/A	N/A	3,128	76.5	19	8,517	23	345,496	27

Sources: FAA OPSNET and ASPM data are for CY 2000. Honolulu is not included in the voluntarily reported ASPM database. ASQP data for February 2001 is from the April edition of DOT's Air Travel Consumer Report. Enplaned passengers are from the 1999 edition of DOT's Airport Activity Statistics of Certificated Route Air Carriers.

individual left the checkpoint and went outside to the front of the terminal building. Stunned passengers and motorists were frightened as a gun battle ensued with police officers right before their eyes. During the exchange of gun fire the individual was wounded and eventually arrested. No other serious injuries resulted from this horrific incident.

FLIGHT CANCELLATIONS

The breakdown of the system plays a large part in the number of flight cancellations as well. On some carriers at some airports during peak times, there is a one-in-ten chance that your flight will be canceled. Even in off-peak times, there is still a strong possibility that your flight may be canceled (see Table 5).

As airlines continue to push the envelope by flying more and more aircraft, the manifestations of the broken system become even more apparent.

Pilots are under great pressure to adhere to schedules in the great rush hour in the skies. A pilot who was fired after refusing to fly during an ice storm was awarded $10 million by a jury. The pilot, a ten-year veteran of a major U.S. carrier, was awarded the money in a lawsuit contending he was fired for turning around his turboprop plane in a storm. The pilot made an attempt to fly from Dallas to Houston but returned to the airport because he thought conditions were unsafe. He was asked to try again, but refused. A statement issued by the carrier stood by their position that the pilot was fired because he did not execute proper procedures during severe ice conditions and failed to follow safety procedures in two earlier incidents.

All of these factors have a direct impact on the passenger and the mood she will carry on board a flight. And as the broken system negatively affects greater numbers of passengers, it plays a larger and larger role in creating a stressful environment that can potentially lead to air rage.

IDENTIFYING THE BROKEN SYSTEM

On July 25, 2000, Jane F. Garvey, FAA administrator, made the following comments before the Senate Committee on Appropriations, Subcommittee on Transportation and Related Agencies Concerning Air Traffic Control Delays.

Table 5. Overall Percentage of Flight Cancellations, November 2000

Airline	Percent of flight cancellations
America West	4.2
United	4.2
Alaska	3.2
American	2.8
Northwest	2.7
Delta	2.6
US Airways	2.0
TWA	1.1
Southwest	0.9
Continental	0.7
Total Average	2.3

Source: Office of Aviation and Proceedings, U.S. Department of Transportation

Delays have significant financial, scheduling, and service consequences for airlines and result in understandable frustration for their passengers. The issue of delays is very complex. There are many conditions that cause delays: bad weather, inoperable runways, airport capacity limitations, aircraft equipment problems, maintenance and crew problems, and, yes air traffic equipment outages and air traffic procedures. . . .

A further factor that complicates air traffic control is that of airline scheduling and airport capacity. At the risk of stating the obvious, air traffic is a dynamic situation. Every procedural enhancement, every step forward in modernization, every improvement in efficiency, cannot be measured in a static environment, but is evaluated in light of daily changes in weather, runway availability, and airline schedules. . . .

Consequently, the installation of an instrument landing systems (ILS), enhanced radar, or a reduction of miles in trail requirements may not necessarily translate into a reduction of airline delays, even if efficiencies are achieved. . . ."

Whether local communities are discussing new runways, new terminals, or new airports, the debate is always heartfelt and emotional. Hard choices will have to be made at all levels of government with communities across the country to ensure that we have the infrastructure in place to accommodate anticipated demand.

With so many pressing and immediate issues it's difficult to get organized and get started. Progress, needless to say, has been slow.

Recently the Office of the Inspector General made headlines when it reported that the FAA has been ineffective in reducing air traffic control operational errors and should approach the problem with an extreme sense of urgency. In a report that was sent to Jane Garvey, the Inspector General's Office stated that operational errors actually *increased* by as much as 51 percent from 1996 to 2000.

These operational errors took place while aircraft were on the ground and in flight, and under the direct control of the FAA. The report indicated that the severity of the problem is difficult to determine because the incidents reported range from minor infractions to extremely dangerous and life-threatening incidents. In the meantime, the FAA is working on a report to identify airports and airspace that have serious congestion problems, in order to project the amount of traffic that can be safely handled in the vicinity of these high-density airports. It is our hope this report will come sooner rather than later, as it would be in everyone's best interest to have less traffic in the air during peak hours of the day.

Incidents on the ground can be just as serious as incidents in the air and are referred to as *runway incursions*. These are occurrences at airports involving an aircraft, people, or objects that create collision hazards or result in aborted landings or takeoffs. For example, if an airport vehicle accidentally crosses an active runway without permission from the control tower, that is an "incident"; if an aircraft was less than one mile from landing, however, it would be considered an "incursion."

THE BROKEN SYSTEM AND AIR RAGE

The air rage offender is often born in the kind of environment created by the broken system. Chaos is one of the primary ingredients for a potential air rage incident. We each may become a little upset, or feel an "air rage sensation," when our flight is delayed or canceled or our baggage is lost.

Many instances of air rage have occurred during these very stressful moments.

In fact, groups of passengers have become angry and upset at the airlines, the government—and God, for that matter. These individuals, who were once law-abiding citizens, now have a common bond. No one likes to be inconvenienced, but it's amazing how many individuals would risk landing in a thunderstorm just to get home. There is never a concept of how serious a situation may be—only the concept of how inconvenienced one may become. Have you ever been told a flight was delayed due to weather at your destination city, and then notice some guy pick up his cell phone and call his wife at home? The response is always something like, "My wife said the weather is fine, what's the problem?"

If more spouses worked for the National Weather Service maybe we could keep the aviation system on schedule. It is always interesting to watch the reaction of passengers, whether it's an elderly couple going on vacation or the CEO of a major corporation, when they are told by a pilot, gate agent, or customer service representative, "This plane is diverting to Appleton, Wisconsin, whether you like it or not, for your safety."

3

ALCOHOL AND DRUGS

It is not surprising that alcohol consumption is associated with a higher incidence of air rage than any other causal or contributing factor. Most airline passengers are either going on or coming from a vacation, or are going away to or returning from a business trip. The vacationers are often in a party mood, in good spirits, and want to continue partying on board. The businessperson is often tired and stressed, and in "need" of a stiff drink. In either situation the ingredients add up to a dangerous cocktail.

The vast majority of people can deal with the uncomfortable aspects of flying, but when under the influence of alcohol, some people become volatile. After a drink or two, most of us have been known to say a little bit more than is necessary. We exaggerate ideas and movements, and we can get a little bit more irate. Some people become violent. The violent ones are Molotov cocktails just waiting to explode.

During a flight to Honolulu, a first-class passenger downed seven vodka miniatures, three Bailey's, and six beers. As he proceeded to the lavatory for the fourth time during the course of the flight, he mistook the cockpit door for the lavatory door. After several unsuccessful attempts to open the door, he was eventually coaxed back to his seat where he proceeded to urinate in the airsick bag. Later, he began to flick food at fellow passengers and then pulled the tie and uniform of a male flight attendant. The first officer came out to try to calm down the situation, and had his hat knocked off and his glasses snatched by the drunken passenger. Not appreciating the reprimand from the first officer, the man decided he didn't like the atmosphere and stepped toward the aft emergency exit. Upon seeing the man approach, a

43

flight attendant stood spread-eagled against the door, screaming for help. One passenger who tried to intervene was kicked in the groin while two other passengers were punched and kicked by the drunken passenger. Finally, a passenger tackled the drunk and, with the help of several others, handcuffed the man to a seat using the linen napkins from first class.

A Pennsylvania man was traveling on a U.S. Airways flight from Pittsburgh to Miami when he became belligerent after drinking several mini-bottles of alcohol. About thirty minutes into the flight, the man allegedly pushed a flight attendant, grabbed two passengers by the throat, and tried to open the door of the plane. Several passengers finally wrestled him to floor, where the crazed passenger was handcuffed and placed in a rear seat of the aircraft. Keith Kenard of Pittsburgh, who helped subdue the drunk, said, "It was a great feeling to finally touch ground. When you're up there, and you've got a guy yelling 'I want out, I want out,' and he's trying to open the doors and can't control him, that's a very scary, isolated feeling."

After his arrest, it was discovered that the offender had been released from a Pennsylvania state prison just a few days earlier. He was supposed to report to a halfway house in Harrisburg. Instead, he boarded the U.S. Airways flight.[1]

THE DOUBLE-EDGED SWORD

In the United States, onboard alcohol service is a double-edged sword. It is a primary source of fuel for air rage, but it is also a great source of revenue. On domestic flights, the sale of alcohol can more than cover the cost of the entire crew for a particular flight. Long-distance flights to popular destinations like Las Vegas and Hawaii can easily turn a nice profit for the carrier.

The same is true for airports. The sales of alcohol constitute a significant portion of their revenue streams. Whether it is served in restaurants, bars, or lounges, or sold at duty-free stores, alcohol is available in every airport.

Moreover, alcohol is also more closely associated with airline travel than any other mode of transportation. Airlines are unique among transportation entities by the fact that on many flights they regularly distribute alcohol free of charge, often without any limits, to their passengers. On domestic flights in the United States, first-class passengers get free drinks. And on almost every international flight—regardless of the carrier—*all* passengers drink for free without limits.

Not surprisingly, a disproportionate number of air rage cases involving alcohol are caused by passengers traveling in the premium classes of service, where alcohol is more readily available both on the ground and in the air. Airline business lounges can be found in almost every airport in the world. Almost universally, they serve alcohol free of charge. At major international hubs, the alcohol flows freely in transfer lounges, as passengers wait to make their next connections.

A British Airways passenger, who admitted to drinking beer and vodka in the waiting area prior to his flight, threatened and abused the cabin crew and other passengers aboard his flight to Newcastle. The passenger told an attendant five minutes into the flight that "he hated flying and asked if he could stay with her in the galley." The flight attendant, Caroline Clement, agreed and then began a conversation with him. After a few seconds, she realized he had been drinking but didn't think he was drunk.

Clement asked him what he did for a living and he leaned toward her face and said he was a terrorist. Clement become concerned about what was happening as the man's language deteriorated and he began to swear at her.

At this point, he asked for another drink and Clement, hoping to steady the situation, served him a vodka and coke. Instead, his behavior further deteriorated and he began to threaten other passengers. The passenger was later arrested and charged with disorderly conduct and being drunk on an airplane.[2]

An off-duty soldier became a hero on a Japan Air Lines (JAL) from Australia to England when he helped cabin crew restrain a dangerously drunk passenger. Private Anthony Barrett was returning from vacation when he became aware of an escalating air rage incident.

"I was requested by the cabin attendants in helping restrain a drunken passenger who had become very obstreperous," the soldier explained.

The drunken man, after being asked to calm down, became aggressive and threatening and air crew were worried that he might attempt to open a door on the jet.

"He was very drunk and abusive and eventually he had to be handcuffed as he was a threat to the passengers and crew on board," Private Barrett continued.

The crew, who identified Barrett as a soldier from his casual fatigues, asked him to help in restraining the man. Mr. Barrett handcuffed the passenger, who was arrested on arrival in Heathrow. As a token of thanks, JAL presented Mr. Barrett with an around-the-world voucher for free travel to the destination of his choice.[3]

ONLY TO EXCESS

Many air rage cases involving alcohol seem to stem from a refusal on the part of flight attendants to keep serving drinks to apparently drunken passengers.

A group of ten or so passengers on board a Continental flight from Cancun to Newark became threatening and boisterous after flight attendants refused to serve alcohol to several apparently intoxicated people on the nearly four-hour flight. Flight attendants became concerned when one of the plane's 173 passengers apparently passed out after drinking too much. At this point, the decision to stop serving drinks was made. Many passengers immediately became indignant and demanded that alcohol service continue. Airline employees said they believe that several of the disruptive passengers were college students on spring break in Mexico.[4]

An Air Canada flight from Edmonton to Toronto turned scary for passengers when a drunk woman who was refused alcohol service from cabin crew threatened another female passenger, stole food off the tray of another, drank her own booze, tried to light a cigarette, and vomited on herself.

Police said the woman, who was drinking before the flight, was grabbed by crew members when she tried to light a cigarette. At one point, she became angry with a female passenger and threatened to "kick her ass." The woman kept yelling and insulting other passengers on the flight. Later, the woman threw up on herself in front of other passengers, who had to be moved to other seats.[5]

On an America West flight from Las Vegas to Fort Lauderdale, fifteen passengers were detained and questioned by the FBI after they became unruly about the alcohol service on the plane. Following an emergency landing in Albuquerque, the FBI was called in to investigate.

According to FBI spokesman Doug Beldon, some in the group of detainees were upset because they felt the free drink coupon they received at the beginning of the flight should have been worth more than one drink. Others got angry because the flight crew considered them drunk and quit serving them. One of the passengers allegedly threw a crumpled beer can and a cup of ice at a flight attendant.[6]

On a Virgin Atlantic flight from Great Britain to Los Angeles, a drunken male passenger flew into a rage when his alcohol service was cut off by a flight attendant. The plane was diverted to Calgary when the man swore and threatened the flight crew and other passengers. The crew restrained him, and when Calgary police boarded the plane to make an arrest, the drunk was already handcuffed. The man, who was traveling with his wife and children, later blamed the stress of a funeral he had attended in England as well as the effects of an antidepressant he had taken prior to boarding.

A passenger on a South African Airways (SAA) flight from London to Johannesburg was arrested after he drunkenly harassed a female passenger and punched a crew member. An SAA spokeswoman said that a woman passenger complained to the crew that the man had harassed her during the flight by asking her for sexual favors. When a flight attendant approached the man, he punched the flight attendant in the ribs. The pilot ordered the man subdued for the rest of the flight, and he was handcuffed by the crew.[7]

A passenger from Singapore on board an American Airlines flight from Miami to London became unruly and caused the aircraft to divert to Logan International Airport in Boston. The passenger, who apparently had too much to drink, became enraged when he was refused more alcohol. Shortly after takeoff, the passenger made several references to being a hijacker, stating, "If I were a hijacker . . . ." The flight attendants immediately reported the passenger's behavior to the flight crew, who had no choice except to take immediate action and declare an emergency.

Boston air traffic control gave priority clearance to the flight and treated the incident as a hijacking. The aircraft landed in Boston without further incident and the passenger was arrested without a struggle. The passenger was charged with interference with flight crew, fined, and deported.

A male passenger aboard an American Airlines flight from Miami to London got out of control after being refused additional alcohol service from a flight attendant. Indignant about the denial, the man ran to the rear galley and tried to grab some bottles of alcohol off a serving cart. When confronted by a female flight attendant, the drunk man lowered his shoulder into her ribcage and sent her flying into a lavatory door. The captain, with the help of a several passengers, was finally able to restrain the man using the cord for a mobile phone located in the back of a seat.

BYOB

The airlines could learn from other places that serve alcohol over long periods—a nightclub, for example—and could instead employ bouncers—who, perhaps, are not as well known for their cheery smiles, politiesness, and willingness to serve—rather than flight attendants.

This may seem extreme, but the problems seen in flight are similar to the problems evident on a Friday night in bars and clubs across the country. Only in these instances, the problems occur at thirty-five thousand feet, in congested airspace, and could have a life-threatening effect on two to three hundred other passengers. Unlike the Friday night reveler, the air rage assailant cannot easily be thrown out the door.

The situations become even worse when the passenger brings his own alcohol onto the plane or comes on board drunk—clear violations of FAA and international flight regulations.

The environment within the cabin may add to the effects of drunkenness because of the effects of air pressure on alcohol in the blood. In most airplane cabins at thirty-five thousand feet, the air pressure is less—sometimes much less—than it is on the ground. The reason is simple: the air is thinner the higher you go. Anyone who travels from sea level to Denver, La Paz, or Albuquerque immediately feels the effects of the higher altitude when getting off the plane. Breathing becomes more difficult and physical activity becomes more strained because of the lack of oxygen. Lower air pressure also eases the process by which alcohol is absorbed into the bloodstream. It is, therefore, a lot easier to get more drunk, more quickly in the air than on the ground.

An American Airlines flight with 260 passengers that departed JFK for San Juan, Puerto Rico, was forced to turn around after a loaded passenger got out of control, pouring liquor on other passengers and screaming he had planted a bomb on board. The man, who was drinking from a large bottle of scotch that he had brought aboard, became enraged when flight attendants asked him to stop splashing alcohol on other passengers. He allegedly started screaming and punching his seat before boasting to attendants about the bomb. The pilot turned back to New York, where the passenger was led of the airplane. No explosives were found.[8]

A woman on a Continental flight from Anchorage to Seattle pleaded

guilty to a felony count of interfering with a flight crew after her behavior
caused the plane to return to Anchorage. The woman's actions included
profane speech, throwing a full can of beer at a flight attendant, hitting a
flight attendant in the chest, and biting the crew's first officer after
punching him several times in the face when he tried to subdue her.

Although the woman took full responsibility for her actions, she also
said she doesn't remember what happened on the plane. She told the court
she was having a blackout caused by beer and liquor that she had consumed before boarding the flight in Anchorage with her boyfriend.

"Um, see I drank beer and that peppermint stuff . . . peppermint
schnapps," she said.

An empty bottle of peppermint schnapps was found in the seat-back
pocket where the woman had been sitting on the plane.

Hours after the plane returned to Anchorage, the woman reportedly
registered a 0.113 on a blood alcohol test. The legal blood alcohol level for
driving in Alaska is 0.10.

The U.S. Attorney prosecuting the case also asked the judge to have the
woman pay restitution to Continental Airlines for the amount of fuel the
plane had to dump when it turned around thirty minutes into the flight.[9]

In one of the more violent air rage incidents in Canadian history, a
Scottish woman brutally assaulted a female flight attendant during a
Canada 3000 flight from Glasgow to Toronto after being refused a drink.
Inspector John Byrne, who investigated the matter, said, "This is one of the
worst cases of air rage we've ever seen. It was a flight from hell."

Byrne said police were called to the airport to meet the flight, which
had two hundred passengers on board, and arrest the female passenger. It
was discovered that the woman had been drinking duty-free booze during
the flight. After being refused a drink from a flight attendant, she began
swearing profusely and challenged her to a fight. According to passengers,
she had her fists up and was ready to duke it out. Other crew members
joined in and told her to settle down. At this point, she passed out on the
aisle of the plane and was lifted to her seat, where she slept for two hours.
After she woke up, she was again refused a drink, charged the attendant,
and punched her twice, bloodying her face.

The drunk woman was finally restrained by the other flight attendants,
who tied her up "hog-style" with plastic restraints. She was sentenced to

four days in jail and sent home to Scotland. "The only place she saw in Canada was the airport and the jail," said Inspector Byrne.[10]

On an American Airlines flight from Dallas to London, the drunken behavior of a man forced the plane to make an emergency landing at Boston's Logan Airport. According to airport spokesman Philip Orlandella, "The man was drinking his own liquor on the plane. He was standing up, making noises, and using vulgarities."

Orlandella said the copilot left the cockpit tried to calm the passenger, but he continued to act out, poking his finger at members of the flight crew.[11]

A businesswoman on a Virgin Atlantic flight from Newark to London's Gatwick was charged with assaulting a flight steward and another flight crew member. Apparently, the woman had been drinking miniature bottles of vodka that she had bought from the duty-free stores at the airport and consumed on board.

A woman who suffers from Hepatitis C was sentenced to ten days in jail after she pleaded guilty to endangering the life of a flight attendant and assaulting others aboard a flight from Paris to Toronto.

About halfway through the seven-hour flight, the woman started yelling at other passengers and punched two flight attendants after she demanded to talk to her husband in Paris.

According to court records, the intoxicated woman bit the hand of one steward. During the air rage incident, the woman became increasingly agitated and aggressive, crawled in the aisle and growled like an animal. She told flight attendants that her husband had killed her children, then changed her story to say that she had killed her children and was going to kill herself.

The judge in the case agreed with the woman's defense lawyer, who claimed that the incident wouldn't have occurred had the passenger not consumed the bottle of cognac she had brought on the plane.[12]

"THE BOOZE MADE ME DO IT!"

The mix of alcohol and the rigors of air travel can cause people to do things they might not normally do.

On an American Airlines flight from Dallas to Manchester, England, two passengers, one male and one female, who didn't know each other previously, were sitting in adjacent seats. During the seven-hour flight, passengers complained that the two got drunk, fondled each other, and removed the woman's pants and top. When airline attendants asked them to stop, they became angry and abusive.

Upon arrival in Manchester, they were arrested. The male was quoted as saying, "We became a little over-familiar that's all." Both had been returning from business trips in the U.S. Their case attracted huge publicity in Britain, and both were fired from their jobs. She was fined $1,599 and he was sentenced to pay $1,987.

At their sentencing, the woman, who left the court with her husband, said in a statement that her behavior "was a matter of regret." The man said his wife and three children had been humiliated. Through his lawyer, he asked for privacy to "rebuild a relationship I nearly threw away through my own drunken stupidity."[13]

On a Singapore Airlines flight from Los Angeles to Singapore via Taipei, a passenger from California slapped a male flight attendant and put him into a headlock after the flight attendant blocked him from entering the cockpit. The male passenger started a commotion on the plane when the cabin crew told him they would no longer serve him alcohol since he had become rowdy and was annoying other passengers.

He then headed to the cockpit and punched the flight attendant, who stopped him at the business-class section. When other passengers and stewards tried to hold him back, the enraged passenger kicked the male steward on the left shin.

On orders from the captain, the stewards used a plastic strip to bind the man's wrists together. Still shouting and trying to get up from this seat, the man was stopped by another steward, who he bit on the right hand.

The man later said his behavior was caused by the effects of the alcohol and the depression he was experiencing because his wife had been recently hospitalized.

A passenger aboard a flight from Glasgow to Cyprus staged the "Full Monty" after he became so drunk on vodka that he didn't know what he was doing.

Cabin crew first became alarmed when they saw the man downing vodka from a bottle. Flight attendants took the bottle from his hands and ushered him to a part of the aircraft where there were empty seats, to sleep off the effects of the drink.

Later, the crew saw he had returned to his original seat and was removing a wet T-shirt and putting a fresh one on. Suddenly, he removed his jogging pants and boxer shorts too, exposing himself to the young children seated near him.

As he appeared in front of the judge, the man claimed to be disgusted with himself but genuinely had no recollection of what had taken place because of the amount of alcohol he had consumed.

A United flight from Tokyo to San Francisco was forced to turn back to Nairta Airport after an intoxicated passenger told flight attendants he had a bomb. The Japanese man was near the rear lavatory of the aircraft, walking up the aisle and smoking a cigarette, when he was told twice to be seated and extinguish the cigarette. After the second warning, the passenger produced an air sickness bag and stated in English that he had a bomb. The captain and the rest of the crew were advised of the situation, and several crew members, with the help of passengers, tackled the man.

Upon arrival at Narita Airport, the suspected device was placed in an aluminum carrier and covered with blankets. The "bomb" was discovered to be a plastic cup filled with trash. The man told police he was only joking and that the six beers he drank before boarding had taken their toll.

A drunken passenger on an Air France flight from Paris to Hong Kong stripped naked, believing he was sleeping in his own bed at home. The man, a Portuguese tourist, became drunk at the airplane's bar and was told to return to his seat. But shortly afterwards, a woman sleeping next to him awoke to find him lying naked next to her.

The crew covered the man with a blanket and let him sleep for two or three hours before waking him up and asking him to put on his clothes. Passengers told the *South Morning Post*, "The cabin was in total chaos. It was so funny yet embarrassing. We wondered how the passenger was given so much alcohol by Air France."[14]

Airline spokeswoman Jose Greenwood said she didn't know how many drinks he had had, but asserted that the airline would not alter its bar practices. "We want people to feel comfortable on our flights, but not to the extent that they walk around in the nude like they're at home," she said.[15]

A United flight from Chicago to Hong Kong was forced to make an emergency landing when a drunken passenger caused havoc on board and threatened the cabin crew. The flight, with almost three hundred people on board, touched down in Alaska so the air rage offender could be taken into custody.

Reportedly, the male passenger became upset when a female flight attendant told him if he did not stop his obnoxious advances towards her she would be forced to notify the captain. When he continued, she reached for the flight attendant's phone. The man ripped the phone from the wall and tussled with other members of the cabin crew. He was eventually subdued and handcuffed by air crew and other passengers.[16]

Two drunken Germans, apparently looking for a toilet during a conference at Frankfurt airport, got on a plane by mistake and flew to Moscow. The twenty-year old men were wandering around the airport when they found themselves on the tarmac and boarded a shuttle bus, which drove to an aircraft bound for the Russian capital.

"They got in and sat in the back of the airplane, which then flew to Moscow," said the Frankfurt state prosecutor, Mr. Job Tilmann. On arrival in Moscow, they noticed it was cold and realized they had no passports, let alone entry visas. Russian police put them on a flight back to Frankfurt, where they met by Federal Border Police who charged them with joyriding.[17]

THE EFFECTS OF ILLEGAL DRUGS

Beyond alcohol, drugs of all kinds—including illegal narcotics and tobacco—are used by millions of airline passengers. The mixture of the rigors of air travel with these chemicals often leads to erratic and dangerous situations. Several of the worst air rage cases have involved individuals under the influence of illegal drugs.

On a recent flight to Seattle, a male passenger jumped up and claimed he was seeing faces in the television screens that told him he should report immediately to Tampa. The man, who passengers later said was sweating heavily, began to pour water over his head and run toward the back of the plane. When he reached the rear door, he tried to kick it in. Terrified passengers afterward explained to authorities that "they thought they would be sucked out like a Hoover." Seven passengers and crewmembers were needed to restrain the man, who was later discovered to be on a bad LSD trip. Had he succeeded in opening the rear door, he may have brought down the Boeing 737 with all 130 passengers on board—killing nearly as many people as died in the Oklahoma City bombing.

A male passenger aboard an America West flight became unruly as the plane was taxiing for departure from Tucson to Los Angeles. The passenger arose from his seat and began to shout racial epithets at a Hispanic mother and her children, who were seated next to him. He then broke an armrest and swung it at a flight attendant before trying to kick in the door to the flight deck. As the plane returned to the gate, the passenger began to shout that the plane would "blow up." Two police officers and a flight attendant were injured subduing the passenger, who was arrested and later discovered to be on a bad acid trip.

On a Delta flight from Atlanta to Tampa, a passenger allegedly jumped up out of his seat and began shouting obscenities at no one in particular. He then broke an armrest off a seat and attempted to kick open the cockpit door. Fortunately, he was distracted by flight attendants and passengers seated near the front of the aircraft and was not able to gain entry. The pilots quickly taxied to the closest gate as the man made repeated attempts to enter the cockpit. Frightened passengers felt helpless as the man screamed that the plane was "hijacked," and would "blow up." The pilots made it back into the gate just as the man allegedly began threatening to use physical violence. Police officers rushed aboard the aircraft and fought with the man until he was subdued. Two police officers and a flight attendant were injured in the incident. The reasons for his behavior were uncertain, although toxicology reports found traces of PCP, marijuana, and cocaine in the man's system.

A Turkish male passenger attempted to hijack an aircraft with a toy panda bear. The passenger stated that he had an explosive device hidden in the teddy bear and demanded to be flown to Tehran's airport, which was closed at the time. The flight crew convinced the man that they didn't have enough fuel to make it to Iran and needed to land the plane immediately in Turkey. The hijacker, convinced of the fuel shortage, allowed the aircraft to land in Turkey. The aircraft was on the ground for only about thirty minutes when he decided to release the twenty passengers seated in the first-class section. The hijacker wanted to be in first class by himself and had been enjoying the service provided by the flight attendants.

Officials in Turkey refused the captain's request for fuel, as Turkish security forces were preparing to make a major assault against the aircraft. Just after he finished his second meal, the hijacker was overpowered by passengers in the coach section of the aircraft. The passengers, armed only with wine bottles, proceeded to beat the man until the Turkish security forces rushed the aircraft and saved the hijacker from certain death. The teddy bear was removed from the aircraft by explosives experts; however, no explosives were found. There were no injuries to the passengers or crew, but the man sustained multiple cuts, bruises, and abrasions. The man's motive was never determined; however, he was reported to be taking illegal drugs at the time.

An individual who purportedly was under the influence of narcotics created a disturbance at the Hartsfield International Airport in Atlanta, Georgia. An individual approached the security checkpoint with a .45 caliber handgun aimed at the back of a ticketed passenger. According to witnesses, the gunman had "words" with the passenger just prior to the incident, and may have been involved a dispute over a parking space in the airport parking facility.

When the individual was challenged at the checkpoint by a security screener, he doused the passenger with gasoline from a plastic bag he had been carrying in his jacket and attempted to force his way through the checkpoint. The individual was immediately apprehended and arrested by police, who were stationed at the checkpoint. The handgun contained eight bullets, and the individual also had matches and a knife in his pocket. The individual was charged with aggravated assault, committing terrorists threats, and carrying gasoline for use as an incendiary device. He was transported to a local jail. Although there was no official motive for his actions, illegal drugs appear to be a contributing factor.

The actions of an Australian man who threatened to open the door on an Ansett Airlines plane during flight and kill a crew member were defended as "the results of a attention deficit hyperactivity disorder and his immature personality, combined with excessive alcohol and use of heroin, cocaine, and marijuana."

Two hours into the flight from Melbourne to Perth, flight attendants stopped serving alcohol to the man after he began bragging to them of his previous air rage conviction. At least three times during the flight, cabin crew were forced to stop him from trying to open the aircraft door.

The passenger also refused to fasten his seatbelt and continually stood up during a period of severe turbulence, using obscene and aggressive language and threatening to kill a flight attendant who approached him.[18]

Shortly after takeoff, an Indian student on board an Air India flight from Calcutta to Dubai began screaming at the woman seated next to him for no apparent reason. When he was asked by other passengers to cease and desist, he became violent and started punching everyone around him. Then, he suddenly announced he was going to "settle the score with everyone" and rushed to the cockpit, yelling, "I have a bomb!"

He was subsequently overpowered by the passengers and crew and was arrested upon the plane's return to Calcutta. Police discovered that he was under the influence of methamphetamines, and the package he was carrying was found to contain fruit.

A man burst into the cockpit of a commuter flight from Toronto to Chicago holding an object in his hands and shouting, "Let us fly to Holland. Over there, narcotics are sold freely." The man, apparently reacting to something that was said, struck the pilot, and a scuffle ensued. The man was eventually overpowered, restrained, and turned over to authorities when the plane landed.

A subsequent investigation revealed the man had been just released from prison. Moreover, it was discovered that the ex-con had been rejected from entry into a methadone clinic earlier that day because of threatening behavior toward a nurse. Using his last dollars, the deranged man purchased an airline ticket under the insane notion that if he could get to Holland, he would be able get his fix.

THE AIRLINES AS DRUG CARRIERS

The preeminence of the global drug trade has led to the use of the air transport system as a primary carrier of illegal drugs. For cabin crews and passengers, the mere presence of "mules" compromises the flight's safety and security. A "mule" is typically someone who either swallows or has surgically implanted within him several sealed condoms of illegal drugs immediately before boarding a flight. Upon arrival, the mules either extract the drugs themselves or have surgery performed to remove them from their bodies. As carriers of illegal narcotics, it is not too difficult to envision such individuals as ominous threats to all those around them. And, again, at thirty-five thousand feet, you can't get off the plane or call the police for help.

Recently a man from Jamaica was arrested in Toronto when he danced what police call the "funky chicken." According to reports, the man was singled out because he displayed typical signs of drug packets bursting inside his body. "We call it the funky chicken because of their frenetic body movements," said customs spokesman Duncan Smith.

Agents offered to call for medical attention, which the man repeatedly refused, but they insisted and ended up saving his life. "The guy died a couple of times. He was in extremely grave condition before being revived at a local hospital," Smith said. The man had ingested 360 grams of cocaine. His companion, who was also arrested, had swallowed 100 grams of hashish and inserted one kilogram of cocaine into her vagina.[19]

A Dutchman stopped at Birmingham (England) International Airport was found to have 101 packages in his stomach. The passenger was stopped as he was passing through the Green Channel at the airport after he had aroused officers' suspicion.

A search of the mule's bags found a bottle of glycerin, a liquid often used to aid in the swallowing of drug parcels. He was taken to a local hospital, where an X-ray showed his stomach was filled with the packages. Customs spokesman Mark Powell said, "It's an awful lot to be carrying inside your stomach. Each package was the size of two thumbs put together."[20]

An Indonesian man was arrested at Japan's Narita Airport after an X-ray examination detected some lumps in his stomach and intestine, which were later found to be wraps of heroin. Found in the man's body were a total of about 290 grams of heroin with an estimated street value of $300,000. The smuggling attempt was perilous at best, as only 0.01 gram of heroin is enough to cause death from shock.

At the customs examination office, officers found a number of aspects exhibited by the passenger to be very suspicious, including his paleness and a tendency to wander around. He later admitted he swallowed thirty-two wraps of heroin powder with orange juice at a Bangkok hotel the previous day.

The mule said he was asked by some Bangkok acquaintances to take heroin to Japan. He said he had accepted the request because his folk craft business back home was not fairing well and he needed the money.[21]

Beyond placing drugs into their bodies for transport, mules also use a wide variety of other methods to try to sneak illegal narcotics into a given country.

A Canadian man was arrested at Tampa International Airport on charges of trying to smuggle three and one-half pounds of cocaine. He had hollowed out wood panels in the bottom of his luggage and stuffed them with packages of cocaine, worth $300,000 on the street. A customs official became suspicious when he thought the bottom of the bag seemed unnaturally hard, said Bob Pritchett, narcotics detective for the airport. Police said Williamson was on his way to Detroit from Jamaica.[22]

Police arrested a Singaporean man attempting to leave Cambodia with thousands of methamphetamine pills strapped to his body after they discovered more than nine thousand pills hidden beneath his pants. An airport spokesman said the man walked through an X-ray that showed he was hiding the methamphetamines around his waist and up his legs.

As technology provides new weapons in the fight against drug smuggling, so the criminals have become more cunning in finding ways to avoid detection.

One man with a wooden leg was stopped at London City Airport and when officers searched the false limb, they found $15,000 worth of marijuana inside.

Drug officers at Pearson International Airport in Toronto were left scratching their heads after seizing nearly five pounds of cocaine hidden in the wig of a Canadian woman returning from the Caribbean. Customs agents and the Royal Canadian Mounted Police (RCMP) found nearly $400,000 worth of cocaine on the woman after a drug-sniffing dog became suspicious of the woman as she attempted to pass through Canadian customs.

Customs spokesman Mark Butler said officers were baffled after they didn't find any drugs on the woman's body. He said officers then became suspicious of the woman's hair.

"We asked her if she was wearing a wig, which officers determined was way too heavy," Butler said. Butler said the cocaine was found sewn into the plastic-lined skullcap of the wig. After the seizure, officers said the woman began complaining of a headache from the weight of the drugs she was carrying on her head during the four-hour flight.[23]

Other methods that have been uncovered by customs officials include an Islamic prayer book that contained 46 grams of heroin, a wooden duck holding cannabis, and a flower in a glass vase which held more than $25,000 worth of cocaine.

In one of the more revolting cases in recent memory, a Colombian couple traveling with their newborn were stopped and searched at Miami

International Airport when flight attendants reported that the baby never moved during the five-hour flight from Bogota. After X-rays by U.S. customs officials, it was discovered that the baby was dead and her lifeless body had been filled with almost ten pounds of cocaine.

The transport of illegal narcotics is not limited to passengers. Ground crews and flight attendants have also been discovered using the airlines to smuggle drugs from one place to another.

Five Air Canada employees who worked as aircraft cleaners at Toronto's Pearson International Airport were among ten people charged in connection with a conspiracy to import almost $8 million worth of illegal drugs from Jamaica.

The drugs, including forty kilograms of cocaine, forty kilos of hash oil and twenty kilos of hashish, were seized by customs officers during a eleven-month investigation.

The drugs—mostly in small one and two-kilogram packets—were hidden inside the paneling of aircraft bathrooms and under seats in Jamaica. They were recovered by Air Canada employees in Toronto called "groomers," who had high security clearance to board and clean the planes.

"It's a pretty easy way to do it," Staff Sergeant Bill Matheson of the RCMP said of using airline workers to smuggle drugs.

"It's not like you have to body-pack it in, where there's a risk to couriers," Matheson said. "The groomers have access to the plane all the time."[24]

Police K-9 units patrolling the service area at Miami International Airport found more than a kilo of cocaine hidden inside an empty food tray. The dogs honed in on a truck filled with empty metal food carts that passengers commonly see flight attendants pushing up and down the aisles. Investigators ripped apart two of the carts and found several packages of cocaine stuffed under the top lid of one cart.[25]

Recently, two Servivensa flight attendants were caught strapping heroin to their bodies while working on flights from the airline's base in Caracas, Venezuela. According to U.S. Attorney Guy Lewis in Miami, a ring of seventeen people, including the flight attendants, smuggled thirty-three to forty-five pounds of heroin per week, with a wholesale value of about $42,000 a pound. The Caracas to Miami flight was the first leg of a distribution ring that ran from Florida to New York and Houston.[26]

NICOTINE ATTACKS

An overwhelming amount of physiological and psychological research suggests that barring smoking for nicotine-addicted passengers can easily lead
to higher levels of stress and increase the likelihood of an air rage incident.

Two smokers on a flight from Las Vegas caused panic when flames
began to billow out of the jacket under which they had been hiding to
smoke. Fellow passengers, seeing the smoke and thinking the aircraft was
on fire, screamed for the cabin crew to help. The fire in the burning jacket
was put out by the crew, who smothered it with blankets and doused it with
soda. The man and woman were detained at the destination city for only an
hour when it was decided by an airline official that "a misunderstanding of
the preflight instructions was responsible for their behavior."

A woman from the Middle East living in the United States was deported
after she bit a flight attendant who caught her smoking on a plane. The
woman was traveling with her three-year-old on a American Eagle flight
from Cleveland to Chicago.

After takeoff, a passenger on the commuter plane saw the female passenger light a cigarette and told her she could not smoke on the plane. The
woman reportedly put out the cigarette, but later went into the bathroom to
light up again. She was caught by a flight attendant, who confiscated her
boarding pass and lighter.

As the flight attendant was on his way to the front of the plane to fill
out a report, the woman followed, yelling at him to return her ticket and
pulling her boarding pass from the flight attendant's hand. After he
ordered the woman back to her seat, he started passing incident report
forms to other passengers. That is when the woman bit him on the right
forearm, breaking the skin. A police officer on board and another passenger were able to restrain the female smoker, who tried unsuccessfully
to bite them as well.

She was later arrested, convicted, sentenced to time already served,
and deported as part of her plea agreement with prosecutors.[27]

On a flight from London's Gatwick to Malaga, Spain, a female flight
attendant was attacked by a male passenger with a vodka bottle after she
discovered him smoking in the lavatory.

According to the flight attendant, Fiona Weir, the flight began calmly enough as the man was warned he would not be served alcohol and could not smoke.

"During the flight, I was doing drink service and this passenger came up the aisle and went to the toilet.

"When he went to the toilet he was in there for a considerable amount of time so I remained in the area to check the toilet.

"When he came out I let him go back to his seat, I never said anything to him, and I checked the toilet and I knew he had been smoking."

Ms. Weir then went to his seat, looked him in the eye and told him she knew he had been smoking and if he did it again he would be in "serious trouble."

For the remainder of the flight, Ms. Weir says, "The male passenger gave me a stream of verbal abuse and persisted during the whole flight to abuse me and my rear crew members, who were female."

When they touched down in Malaga, the male passenger was informed by cabin crew that he was going to be arrested by waiting police. At this point, he rushed toward Ms. Weir, smashed a vodka bottle over her head, and raked its jagged edges across her body as she cowered in the galley in the back of the plane.

Four passengers leaped on the man as she opened the rear door, staggered down steps, and collapsed on the tarmac at Malaga Airport. From her hospital bed, Ms. Weir said: "I just knew if I didn't get out of the aircraft, he was going to kill me." She suffered ten stitches in her back and eight in her arm. She also had a badly bruised face and head.[28]

Needless to say, the abuse of alcohol, the taking of illegal drugs, the transport of illegal narcotics, and the inability to smoke have become some of the most prevalent factors contributing to the rise of air rage incidents in recent years. Most people would agree that they are probably the easiest causes of air rage to identify and explain. Still, there are other factors that can lead directly to an air rage incident. To truly understand the scope and magnitude of the air rage crisis, these other factors must be explored as well.

4

MENTAL ILLNESS

Although Western societies are beginning to pay more attention to mental illness, experts agree that it is still a widely underdiagnosed disease. Given the vast number of people with mental illness, no one should be surprised that it can create problems in the cramped and stressful environment of an airplane.

In one of the more frightening examples of mental illness precipitating air rage, an apparently deranged passenger broke into the cockpit of a British Airways jumbo jet and grabbed the controls, sending the plane plummeting toward the ground before the crew regained control.

According to statements from passengers and crew, the man, after barging into the cockpit, disengaged the autopilot, and sent the plane hurtling into a ten-thousand-foot dive. The crew struggled with the man, who sent the plane into a second dive before the crew finally recovered command of the aircraft.

Many of the 379 passengers aboard the Boeing 747-400 from London to Nairobi screamed and prayed as they were jolted out of their early-morning slumber to find hysteria sweeping the cabin.

For more than two minutes, passengers believed they were going to die as the plane continued to plummet. Finally, after what have must seemed like an eternity, the man was overpowered by first-class passengers and flight crew.

During the melee, the intruder bit the ear of the captain and injured four other passengers and a crew member. The first officer was eventually able to get the man out of the cockpit and the reserve officer was able to fly the aircraft.

Aviation experts believe that had the incident raged on for another four or five seconds, the copilot would not have been able to regain control of the plane because the aircraft was nearly on its back.

The results of the medical examinations conducted on the passenger showed that the twenty-seven-year-old Kenyan was mentally disturbed. Passengers said they saw the perpetrator wandering around one section of the plane for about thirty minutes before he made his way toward the cockpit and burst in, lunging for the controls.

One hour into a recent flight from Miami to New York, a young couple sitting in coach class calmly asked the flight attendant if they could move into the two empty seats in the first-class section because "They believed the elderly woman sitting in the aisle next them was trying to kill them." The attendant, believing they were joking, politely said "no" and continued serving drinks. At this point, a seemingly normal trip became a near-disaster. The girlfriend, incredulous that she was denied an upgrade, became enraged. Screaming obscenities at the top of her lungs, she jumped up from her seat and made a mad dash, on her knees, for first class.

Following his girlfriend's lead, the man stood up and announced to everyone that the overhead compartments were filled with machine guns and that she was carrying a bomb. As his girlfriend continued to crawl toward the front of the plane, the boyfriend grabbed two coffeepots and yelled, "These are my weapons!" as he threw coffee on a flight attendant and burned her. Reaching first class, the man kicked a hole in the cockpit door and the woman grabbed the emergency exit handle, shouting, "We're taking this plane down!" Fortunately, four male passengers tackled the boyfriend before he could do anything else, beating him unconscious, while two other flight attendants subdued the woman and then sat on her until the flight could be diverted to Atlanta. Upon arrival, the two were sent to a hospital for observation. They were released after it was discovered that they were both under psychiatric evaluation in their hometown. Their family doctor had ordered them to take their medication and stay within five miles of their residence. Unfortunately, they had the urge to travel and acted upon it.

Mental illness is a general term that refers to a group of illnesses that affect the brain, in the same way that heart disease refers to a group of illnesses affecting the heart. Mental illness may influence the way a person thinks, behaves, responds, and interacts with other people. And, like heart diseases, for example, mental illnesses can vary in severity and type. Many people suffering from mental illness may not look as though they are ill or have something wrong, while others may appear to be confused, agitated, or withdrawn.

All of us have oddities and most of us get through life despite them. Some sufferers of mental illness may spend an entire lifetime completely unaware of their affliction. Others may display problematic characteristics at an early age. For still others, mental illness can be transient—it can come and go throughout the duration of their lives. Some people experience their illness only once and fully recover. In others, it recurs throughout their lives. Whatever the case, it is a myth that mental illness is a weakness or defect in character and that sufferers can get better simply "by pulling themselves up by their bootstraps." Mental illnesses are as real as heart disease and cancer—they require treatment.

Some of the more commonly known psychiatric disorders are:

- Depression
- Manic depression (also known as bipolar disorder)
- Anxiety disorders, including specific phobias (fears), social phobia, panic disorder, agoraphobia, claustrophobia, obsessive compulsive disorder, and generalized anxiety disorder
- Dementia
- Eating disorders, such as bulimia and anorexia
- Sleep disorders
- Attention deficit/hyperactivity disorders
- Learning disorders
- Sexual disorders
- Dissociative disorders, such as multiple personality disorder
- Personality disorders, such as borderline personality disorder and antisocial personality disorder
- Schizophrenia and other psychotic disorders, such as delusion[1]

THE FEAR OF FLYING

According Dr. R. Reid Wilson, one of the foremost authorities on the fear of flying, one in every six adults is phobic about air travel.[2] He lists the reasons people fear flying:

- Panic attacks
- Embarrassing self
- Weather
- Traveling more than a certain distance
- Closed-in spaces
- Being trapped (door closing)
- Heights
- Being out of control
- Turbulence
- Trusting air traffic controllers
- Crowds
- Crashing
- Takeoffs
- Trusting airline industry
- Stuffiness
- Dying trusting
- Landings
- The mechanics
- Nausea
- Being far away from loved ones
- Flying over water
- Trusting the integrity of the plane

In addition to these reasons, Dr. Wilson, like other experts on the subject, recognizes that heavy media coverage of airline crashes contributes to the problem of fear of flying. Dr. Arnold Barnett, a researcher at the Massachusetts Institute of Technology, compared the number of front-page stories in the *New York Times* that addressed six sources of death and tragedy: AIDS, automobiles, cancer, homicide, suicide, and airplane crashes. Over the period of a year, stories about airline accidents far outnumbered stories about any other of the five sources of death.

When considered on a per-death basis, the number of airline stories was sixty times the number of stories on AIDS and more than eight thousand times the number of stories about cancer, the nation's number two killer.[3]

An Alaska Airlines passenger, extremely fearful about his first flight, triggered a health scare after vomiting blood, splashing seven passengers and telling crew members he that might be infected with hepatitis C.

A TWA flight from Rome to New York was diverted to Shannon, Ireland, when a note was discovered in the lavatory stating a "bomb" would explode. The aircraft landed safely in Ireland, and a search yielded no explosives. During a continuation of the flight the next day, a small fire broke out in a lavatory. It was quickly extinguished and no damage resulted. The plane landed safely at its destination in New York.

An immigration officer noticed that the handwriting of a seventeen-year-old Egyptian passenger was similar to the handwriting on the bomb threat note. The youth admitted that he wrote the note and started the fire. It seems his motive was to keep from going to the United States and return to Egypt since he was terrified of flying.

PSYCHOTHERAPEUTIC MEDICATIONS AND THE RIGORS OF AIR TRAVEL

Fortunately, over the past thirty years, psychiatric research has made great strides in the precise diagnosis and successful treatment of many mental illnesses. In the past, severely mentally ill people were warehoused in public institutions because they were feared to be disruptive or potentially harmful to themselves and others. Today, most people who suffer from a mental illness—including those that can be extremely debilitating, such as schizophrenia—can be treated effectively and lead full and active lives.

Some disorders are mild, while others are serious and long lasting. Even the worst conditions can often be helped through psychotherapy and medication.

Compared to other types of treatment, psychotherapeutic medications are relative newcomers in the fight against mental illness. It was only about thirty-five years ago that the first one, chlorpromazine, was introduced. But considering the short time they've been around, psychotherapeutic medications have made dramatic changes in the treatment of mental disorders. People who, years ago, might have spent much of their lives in mental hospitals because of crippling mental illness may now go in only for brief treatment, or might receive all their treatment on an outpatient clinical basis.

Psychotherapeutic medications also may make other kinds of treatment more effective. Someone who is too depressed to talk, for instance, can't get much benefit from psychotherapy or counseling; but often, the right medication will improve symptoms so that the person can respond better to other therapies.

Another benefit of these medications is an increased understanding of the causes of mental illness. Scientists have learned a great deal more about the workings of the brain as a result of their investigations into how psychotherapeutic medications relieve disorders such as psychosis, depression, anxiety, obsessive compulsive disorder, and panic disorder.

Just as aspirin can reduce a fever without clearing up the infection that causes it, psychotherapeutic medications act by controlling symptoms. Like most drugs used in medicine, they correct or compensate for some malfunction in the body. Psychotherapeutic medications do not cure mental illness, but they do lessen its burden. These medications can help a person get on with life despite some mental pain and, for some, difficulty coping with problems. For example, drugs like chlorpromazine can turn off the "voices" heard by some people with schizophrenia and help them to perceive reality more accurately. And antidepressants can lift the dark, heavy moods of depression.

How long someone must take a psychotherapeutic medication depends on the disorder. Many depressed and anxious people may need medication for a single period—perhaps for several months—and then never have to take it again. For some conditions, such as schizophrenia or manic-depressive illness, medication may have to be taken indefinitely or, perhaps, intermittently.

Like any medication, psychotherapeutic medications do not produce the same effect in everyone. Some people may respond better to one medication than another. Some may need larger dosages than others do. Some experience annoying side effects, while others do not.

The development of psychotherapeutic medications in the treatment of mental illness is relatively recent; consequently, not a lot of research has been done on how the environment inside an airplane may affect those individuals who are taking or in need of a particular medication. Therefore, the negative physiological and psychological impacts of these drugs or their absence on airline passengers are simply not known.

Because of the sheer volume of legal prescriptions taken by millions of people, research cannot possibly determine which medications will affect which people during a flight. Therefore, the negative physiological and psychological impacts of these drugs on airline passengers are simply not known until it's too late. Moreover, the absence of needed prescribed drugs could be equally devastating.

Aboard a flight to Portland, Oregon, a seemingly normal, well-dressed businessman attempted, without warning, to yank open a pressurized cabin door at thirty thousand feet. When he realized the door wouldn't open, he torched a magazine and screamed, "God does not exist. I am on my way to Key West to meet extraterrestrials who have recognized me as the Supreme Being." Two passengers helped the flight crew subdue the man. It was later discovered the man had placed his antidepressant medication into his checked luggage and had failed to take the tablets every four hours as prescribed by his physician.

A Florida man was sentenced to six months in prison for causing a disturbance that injured four people and forced the emergency landing of a Delta Airlines flight at Las Vegas.

The man had been diagnosed as a schizophrenic about five years before the incident, but, according to court records, medication had succeeded in controlling his behavior during that period.

An FBI spokesman said the man became upset on the airplane after a flight attendant refused to serve him a beverage before his turn. He immediately stood up and tipped over the serving tray, spilling hot coffee on a woman and her seventeen-month-old child. He then proceeded to strike a twelve-year-old girl in the head and did the same to another woman.

The man's attorney said the incident occurred after a trip to Vietnam with his mother. As he was departing to return to the United States, customs officials in Vietnam had confiscated his medication, and this caused him to be disoriented on the flight from Los Angeles to Atlanta.[4]

An unemployed Italian passenger on a flight from Rome to London's Gatwick Airport was convicted of drugging a fellow airline passenger into a coma during the flight in order to rob him. The perpetrator was found guilty of slipping the sleeping drug Flurazepam into the drink of a businessman.

The court later heard from the victim, a Japanese businessman, who could not be awakened on board the flight since he was comatose. After the flight, he was taken to a local hospital. The victim said $200 had been taken from his jacket, which was stored in the overhead bin, after he collapsed on the Alitalia flight.

The jury needed only two hours to convict the man of theft and of administering a noxious substance. The judge ordered him to be admitted to a mental hospital. He said that the man had been diagnosed as suffering from a bipolar mood disorder, or manic depression, and his medication was adversely affected by the cabin environment.[5]

A Russian national from Dagestan who commandeered a plane to Israel had the hijacking charges against him lifted because doctors concluded he is a schizophrenic. Court doctors, who examined the twenty-seven-year-old man for more than three months, determined that he was not responsible for his actions because of his mental illness. The man had no previous criminal record.

THE RIGORS OF AIR TRAVEL AND MENTAL ILLNESS

While we know that many mental illnesses are caused by a physical dysfunction of the brain, we do not know exactly what triggers the illness. However, we are beginning to see the strong role that stress may play. Stress may trigger some mental illnesses or may prolong episodes. Stress can also result from a person's developing a mental illness. In short, the relationship between stress and mental illness is complex. People react differently to stress: some respond psychologically with mental anguish while others might respond physically, with elevated blood pressure, for example.

Almost everyone, even the most seasoned passenger, experiences anxiety at one time or another during the air travel experience. Whether it is "butterflies in the stomach" during a period of turbulence, or sweaty palms before takeoff or touchdown, or a reddening of the face when the connecting flight is delayed, anxiety is seemingly commonplace. Other symptoms of anxiety may include irritability, uneasiness, jumpiness, feelings of apprehension, rapid or irregular heartbeat, stomachache, nausea, faintness, and breathing problems.

Nevertheless, anxiety is often manageable and mild. But sometimes it can present serious problems. Phobias, which are persistent, irrational fears and are characterized by avoidance of certain objects, places, and things, sometimes accompany anxiety. A panic attack is a severe form of anxiety that may occur suddenly and is marked by symptoms of nervousness, breathlessness, pounding heart, and sweating. Sometimes a fear of death takes over. Antianxiety medications help to calm and relax the anxious person and subdue the troubling symptoms.

Still, for those individuals who suffer from mental illness, the realities and anxieties associated with air travel may prove to be too much to handle.

A U.S. citizen lost control on a parked British Airways flight from Hamburg to London when he found out the plane would be landing at Heathrow Airport instead of Gatwick. The man was charged with assaulting a flight attendant by slapping her in the face. After the aircraft pulled back into the gate, the pilot ordered him off the plane.

As he was being escorted off the plane by police into the terminal, the man grabbed the officer's gun out of its holster. The man aimed the gun at the officer, then at himself, pulling the trigger twice each time, but, luckily, the gun did not fire. Tests later revealed the passenger was not drunk or under the influence of any chemical substance.

A flight traveling from Phoenix to Austin had to make an unscheduled landing because of the actions of a distressed, unruly passenger. The interesting point in this case was the fact that the passenger happened to be a pilot for a rival airline.

Reportedly, the passenger, who had been a pilot for thirteen years, was yelling "get away from me" over and over to flight attendants and those seated immediately around him. Detective Sergeant Philip Young of the Tucson Airport told the *Arizona Daily Star* that man was "yelling and screaming and speaking in ways that didn't make a lot of sense." When the man was arrested for disorderly conduct, Young said, he resisted verbally but not physically.

It turned out that the man had been going though some marital problems and had recently lost a friend who committed suicide.[6]

An Australian woman became violent and was restrained three hours into a thirteen-hour flight from Sydney to San Francisco because she said "she was hearing people talking in her headphones and it was driving her crazy."

The woman, who was traveling with her son and nephew, allegedly stopped a flight attendant to complain about "voices" in her headphones. According to Officer Henry Friedlander, a spokesman for the San Francisco Police Department's airport bureau, the woman then "began to act very erratically, yelling, and banging her head against the aircraft walls."

Cabin crew members decided to restrain the woman, and called in the chief pilot. She physically fought off the crew, biting and punching them as they put her in plastic restraints, from which she broke loose and had to be restrained again.

A doctor on the flight gave the woman injections of Valium and an antidepressant, but she remained combative, injuring the hands of one of the crew members.

Fire and ambulance personnel who responded when the flight landed called police, who said they found the woman cuffed, collapsed, and unresponsive in a back row. As police moved in, she allegedly became violent again, injuring one of the officers.

Friedlander said the woman was taken to San Mateo County General Hospital for psychiatric evaluation.[7]

A Southwest Airlines flight from Kansas City to Oakland, California, was forced to make an emergency landing when an unruly passenger punched a flight attendant in the chest. The male passenger allegedly became agitated, started yelling unintelligibly, and struck the flight attendant with his fist.

After the attack, the flight attendant who was struck and several other passengers, at least one of whom was an off-duty police officer, held the man in the back of the plane. According to FBI spokesperson Kevin Caudle, the man had to be physically held on the floor of the plane until it could make an emergency landing in Las Vegas.

The alleged assailant was on his way home from a business conference in Washington, D.C., when the incident occurred. "The cause is unknown, but he had not been drinking—he was not intoxicated," Caudle said.[8]

A businessman traveling in first class on a flight from New York to Los Angeles eventually pleaded guilty to threatening female flight attendants with assault unless they posed for indecent pictures in the galley of the cabin. The man, who also spent most of the flight watching a pornographic video on his laptop, later told authorities he was sexually repressed because his mistress left him when his wife sued for divorce.

OTHER FORMS OF MENTAL ILLNESS AND THE EXPRESSION OF AIR RAGE

Beyond phobias, anxieties, and the effects of psychotherapeutic medication, mental illness often rears it head in the form of other dysfunctions.

A fifteen-year-old English girl, who was traveling alone, was sexually assaulted by a drunken passenger on a long-haul flight from Kuala Lumpur to Amsterdam on KLM. Her parents had bought an unaccompanied minor ticket, expecting the cabin crew to keep a close eye on their daughter during the sixteen-hour flight.

But she was placed in the center of the aircraft next to two men and woke up two hours later to find one of them touching her leg. The passenger responsible was arrested when the aircraft landed in Amsterdam.

The family won an unprecedented legal ruling in favor of their bid to claim damages from KLM for psychological damage suffered by their daughter. The goings on of this flight essentially caused mental illness. The judge ruled that the depression she suffered could be regarded as an injury under the Warsaw Convention, which covers accidents on aircraft.[9]

A British man who was driven to the end of his rope by the noise from low-flying aircraft called the airport and threatened to attack staff and pilots.

One evening, the enraged man allegedly telephoned the air traffic control tower threatening to kill a pilot. After his arrest, the court heard that the man had allegedly said, "If I hear another plane I will come to the airport and stab the first pilot I see."

When he was arrested, the man admitted to police that he had called the tower and threatened to stab a pilot, but he said he never intended to carry out the threat.

The man's defense attorney admitted her client had reached his limit, but was seeking help from a doctor. She further told the court that he had an IQ between 58 and 71 and he was now taking medication administered by a psychiatrist, which seemed to help him.[10]

An Italian male hijacked a flight en route from Marseille's Provence Airport to Orly Airport in Paris and diverted the Airbus A-320 aircraft to Paris's Charles de Gaulle Airport. The hijacker claimed to have an explosive device in his carry-on bag that he could detonate using a remote control. Upon landing in Paris, the hijacker demanded a televised news conference to promote his new political movement for the unification of Europe. He also used a mobile phone to call the French news service Agence France-Presse. The hijacker surrendered after several hours of negotiations; he was later determined to be mentally ill. No one was injured in the incident.

An Indonesian Special Forces officer fired into a crowd at Timika Airport in Indonesia, killing several passengers and wounding at least a dozen others. The officer had been a member of a unit deployed there after rioting had erupted near the airport. According to reports, the officer is believed to have been under a lot of stress and in a state of depression after hearing that two of his friends were killed the previous day. Indonesian authorities were horrified at the death toll and destruction at the airport, which was generally considered to be a safe haven. The man was put under house arrest where he was evaluated for six months by a team of psychiatrists.

Recently, a Spanish airliner was under the control of an air rage offender from Seville to Barcelona, Spain. During the flight, a male passenger held up a remote control device and threatened to blow up the plane, stating that he could detonate a bomb that he had placed in his suitcase, which was located in the aircraft's cargo hold. The hijacker demanded to be flown to Athens, Greece, but later changed his mind and demanded to be flown to Tel Aviv, Israel.

The flight crew convinced the man that they needed additional fuel and would have to divert to another city. The man agreed and the aircraft diverted to Valencia, Spain. While the aircraft was being fueled the hijacker released approximately twenty passengers, mostly children. After several hours, Spanish authorities identified the man as a psychiatric patient.

In an attempt to resolve the situation peacefully, the man spoke for several hours with his psychiatrist, who eventually convinced him that he should surrender. None of the passengers or crew were injured during the incident. A search of the plane and baggage in the cargo hold did not reveal an explosive device and the remote control device the man held in his hand was a television remote control.

A Chinese airliner was taken over by a Chinese man during a domestic flight from Chongqing, Sichuan Province, to Zhuhai, Guangdong Province. The man demanded that he be flown to Taiwan or he would blow up the aircraft with the explosives contained in his attaché case.

According to reports, the pilot put the aircraft in a steep dive, which caused the hijacker to lose his balance and send the attaché case airborne, over the heads of several passengers. Security guards and passengers then overpowered the hijacker before he could get back on his feet. Fortunately, there were no explosives found in the attaché case, which landed several rows away. The man was handcuffed to a seat until the flight could be diverted to Baiyun Airport in Guangzhou Province, where he was turned over to the authorities. There were no reported injuries as a result of the incident. It was reported that the individual had apparently been treated and released from a psychiatric hospital just prior to the incident.

A grounded Air Botswana pilot took an ATR-42 turboprop passenger plane without permission and crashed it into the apron at Sir Seretse Khama

International Airport in Gaborone. The pilot, who had been grounded by the airline's management because of his ill health, was angry because the airline would not reinstate him. After stealing the plane, the pilot began circling Gabarone. He then contacted the air traffic control center and indicated his intention to commit suicide.

During the two hours he circled the capital city, the pilot demanded to speak to Botswana's vice president, Ian Khama. As the pilot's call was about to be put through to Khama's office the plane began to run out of fuel. The pilot then began threatening to run into buildings or other targets on the ground. At one point, he contemplated crashing into the Air Botswana office building near the airport but decided against it when he learned there were people inside. Finally, the pilot gave authorities time to clear the area near the terminal, and he crash-landed into two other ATR planes sitting empty on the apron, killing himself.

On a flight from Nicaragua to Costa Rica, a Nicaraguan man attempted to take over an aircraft shortly after takeoff. The man doused a passenger and a portion of the aircraft's interior with gasoline and threatened to use his cigarette lighter. The man demanded that the aircraft be flown to San Andres Island, Columbia, however, the pilots told the man they did not have enough fuel and convinced him to go to Puerto Limon, Costa Rica.

According to Costa Rican authorities, the man was removed from the aircraft without incident when the aircraft landed. There was no injuries to the passengers or crew during the entire incident. The man was reported to be mentally unstable and was identified as an unemployed drug addict from Nicaragua. He was kept under psychiatric evaluation for several months and eventually released.

On January 12, 1999, Southwest Airlines Flight 923 from San Diego to San Jose, California, was diverted to the Burbank-Glendale-Pasadena Airport after a passenger threatened to kill other passengers. The passenger had boarded the plane in San Diego and fell asleep. After awakening following departure, he asked a flight attendant their destination. Upon being told, he replied that the plane was going to Hollywood, California, or he would begin killing people. The pilot stated that there was no airport in Hollywood, and he landed the plane in Burbank. The threatening passenger was arrested when the plane landed. He had no weapon and there were no injuries to the seventy-four passengers and five crew members onboard.

The individual was arraigned before a U.S. magistrate on charges of air piracy and interference with a flight crew member. He was also ordered to undergo a psychiatric examination and was found to be manic-depressive. In August, he pleaded guilty to a felony charge of interfering with a flight crew and in November was sentenced to serve two years in a federal prison.

Al Nippon Airways (ANA) flight 61 was hijacked by Yuji Nishizawa on July 23, 1999. The Boeing 747-400 aircraft carried 503 passengers and fourteen crew on a domestic flight from Tokyo's Haneda Airport to Sapporo. On the morning of the hijacking, Nishizawa had taken two JAL flights—from Tokyo to Osaka and back. He checked a bag containing two knives and carried another bag with him on the flight to Osaka. On the return flight to Tokyo, Nishizawa reportedly asked a flight attendant to allow him to see the cockpit of the 747-400 plane, probably as part of his plan. JAL authorizes cockpit tours on some flights, whereas ANA does not permit this practice on its domestic flights.

Upon returning to Haneda Airport, Nishizawa claimed his checked baggage and proceeded to the ANA departure gate to present his ticket for flight 61. He was not required to exit the baggage claim area and reenter through the normal departure ticketing and security procedures. In this way, Nishizawa was able to board flight 61 without having to pass through a screening checkpoint for carry-on bags. He carried with him his two bags, one of which contained the two knives.

ANA flight 61 departed Haneda Airport at 11:23 A.M. Approximately two minutes after takeoff, Nishizawa, seated in the aft section of the upper deck, stood up. When a flight attendant approached to tell him to be seated, he produced an eight-inch kitchen knife and demanded to be taken to the cockpit. He forced the flight attendant to knock on the door and pushed his way in when the door was opened. Once inside the cockpit the hijacker ordered the first officer to leave and then took his seat. Nishizawa gave the pilot instructions to fly to several different places: first to Yokosuka, a U.S. Navy base south of Tokyo; then to Oshima in the Izu Islands south of Yokosuka; and finally to Yokota Air Base. Complying with the hijacker's demands, the pilot declared an emergency with Tokyo flight control at 11:25 A.M. and turned the plane to the south. Meanwhile, the first officer and flight attendants cleared most passengers from the upper deck. Several ANA crew members who traveling as passengers on the flight on board joined with the first officer in attempting to hear what was taking place in the cockpit.

The pilot discussed heading and altitudes with Tokyo Flight Control between 11:25 A.M. and 11:46 A.M. He kept the transmit button pressed to enable his conversations with Nishizawa to be heard. As the plane flew over Kanagawa Province en route to Yokota Air Base, Nishizawa reportedly asked to fly the plane. Some reports suggest that he also told the pilot that he wanted to land the plane at Yokota. When the pilot refused, Nishizawa began to stab him in the neck. The pilot sustained multiple stab wounds, which resulted in such massive bleeding that he died almost instantly. As the attack was taking place, the plane repeatedly pitched up and down. Nishizawa took the controls from the copilot's seat and attempted to disengage the autopilot and descend into Yokota. The first officer and others outside the door rushed into the flight deck when they heard the plane's ground proximity warning alarm. Nishizawa was subdued as he fumbled with the controls, with the plane at an altitude of approximately six hundred feet. One ANA pilot took control and stopped the steep dive, while others tied Nishizawa to a seat with neckties and belts. The first officer then assumed control of the plane and returned to Haneda Airport, where all three runways had been closed in preparation for the emergency. The plane landed safely at 12:16 A.M. Police immediately entered the plane and the hijacker was taken into custody. There were no other injuries to crew members or passengers.

It is believed that Nishizawa hijacked the plane because, in his perception, Haneda Airport officials had failed to heed his warnings about security problems. He had claimed that these problems made Japanese airliners easy prey for hijackers. Nishizawa, as a student, reportedly held a part-time cargo handling position at Haneda Airport and gained some familiarity with the airport's operations. According to Japanese Transport Ministry officials, Nishizawa, in a letter, pointed out faults in security measures at Japanese airports. He also reportedly demanded compensation for his "investigations" into security problems.

Nishizawa also reportedly told investigators that he hijacked the plane because he wanted to fly a jumbo jet. He boasted of his piloting ability in flight simulation games. It was his experience and familiarity with these games that may have led him to believe that he could safely pilot a large aircraft. Police suspect that Nishizawa's repeated playing of simulation games and reading aeronautics books played a role not only in his decision to hijack the plane, but also in a plan to fly a plane under the Rainbow Bridge, which crosses Tokyo Bay.

It remains unclear why Nishizawa wanted to be flown to Yokosuka or Yokota Air Base. Some reports suggest that he was going to force the plane to land at the air base and then commit suicide. Police speculate that he was going to use one of the two knives he carried to kill himself.

On December 19, 1999, Nishizawa pleaded guilty to hijacking the aircraft and to killing the pilot. His lawyers have insisted that he is mentally ill and suffered a nervous breakdown when he committed the hijacking. Nishizawa faces a possible death penalty sentence, which is allowed under Japan's antihijacking law for incidents that result in fatalities.

An individual armed with only a pocketknife seized control of a commuter aircraft at Panama's international airport. The individual apparently followed a vehicle through a security gate and drove right up to the aircraft. Reportedly, the individual removed luggage from the trunk of his car and approached the aircraft waving his pocket knife. The would-be hijacker rushed the aircraft before anyone realized what was happening and took the pilot, copilot, and flight attendant hostage.

The terminal was cordoned off and police authorities boarded the aircraft, negotiating for several hours. The individual finally agreed to close his pocket knife and release the hostages, who were unharmed. The individual was apparently distraught over a relationship and just "needed to get away for a few days."

An Ohio man who pleaded guilty to charges he sexually assaulted a seven-year-old girl aboard a Northwest Airlines flight was sentenced to six months in prison. A federal judge in Birmingham, Alabama, sentenced the man after he entered a guilty plea to assaulting the girl while she was traveling alone from Birmingham to see her father in New Jersey.

The Birmingham judge ordered the man to pay a $5,000 fine, with interest, and $400 in restitution to the girl's parents.[11]

A Taiwanese man who was apparently suffering from mental illness attempted to set a fire on board a Chinese airliner. Only minutes after the Boeing 727 took off, the passenger got out of his seat and began to douse the cabin with gasoline, which he had carried on board in two tea bottles. One of the flight attendants smelled the odor in the back of the aircraft and notified the captain. Two elderly passengers seated near the rear of the aircraft screamed when they saw the man preparing to light the gasoline with a cigarette lighter.

Fortunately, a security guard on board heard the commotion rushed over, and tackled the man in the aisle. In addition, four other passengers assisted in subduing the man before he was able to start the fire. The pilot diverted the aircraft and made an emergency landing at the nearest airport, where the suspect was taken into custody. The man reportedly told the authorities that he was trying to kill himself. There were no injuries to passengers and crew.

A lone individual commandeered a Portuguese airliner at Pearson International Airport in Toronto. As passengers boarded the aircraft for a flight to Lisbon, Portugal, the Toronto resident forced his way past a security checkpoint and onto the plane. He ran into the cockpit, locked the door behind him and ordered the flight crew to take him to Chicago, Illinois. The individual had no weapon and was almost unintelligible as he added further demands. He soon became disoriented and after only a few minutes allowed a crew member to unlock the cockpit door. Toronto authorities subdued the individual without a struggle. There were no injuries during the brief commandeering, and no weapons or explosives were found. The individual was charged with attempted hijacking and endangering the flight crew, but the charges were eventually dropped. When the individual appeared in court, the results of his psychiatric evaluation were revealed, and it was determined that he could not be held criminally responsible.

A Chinese man, who was reportedly upset because his wife had left him and purportedly stole all their money, took over a domestic Xiamen Airlines flight. The man attempted to divert the flight to Taiwan, insisting that he had explosives in his pocket. The pilot agreed to divert the plane but instead continued on to the original destination of Xiamen, so none of the passengers would be inconvenienced. Just before landing crew members, and passengers quickly subdued the man, who was not aware that the aircraft was landing in Xiamen. The aircraft landed safely and the man was taken into custody by the Chinese authorities.

A Taiwanese man attempted to take over a Boeing 757 aircraft during a flight from Kaohsiung to Taipei, Taiwan. The air rage offender doused himself with gasoline and demanded to be flown to China. The man reportedly told the pilot that he was a victim of political oppression and wanted political asylum. The aircraft changed course and was granted permission to proceed to Xiamen, China. During the two-hour flight diversion several irate passengers, upset over the inconvenience of stopping over in China, threatened to take out their cigarette lighters and set the man on fire. Cabin crew members stood by with fire extinguishers as the man sat outside the cockpit door. The aircraft landed safely and the air rage offender was taken into custody by the Chinese authorities. The man, a former journalist, had reportedly been fired from his job at a Taiwanese newspaper for disciplinary problems. According to Chinese authorities, the man will undergo a psychiatric evaluation before facing criminal charges.

5

THE ADVENT OF
CATTLE CLASS

The din of complaints about airline service is becoming deafening. From gripes aired on Web sites to the passenger rights movement to letters sent to governments, airline passengers appear more irritated than ever. Web sites with names like TravelProblems.com, PassengerRights.com, and ticked.com, as well as deltasucks.com, untied.com, and NorthWorstAir.org, are attracting tens of thousands of visitors. Passenger complaints filed with the U.S. Department of Transportation more than doubled in 2000, to over twenty-five thousand, after surging more than 25 percent in the previous year.

In many ways air travel has become like herding cattle into a barn— the more cows you put in, the more edgy they will become. The most stark example of the "cattle-class" mentality might well have occurred during the blizzard of January 2, 1999, when thousands of passengers were stranded in planes on runways at Detroit's airport for as long as ten hours, with little food or water and overflowing toilets. The government assailed Northwest Airlines for being poorly prepared and for continuing to send planes to Detroit with the storm unfolding. The uproar spawned lawsuits and energized national support for passenger rights legislation.

Though the blizzard dumped twelve inches of snow on Detroit Metropolitan Airport on New Year's weekend that year, Northwest officials decided to continue running flights in and out of the airport while other major airlines shut down.

Northwest Airlines eventually agreed to pay $7.1 million to thousands of passengers stranded on the Detroit tarmac during the snowstorm.

"We decided it was time to reach a settlement, to put this behind us and

81

move forward," Northwest spokeswoman Cathy Peach said. "It was a very unusual weather situation. There's no doubt that people were uncomfortable and inconvenienced, but certainly their safety was never compromised."[1]

However, in an internal report that was part of the lawsuit, the airline acknowledged it had no emergency plan for its Minneapolis headquarters to follow, passengers were forced to remain inside the planes for too long, and its flight planners had sent too many planes into the storm-crippled airport.

As the weather worsened, arriving planes began skidding on taxiways and blocking alleys between gates. An engine on a 747 struck a snowbank.

By Sunday afternoon, thirty-six Northwest flights had landed and twenty-nine were still on taxiways waiting for gates. Inside the planes, food ran out and in some cases water wasn't available. Several planes also had lavatories overflow. One passenger went into diabetic shock, and another complained of heart attack symptoms.

Later that evening, the captain of a 757 waiting for a gate sent an electronic message to Northwest officials: "Would U pass on that the next problem they will have to deal with is blown slides. This is not a joke." The captain was threatening to taxi to a cargo carrier's ramp and deploy the plane's emergency slides to let passengers off.[2]

On another plane, pilot Peter Stabler called Northwest CEO John Dasburg at home and pleaded for help. The airline's crew management efforts also failed. Pilots and flight attendants scheduled for departing flights that day were snowed in and couldn't make it to the airport. But the airline's phone system was so overloaded they couldn't get word to their supervisors that they wouldn't be able to show up for work. In several instances, passengers boarded planes that had no flight crew. Those planes occupied gates sorely needed by incoming flights.

The crew members got through to Northwest communications officials who failed to pass on the information those pilots and flight attendants wouldn't be showing up.

In a report critical of how Northwest handled the blizzard, the U.S. Department of Transportation's inspector general's office noted that Northwest had no plan to guide itself in such an emergency.

Still, although it easy to blame the airlines for all of the problems related to poor service, other entities—including government agencies, passengers, and Mother Nature herself—are also responsible for the cattle-class condition of commercial air travel. It should be remembered that blizzards of this magnitude do not happen every day. Moreover, Northwest Airlines has an excellent safety record.

HOW DID WE GET HERE?

Sophisticated television commercials almost always portray a luxurious first-class or business-class experience—not the cramped, sometimes meal-less misadventures had by many in the back of the plane.

But traveling by airplane wasn't always like this. Many of us can remember the days when flying was viewed as a luxury.

Airline service and the quality of the flying experience began to deteriorate in the United States when the industry was deregulated in 1978. Increased competition among carriers forced them to cut corners in order to remain profitable. However, until the early 1990s, most travelers would probably agree that the experience of air travel was still generally a positive one, although relatively expensive. Then in 1992, almost overnight, everything seemed to change.

The arrival into the U.S. marketplace of cut-rate carriers like Midway and ValuJet, and the explosive growth of Southwest Airlines, dramatically altered the nature of the airline business. As a result of the increased competition from these bargain carriers, fares had to be substantially cut by every other airline in order to compete. Many consumers soon discovered a ticket in 1992 could be bought for 70 percent less than the price of the exact same ticket a year earlier!

The result of the tremendous discounts in the cost of airline tickets meant that the airlines were now forced to earn profits not from charging a small group of travelers higher prices, as they had in the past, but from increasing their number of customers and charging them less. In a few short months, the airlines and air travel went from a being personalized experience, like shopping at Herrod's or Nordstrom's, to enduring the masses and the lines at Wal-Mart.

However, air rage is not restricted to the economy-class traveler, assumed to be frustrated by the crowded, cramped conditions. First-class and business-class passengers can be especially aggressive and demanding, as they have higher expectations of service. Many of the people who are frequent fliers are accustomed to giving orders, not accepting them—especially from cabin staff and other passengers.

One of the more publicized cases of a first-class passenger treating the others around him like "have-nots" happened on a TWA flight from New York to San Francisco. The first-class passenger became agitated when he spotted an economy-class passenger standing in line to use the restroom in "his" section. The female passenger waiting to use the restroom had left her coach seat at the direction of the flight attendant, as serving carts blocked the aisle to the lavatory at the rear of the plane.

According to court records, the first-class passenger allegedly grabbed the coach passenger—who was slight, dark, and of Spanish-Filipino descent—and shoved her out of line while calling her a "chink slut" and a whore. The first-class passenger was wearing a navy wool pinstriped suit, and told her she had no right to be in first-class wearing jeans. He said, "Get out of first-class where *you* don't belong. Someone like *you* would dirty the first-class bathroom."

The woman sued the man for, among other things, battery and slander. The man filed two countersuits, including the claim that his first-class ticket gave him legal right to use the first-class bathroom, and that the woman from coach class had trespassed on that right by obstructing his access.

For more than three years, two of the largest law firms in San Francisco slugged it out over the incident. Finally, after a number of appeals, a federal judge threw out the man's countersuits and ordered him to pay damages and attorney costs to the woman. In addition, the first-class passenger's law firm was ordered to pay nearly $5,000 for crossing the line from creative advocacy into "pettifoggery" and silliness.[3]

A prominent Cambodian businessman shot out the tires of a Boeing 737 aircraft after a dispute over an alleged late-arriving flight and lost luggage. Upon arrival at Phnom Penh's Pochentong Airport, the businessman borrowed an automatic weapon from his bodyguard, who was waiting for him at a VIP lounge. The businessman returned to the tarmac and opened fire on the aircraft.

In a later interview, the businessman stated that he was angry at the pilots because the pilot was allegedly rude to him when he boarded the aircraft at the last minute in Hong Kong. In addition, the businessman complained that the flight was late, and the airline lost his luggage and only agreed to pay a fraction of the cost to replace the items.

Several crew members and passengers were still on board the aircraft at the time of the shooting, but fortunately no one was injured. The aircraft was grounded for two days until the nose gear of the aircraft could be replaced.

OPENING UP AIR TRAVEL TO EVERYBODY

Unlike hunger, war, chronic poverty, drought, or any other number of catastrophes that face billions of human beings on a daily basis, the problems confronting air travelers are often by-products of prosperity. Today, because of the availability of cheaper flights to more places than ever before, air travel has become a real possibility for hundreds of millions of people around the world.

Because of this, flying has moved from being the exclusive territory of the "jet set" to a form of transportation that millions of people in developed countries can easily and readily use.

The openness and affordability of air travel has brought the public, with all of its baggage—in every sense of the word—to the once hallowed halls of the world's airports. When walking through a terminal in any major airport, one immediately gets the impression that he is merely one of the masses. Like going to the mall or driving on the freeway, air travel has brought all of the elements of society closer to us. Unfortunately, some of those elements are not the best intentioned, brightest, or most considerate.

In recent years, the numbers of thefts, rapes, and assaults in airports and on airplanes have all increased in proportion to the rise in the number of passengers. This is not surprising, given the sheer volume of people choosing air travel. Atlanta's Hartsfield Airport, one of the world's busiest, handles more than 73.5 million passengers annually. If you add in the airport's thousands of employees as well as visitors and others, it becomes clear that airports like Hartsfield are some of the most crowded and bustling places anywhere.

Toronto's Pearson International Airport, Canada's busiest, has been dealing with the rise of prostitutes working the terminals. Some of these enterprising women claim they can earn $1,500 a day for having sex with travelers—much more than they could ever hope to make on the streets.

Another issue raised by flight attendants and other airline employees is the growing number of people who are not sophisticated travelers.

A women on board an Alaska Airlines flight from Portland, Oregon, to

Anchorage, Alaska, was placed on probation for two years, ordered to perform community service, and fined over $900.00 for reckless endangerment, after she compromised the safety of fellow passengers. The women had placed a loaded .357 caliber weapon in her checked baggage, and apparently failed to declare it and remove the bullets before attempting to transport it.

The weapon discharged inside her luggage as it was being loaded into the cargo hold by an airline baggage handler. The bullet shot up through the cabin floor barely missing a passenger's foot, and stopped inside a diaper bag after tearing through a photo album. Fortunately, no one was injured in the incident, which caused the aircraft to be grounded for several days for maintenance repairs.

The woman was very sorry for what she had done and later stated that she "didn't realize that the weapon was loaded." The FAA has strict guidelines that all airlines must follow when transporting firearms. The air carrier must be notified and the weapon formally declared. The weapon must also be unloaded and confined to a locked, hard-sided case, and ammunition must be keep secured in a separate container.

In a related story, another Alaska Airlines passenger failed to declare his shotgun on a flight from Seattle to Los Angeles. The weapon was discovered with the aid of X-ray equipment and a bomb-sniffing dog, who helped police to immediately seize the checked bag. Seattle police officials then cordoned off an area of approximately two hundred feet around the bag and began a partial evacuation of remaining passengers in the area. The bag was then subjected to a CTX X-Ray scanner, which utilizes CAT scan technology by taking precise X-ray slices of the bag and feeding it to a computer for analysis. It was quickly determined that it was a shotgun and the bomb-sniffing dog had responded to gunpowder residue.

According to reports, the owner of the bag was not remorseful, nor did he have any intention of declaring the weapon as per FAA regulations. The owner of the weapon was taken into custody by the Seattle/Tacoma Police Department and released shortly after being charged with "obstruction" for his failure to cooperate with authorities. In addition, charges are pending with the FAA for his failure to declare a firearm, which could carry a substantial fine. It's unnerving sometimes to witness the audacity of some passengers who feel the rules don't apply to them and are only in place as an inconvenience, violating their rights as Americans.

For years, one of the largest regional carriers in the southern United States reported that plastic trash bags were the suitcase of choice for many of its customers.

Other passengers, when traveling on an "Super" MD-80 aircraft, as described on their ticket, ask the flight attendants at what time they will be receiving their "supper," and would it be at eight o'clock.

A flight attendant on a flight from Biloxi, Mississippi, reported a passenger became incredulous when she would not allow him to pay for a three-dollar beer with food stamps.

On an oversold flight to Chicago, a gate agent told of a passenger who was ecstatic at the opportunity to receive a $250 voucher for waiting for the next flight because, as he exclaimed, "That's more than I make in a whole month on selling my plasma."

Many passengers have become frustrated when they have pressed the flight attendant call button and shouted at the air vent, mistakenly believing it is an intercom system.

After confirming flight reservations and departure and arrival times for a flight from Los Angeles to New York, a passenger demanded that the ticket agent explain why it took eight and one-half hours to travel to New York but only two and one-half hours on the return flight to Los Angeles.

A woman who was assigned a window seat refused to sit down because she thought the wind coming from outside would mess up her new hairstyle. After fifteen minutes of explanation from the plane's captain, the woman finally took her seat next to the window.

A flight attendant, when performing her final preflight safety check, noticed a female passenger had placed the plug end of a headset into her nose, erroneously thinking it was a connection for oxygen.

While still in the gate area, awaiting his flight, a nervous passenger asked an agent if the plane would be boarded in alphabetical order.

On a flight to Jacksonville, a woman traveling with her newborn was told by a flight attendant that the baby's car seat had to be placed in the overhead bin. When the flight attendant returned, she discovered the woman had placed the car seat *with the baby inside* into the overhead bin.

The lack of common courtesy and decency also are on the rise. Many passengers complain of their seat companions taking over the entire arm rest or dropping their seats back when they have a drink or a meal on the tray table, spilling drinks and food everywhere. Others complain about out-of-control children, wandering dogs or cats, and people who spend way too much time in the lavatory.

An obese American passenger on a Sabena flight from New York to Brussels got violent when he couldn't succeed in completely folding down the tray table on which his meal was to be placed because of his corpulence. In an unpleasant tone, the man demanded a flight attendant do something. She suggested the man place the tray of food on his lap. He refused. The flight attendant then offered another seemingly reasonable solution: the man could come to the area reserved for the flight crew and eat his meal there.

In response, the passenger threw his headset at her. A disruption ensued requiring the captain to leave the cockpit to intervene. The situation escalated as passengers, flight attendants, and the captain were treated to a mouthful of insults from the passenger. Finally the captain, seeing no other solution, ordered an emergency landing and had the man removed from the plane by awaiting police.

Indignant about the possibility of arrest, the obese man refused to move when police officers boarded the plane. It took eight individuals—three police officers and five male passengers—to lift, drag, and finally push the man off the plane.

In a terminal at a Chicago airport, a man was caught by a gate agent urinating in a drinking fountain.

On a flight from Dallas, one of the authors lowered his tray table to find a used diaper left by a previous passenger.

Whatever the case, the opening up of air travel to more and more people has added to the cattle-class experience.

THE PHYSICAL STRESS OF CATTLE CLASS

It has only been in the last few years that the physical effects of air travel have come to be understood. Solar radiation, the rise of incidents of deep-vein thrombosis, and perceptions about bad air all have an impact on flight crews and passengers. What exact role these have on people's behavior, however, is still not clear. Nevertheless, they are all part of the flying experience.

Solar radiation

Everyone is continuously exposed to cosmic rays and radiation from radioactive materials in the atmosphere, whether they are flying or not. Even the human body contains radioactive substances, which include radioisotopes of potassium, cesium, radium, carbon, hydrogen, polonium, bismuth, radon, uranium, and other elements. Both cosmic and earth radiation vary from place to place, although humankind has always lived with this "background" radiation.

Our exposure to radiation has increased in frequency and magnitude of dose in recent years, especially in therapeutic applications from X-rays. Exposure to radiation in diagnostic X-ray procedures is particularly widespread; it is the largest and most significant exposure for the general population. Other sources of radiation include effluents from nuclear and other facilities processing or using radionuclides, luminous clocks or watches and signs, and electronic devices utilizing high accelerating voltages and beam currents.

Radiation from the sun, also known as solar radiation, is mainly absorbed by different layers of the atmosphere before it hits the earth. However, at higher altitudes, the atmosphere is thinner and offers less protection.

In 1994, the Federal Aviation Administration issued an advisory circular to all U.S. carriers. It recommended that the airlines inform crew members about radiation exposure and known associated health risks. According to Dr. Robert Barish, medical physicist and author of the benchmark book *The Invisible Passenger—Radiation Risks for People Who Fly*, travelers who fly more than seventy-five thousand miles a year are exposed to radiation doses equal to the maximum permissible doses for radiation workers in nuclear plants or hospitals.

The earth is constantly bombarded by radiation from solar flares, but, says Dr. Barish, the intensity of the radiation is amplified even more during a "solarmax." A solarmax is the peak of the solar cycle that occurs only every eleven years. The year 2000 was a solarmax year.

During these and other periods of hypersolar activity, Dr. Barsih says, "Air travelers can get the equivalent of a chest X-ray every two to four hours on a normal long-distance flight."

Whether this increased radiation affects our health and behavior is a matter for future inquiry.

DVT—Economy-class syndrome

"Economy-class syndrome," a term introduced in 1977 by Drs. Symington and Stack in an article published in the *British Journal of the Chest*, is the widely used term for deep-vein thrombosis (DVT). DVT is a disease of the circulation, occurring most often in people who have not been able to exercise normally. Blood passing through the deepest veins in the calves and thighs flows relatively slowly: When a DVT occurs it moves so slowly that it forms a solid clot which becomes wedged in the vein.

The likelihood of DVT is dramatically increased on a flight because of the cramped conditions most passengers find themselves in. As people have been gotten bigger and the space between most seats has gotten smaller, a passenger's legs are often placed in unnatural positions for long periods at a time. Anyone who has flown in economy class will agree that there are times when their knees ride up into their chest because of the small spaces. The result of this strain can be the clotting that leads to DVT.

Quite often there are no symptoms at all. Where they do exist, there may be pain or tenderness in the leg and raised skin temperature around the area. Sudden swelling in one leg may be the first sign. Occasionally some of the surface veins are more visible through the skin. There may also be pain on flexing the foot upward. There is particular risk with air travel because of the combination of inactivity and dehydration, which makes the blood more sticky.[4]

DVT begins with the collection of stagnant pooled blood in the deep leg veins. During a period of only a few hours, if the legs are not exercised, blood clots can form. DVTs themselves are not life threatening but they are associated with complications that can be fatal. The most common serious complication is a pulmonary embolism, which occurs in between one in three and one in four cases of DVT. A piece of the clot lodged in the leg vein breaks off and travels through the body to the lung, where it becomes lodged again, causing severe breathing difficulties. Untreated, up to one in ten people who suffer a pulmonary embolism die as a result.

More rarely, a part of the clot may also lodge in other organs including the brain, where it leads to a stroke. One less serious complication is post-thrombotic syndrome, which affects many people after a DVT due to damage to the valves along the length of the vein. It can cause pain, swelling, and ulceration of the skin around the area.

Approximately two-thirds of people with a DVT need to be cared for in hospital in the initial stages. The aim is to dissolve the clot and, in the longer term, prevent other clots from forming.

One of the more famous people to suffer DVT was former U.S. Vice President Dan Quayle who, in November 1994, developed a blood clot in his left leg following a series of airplane flights. Parts of the blood clot broke away and migrated to both of his lungs. Quayle, then only forty-seven years old, complained of breathlessness and was diagnosed with "walking pneumonia." The following day, his condition worsened and he was admitted to the hospital. After further tests, doctors rediagnosed his condition as a pulmonary embolism, which can be fatal. Quayle was given a series of blood thinners and released from the hospital after eight days.[5]

At least one person a month dies of a blood clot on the lungs on arrival at Heathrow Airport, say doctors. British airlines are concerned about the incidence of cases of DVT and British Airways has started issuing information to passengers about how to prevent the condition. Getting up and walking regularly during the flight, avoiding alcohol, and drinking plenty of water are the some of the more widely prescribed ways for avoiding DVT.

DVT victims arriving at Heathrow are taken to Ashford Hospital in Middlesex for treatment. John Belstead, an accident and emergency consultant at Ashford, said his department had dealt with thirty passenger deaths in the last three years.

He said, "These are people who die as they get off the aircraft. Around one million people come into Heathrow on long-haul flights each month so it may not seem much compared to crossing the road. But it is something that airlines can help prevent."

But Mr. Belstead said patients who had traveled in more spacious seating had also developed problems. He said the problem was simply related to sitting still for long periods of time, and for this reason people on long overnight flights were at higher risk. The clots are dangerous when they block blood vessels in the leg, or worse, in the lungs.

In Australia, eight hundred people are suing airlines because they developed blood clots during long flights. Most passengers who suffer the condition go to their general practitioner after a few days or weeks, Mr. Belstead said. Another problem in tracing the extent of the condition is that not all hospitals record whether blood clot patients have been on a plane.

According to a study conducted by the clinic at Tokyo's Narita Airport, 25 passengers have died of "economy-class syndrome" over the past eight years. Dr. Toshiro Makino, head of the New Tokyo International Airport Clinic, says more than 100 to 150 passengers arriving in Tokyo each year are treated for the problem; of that number, 50 to 60 cases are regarded as serious.[6]

Carry-on baggage

Despite attempts by international aviation organizations to require airlines to limit the size and number of carry-ons, the demands placed on overhead compartments by passengers continue to exceed their capacity. Almost every traveler on every commercial flight can attest to the staggering amount of luggage carried on by some of their fellow passengers.

Passengers who prefer to carry their baggage aboard the aircraft do so not only to avoid having to wait to retrieve their luggage on arrival, but to avoid the possibility of loss, theft, or damage. Carrying your own luggage has been made easier because many suitcases feature integral wheels and telescoping handles that make it easier to maneuver inside airport terminals and down cabin aisles.[7]

Further, the growing use of E-tickets, which require the passenger only to present themselves at the departure gate, encourage time-strapped travelers to take their bags with them. As a result, passengers are arriving at the departure gate with larger and more numerous bags.

Beyond larger and more numerous suitcases, the kinds of items people try to carry on is sometimes impossible to believe. On his many travels, one of the authors has witnessed passengers trying to stuff everything from a rack of elk antlers to an adult bicycle to a pair of snowshoes to a used camel saddle into the overheard compartments. In parts of Africa and South Asia, he has also seen passengers carry on live goats and chickens.

The ITF estimates that cabin baggage issues trigger approximately 10 to 15 percent of all air rage incidents.[8] Moreover, according to the ITF, the need to transfer excess carry-ons to the cargo hold, or to ensure the safe stowage on board, is the single biggest cause of delays to departure, and such delays can themselves fuel air rage.

Baggage falling from overhead compartments is another problem that exacerbates the cattle-class experience. Research has shown that among the fourteen largest U.S. carriers, there an estimated forty-five thousand baggage-storage incidents annually that cause injury. Worldwide, it is estimated there are ten thousand injuries a year, or an average of one every hour.[9]

Lack of uniform standards makes the problem even worse. Not only is there confusion about how much and what kind of carry-on baggage should be permitted on an airplane, but passengers are also confused about what kind of carry-on baggage they are allowed to take.

Organizations like the ITF are quick to point out that the confusion of different carry-on requirements from each airline makes a bad situation worse. They argue passengers are left uncertain as to what constitutes a reasonable cabin baggage allowance for their flight, and that the best way to resolve the problem is to have the industry create a uniform regulatory limit on the kind and the amount of carry-on baggage allowed on board. Still, we seem a long way away from agreeing on a standard carry-on policy.

In an editorial pleading for such a common policy, *USA Today* blamed the FAA for failing to act, saying, "The best course would be for airlines to agree on a common standard. But that approach has already failed. By failing to take action, the FAA has once again shown that it is more inclined to follow the industry it is supposed to regulate than to lead it."[10]

FAA administrator Jane F. Garvey responded to the editorial on the same day saying, "Carry-on baggage is not a one-size-fits-all issue that lends itself to across-the-board regulations. Rather, it is an issue in which flexibility to adjust to wide differences in the industry is the most logical course."[11]

Some airlines and the courts seem to feel the same way. After spending more than $12 million on bigger overhead bins that can handle larger carry-on bags, Continental Airlines wasn't about to let luggage-sizing templates that a competitor installed at security checkpoints undercut its competitive advantage. So it sued the rival, United Airlines, which had set up the templates at its hub at Dulles International Airport.

A federal judge ruled in Continental's favor, saying that United conspired with other airlines to violate antitrust laws by installing the baggage templates at Dulles—where Continental has just one gate, versus more than thirty for United.

U.S. District Judge T.S. Ellis, sitting in Alexandria, Virginia, ruled in a summary judgment that United's placement of the templates at security checkpoints at Dulles was "an unreasonable restraint of trade that caused [Continental] antitrust injury."

"If there is any proof of failure in the market to be gleaned from the record," the judge wrote, "it is of United's failure to provide what its customers desire.

"The common thread uniting all three of [United's] suggested procompetitive effects—i.e., improved on-time performance, safety, and passenger convenience and comfort—is the fact that some airlines are not able (or willing) to provide onboard storage capacity and carry-on baggage policies the flying public wants."

A spokeswoman said United is "very disappointed and a bit surprised" by the ruling. "We have always been supportive of the baggage templates, and think it has been beneficial to our customers," said Whitney Staley, adding that delays "due to baggage and slow boarding have decreased over 70 percent" with templates.[12]

Air quality in the cabin

Early airliners used 100 percent outside air. This type of system continually exhausted all cabin air through outflow valves while the cabin was pressurized and replenished with outside air.

Beginning in the 1970s and continuing until the present day, designs in air recirculation were developed to make airplanes more fuel efficient. On planes with air recirculation, some of the air exiting the cabin is filtered and reintroduced into the air-mix chamber. The remainder of the air exiting the cabin is ducted overboard. Because outside air supplied to the cabin is taken from the aircraft's engines, any reduction in air usage increases the engine's efficiency and reduces fuel consumption and operating costs.[13]

Joe Lundquist, vice president of technology at Pall Corporation, a major manufacturer of air-filtration systems for large aircraft, says that in recent years there has been a trend toward reducing the amount of outside air entering the cabins.

Fuel savings have encouraged manufacturers and airlines to design systems that meet cabin air-quality requirements while using different combinations of outside air and recirculated air. An analysis by Pall Corporation found that airlines can save tens of thousands of dollars per year for every plane that uses cabin air recirculation.[14]

And it is here that the debate starts over the quality of the air inside a cabin. The FAA merely requires that cabins be "ventilated" at that levels of carbon dioxide be kept within a certain range. Cris Bisgard, M.D., of Delta Airlines says, "If you compare air quality in an aircraft cabin to a standard office building, the airplane has far more air exchanges per hour than an office, and the air that comes into the aircraft cabin is sterile."[15]

Judith Andersen Murawski, an industrial hygienist for the Association of Flight Attendants completely disagrees. She says the airlines reduce the amount of fresh air "just because they want to save money."[16]

Whatever the case, most passengers perceive the quality of the air in a cabin to be poor. And, because of this perception, rightly or wrongly, many passengers believe they have another annoyance to bear in cattle class.

DEPORTING ILLEGAL IMMIGRANTS

Whereas the quality of air aboard planes is a debatable issue, one element of cattle class that invariably puts the safety and security of passengers at risk is the use of the airlines for the deportation of illegal immigrants. Internal reports from the Immigration and Naturalization Service (INS) suggest more than seventy thousand illegal immigrants were deported from the United States on commercial flights during the year 2000. These illegal immigrants, more than half whom have been indicted or involved in criminal activity, are placed on planes by armed INS agents.

Whether waiting in the gate area or approaching the aircraft by vehicle, INS policy requires the deportees to be handcuffed and, for the more violent types, placed in leg-irons. In addition, INS policy mandates that two agents be present with the deportee at all times prior to the transfer onto the aircraft. Frighteningly, however, the vast majority of the deportees travel unescorted to their final destination. INS policy currently states that agents "should" escort groups of eleven or more deportees; groups of ten or fewer travel unescorted.

In almost every case, the agents board the aircraft with the deportees prior to the general boarding of the rest of the passengers. The INS agents remain with the deportees until the plane has been completely boarded. Then, right before the cabin door is closed, the handcuffs and leg-irons are removed and the INS agents get off the plane. So, for the next several hours, the deportees, who just a few minutes earlier were wearing handcuffs and under the supervision of armed guards, are left to wander the cabin like any other passenger. This becomes an accident waiting to happen.

On a flight from San Diego to El Salvador, two dozen unescorted criminal deportees, just out of jail, stole liquor from a service cart and got drunk. A twelve-year-old girl, traveling alone to visit relatives and seated amid the criminals, was inappropriately touched by several of the men before a flight attendant discovered the situation and reseated the girl.

The use of commercial airlines to deport illegal immigrants is not unique to the United States. Many Western European nations also use the same system, although they are more likely than the United States to escort the deportee to the final destination. Still, things can invariably go wrong.

A Nigerian man being deported from Belgium recently threatened the safety of a Sabena flight from Brussels to Abidjan, Ivory Coast. The deportee, who had tried to enter Belgium using false documents, was accompanied on the flight by two Belgian police officers. Throughout the boarding, the man protested loudly and violently about his deportation. However, once the plane was airborne, the officers received permission from the pilot to gradually release the deportee from his restraints.

When the flight was somewhere above Toulouse, France, all of the man's restraints had been removed by the officers. At once, the deportee began to slap nearby passengers, jumped away from his escorts, and ran to the cockpit, which was unlocked.

The man managed to enter the flight deck, where he demanded that the two pilots land the plane immediately. He threatened to operate as many of the control buttons, knobs, switches, and handles as he could if his demand was not met. The pilots convinced him that a landing at Toulouse would be technically impossible and offered to land at Marrakech, Morocco. When the Nigerian, who apparently wanted to avoid returning to Africa at all costs, refused to allow the landing at Marrakech, the pilots diverted to Spain. After dumping excess fuel, the flight landed in Malaga, where the man was overpowered by Spanish police and taken into custody.

A Saudi Arabian airliner was taken over on a flight from Jeddah to Addis Ababa, Ethiopia. The perpetrator was an Ethiopian national who had attempted, but failed, to find work in Saudi Arabia and was being returned. The perpetrator, who was described as very distraught and mentally unstable, used a small letter opener as a weapon in trying to reroute the plane. The flight attendants assisted in calming the man down and aircraft continued on to Ethiopia as scheduled. When the aircraft landed the man was taken into custody calmly and without further incident.

Another Ethiopian man on board an Olympic Airlines flight took a flight attendant hostage and threatened her with a knife from a food service tray. The incident took place when the aircraft was on final approach to Hellenikon Airport in Athens. The remaining passengers, stunned by the sudden burst of violence, sat motionless as the aircraft taxied to a remote parking area. The Ethiopian man had apparently just been deported from Australia and was being returned to Ethiopia via Greece. The man demanded to speak to representatives of the United Nations and the media, but his request was denied. Shortly, thereafter, the man released the passengers and crew and surrendered to Greek authorities.

The simple fact that deportees are being forced to go against their will to a place they wanted to get away from automatically puts them in the category of potential air rage offender—regardless of whether they have a criminal background or not. Many illegal immigrants have risked life and limb to enter a new country and are understandably quite upset when they are compelled to return to their home country. Some may face prison or political retribution, or worse. Other might simply not want to face the shame of coming home a failure. As a result, these passengers may feel they have little or nothing to lose.

Although every commercial flight that carries deportees is under the threat of this kind of air rage incident, the risk is even greater on small, regional aircraft that do not carry a flight attendant. Because of the lack of a cabin presence, the flight crew is unable to monitor and control what happens in the cabin and they are the last to know if a problem has erupted.[17]

One may wonder why the INS and the airlines permit this problem to go on while not doing anything about it. The answers are relatively simple.

First, the INS is under tremendous pressure by leaders in Washington to deport as many illegal immigrants as possible. More than one million illegal immigrants are deported each year via bus or other ground transportation. Still, there are not enough transport facilities available to handle all the deportees rounded up annually by the INS. As a result, the agency, which is already understaffed, is forced to use whatever means necessary—including the commercial carriers.

Secondly, under U.S. law, if an illegal alien arrives in the United States via a commercial airline, it is the responsibility of the airline to transport that individual back to his home country.

The deportation of illegal immigrants also puts passengers in close quarters of communicable diseases. As the deportee has entered the country illegally, he has not undergone the stringent health examinations required of all legal visitors to most developed countries. Therefore, it is not known if deportees are carrying infirmities and ailments such as tuberculosis, cholera, yellow fever, and others.

Over the past years, tuberculosis has reemerged at the world's deadliest infectious disease and one of the planet's leading causes of death—over three million cases annually. In 1999, World Health Organization (WHO) officials said that tuberculosis posed a global health emergency.[18] According to the Centers for Disease Control, an estimated 4 to 6 percent of the population in the United States is TST positive (meaning they show tuberculosis infection when tested with a tuberculin skin test), and in developing countries the estimated prevalence of infection ranges from 19.4 percent in the Eastern Mediterranean region to 43.8 percent in the Western Pacific region. WHO reported in 1997 that one-third of the world's population has tuberculosis and is at risk of developing an active infection in the future.[19]

Health experts readily admit the environment of the airline cabin is most conducive to the spreading of infectious diseases such as tuberculosis. The airlines seem to tacitly agree as well.

In November 1998, the International Air Transport Association (IATA), which represents the airline industry on a global scale, published a nonbinding recommended practice for member airlines to consider in responding to any passenger with an infectious disease.

The guidelines suggest that IATA's member airlines advise the public not to travel with an infectious disease because of the possibility of exposing other people:

> Member airlines should inform passengers through their public relations, literature, etc. that passengers who know they have an infectious disease should not travel by air, as they can expose other passengers and crewmembers to such infectious disease.[20]

Unfortunately, however, the transport of deportees does not fall under this dictum.

So once again, when it comes to the spreading of disease, it seems the animals traveling in the cargo hold have it better than the humans in cattle class. International flight standards for most of the world's airports requires the entire cargo hold of an arriving airplane to be disinfected with concentrated sprays and/or liquids if animals are on board.

ANOTHER DAY AT THE ZOO

It is not a mere coincidence that the term "cattle class" concerns itself with the other members of the food chain.

A few months ago, police shut down Baltimore-Washington International Airport for nearly three hours—causing dozens of delays and cancellations—after a security agent spotted a suspicious bag being carried by a passenger. The airport was evacuated around 6 A.M. when the staff at the security X-ray machine saw what they believed to be an explosive device in a small, soft-sided black suitcase.

Officials asked the bag's owner what he had packed inside. He seemed unable to recall. Then, after he began to move uncontrollably, security agents looked further and discovered two twelve-inch baby pythons up his sleeve. The man said he was simply keeping the snakes warm so as to prepare them for their cross-country flight. Police said it was unclear whether the possession of snakes was a breach of airport security or airline policy. The man was released without his suspicious suitcase, but he got to keep the snakes.[21]

The presence of a three-hundred-pound Vietnamese potbellied pig in first class on a U.S. Airways flight from Philadelphia to Seattle may be one of the best examples of how low the status of air travel has sunk in recent years.

After producing a note from a doctor, a female passenger brought the sow onto the plane, claiming it was a therapeutic companion pet. It seemed the woman had a heart condition so severe that she needed the companionship of her pig to relieve stress. Under FAA regulations, airlines must permit service animals to accompany passengers to their seats. So the pig flew first class across the country, for free.

Nevertheless, things didn't seem to work out quite as well as might have been expected. According to the U.S. Airways report filed with the FAA, the pig got out of control as the plane was approaching Seattle, ran through the aisles, and, like so many human perpetrators of air rage, tried to break into the cockpit. When the swine was unable to break through the door, it took refuge in the plane's forward galley. It had to be lured off the craft with tossed food, then dragged into the main terminal by its handler.

Upon further review, the FAA determined that the airline had done the right thing in allowing the pig on the plane. According to FAA spokesman Jim Peters, "U.S. Airways and its personnel acted in a reasonable and thoughtful manner, based on a legitimate request to transport a qualified individual with a disability and her service animal. We consider the matter closed."

Like the three-hundred-pound pig, other animals seem to fare quite well on commercial flights. According to strict aviation guidelines for dogs traveling in the cargo hold, canines are given more leg room on planes than humans. Unlike their counterparts in cattle class, dogs must be able to turn around in comfort. This means that dogs must be held in containers twice their width, enabling them to stretch, turn around, and ensure their circulation does not suffer. By contrast, the minimum amount of space required for humans is twenty-six inches between the back of the seat cushion and the seat in front—and this is before the person in front reclines her seat.

Horses also fare much better when it comes to waiting time. Horses are not allowed to be on board an aircraft for more than thirty minutes before takeoff, or after landing.

With the advent of cattle class, nobody seems to win. It is reality and it is here to stay.

6

WHO'S REPORTING
AIR RAGE?

If the problem of air rage is to be ever dealt with properly, the quality and quantity of information concerning such incidents needs to be dramatically improved. This is necessary not only to evaluate the magnitude and scope of the air rage problem, but also to determine the effectiveness of any solutions that might be implemented. Unfortunately, the current state of data and research on air rage is abysmal.

A seemingly normal pair of businessmen on a small commuter plane bound for Chicago put the lives of their fellow passengers at risk when they began wrestling and fell into the aisle. As they rolled around the small plane, the aircraft's nose pitched upward. The female captain screamed at the passengers to get back in their seats while she took dramatic corrective action to avoid a catastrophe.

In order to keep the plane from diverting off its course, the pilot professionally applied a number of techniques to regain control of the aircraft. Fortunately, she was able to safely land the plane.

Upon landing, the two brawlers were asked to disembark the aircraft, where they were greeted by a customer service agent who booked their return flight on a different airline!

On a commuter flight from Toronto, a man who claimed his reading light was not working took out the in-flight magazine and lit it on fire so he could finish reading the newspaper. Smoke immediately filled the cabin and forced the pilot to make an emergency landing in the middle of a turbulent thunderstorm. Upon arrival at the gate, the arsonist was greeted by airport security who, after they were convinced by his story, photocopied his driver's license and allowed him to walk away without any charges.

In these and thousands of other cases, the reporting procedures are woefully inadequate. This is not the fault of any single group of individuals. In fact, the vast majority of airline executives, ground and flight personnel, international aviation organizations, FAA employees, and law enforcement officials are all quite concerned about the increase in and intensity of air rage occurrences.

Each of these groups is adversely affected when air rage occurs. Airline executives are concerned because air rage frequently damages the image and efficiency of their corporations. Ground and flight personnel suffer—emotionally as well as physically—as they serve on the front lines against air rage attackers. International aviation organizations, deeply anxious about maintaining the integrity of their industry, become understandably upset when they hear how air rage negatively influences the public's perception of air travel. FAA employees often feel powerless and feel a loss of morale when they hear of another passenger committing air rage. Law enforcement officials often feel frustrated that their hands are tied when they attempt to prosecute an air rage perpetrator. None of these groups is responsible for air rage. Those individuals who commit air rage are ultimately responsible for their actions.

Frankly, nobody ever believed air rage would become the problem that it is today. As discussed earlier, there was a time, not too long ago, when airline travel was the ultimate in privilege and luxury. It was never conceivable, rightly or wrongly, that airline passengers would commit the kinds of crimes described here. Those who traveled by airplane and those who served them were perceived to be part of an exclusive fraternity—select members of an elite club who were able to fulfill the dream of global travel.

Yet since the deregulation of the airlines in the United States and many other parts of the world, the last twenty years have seen a much different kind of air travel experience. And even though deregulation is a not a recent phenomenon, traditional conceptions and assumptions die hard. This has been fundamental to the lack of common standards in reporting and documenting cases of air rage.

The failure to closely analyze and document the problem of air rage is not a conspiracy in the sense of a cover-up. It is not a conscious decision to bury the truth. It isn't even a tacit conspiracy on the part of governments, airlines, or other aviation entities to hide the problem. Moreover, it is not a lack of recognition of the prevalence of the problem. Instead, it is a failure of imagination.

Bluntly put, there is simply no one who really handles the problem well because no one ever imagined it would become the problem that it is. And as a result, no standard, consistent mechanisms were ever created to manage and deal with the air rage crisis.

THE AIRLINES AND THE REPORTING OF AIR RAGE

For the first time, because of the sheer volume of air rage incidents, airlines are beginning to be held accountable by distraught passengers who have filed complaints with the FAA about being intimidated and held hostage throughout a flight due to air rage committed by fellow passengers. For a long time, airlines managed to brush most of these incidents aside using the familiar excuse that they were unable to locate the incident reports, therefore it must not have happened. This lack of critical information put the FAA in the difficult, if not impossible, position of tracking down air rage offenders. In nearly all cases, the perpetrator was allowed to go free, the airline took no responsibility, and passengers who complained were merely sent a letter of apology and a $100 travel voucher. Seemingly, everyone was satisfied. And, as a result, the air rage problem was never really addressed. It was merely a customer service issue.

Although changes are beginning to take place, again because of the scale of the air rage crisis, there is still a long way to go. In fact, cockpit crews and flight attendants are still often discouraged by airlines from reporting cases of air rage in an effort to keep an aircraft as close to schedule as possible. Filling out police reports and waiting for the FAA or FBI could delay an aircraft for hours, costing the airline tens of thousands of dollars in misconnected passengers. In addition to the monetary costs, the negative publicity generated by a serious incident of air rage can have a lasting impact on the air carrier.

THE FEDERAL AVIATION ADMINISTRATION AND THE REPORTING OF AIR RAGE

On the FAA Web site (www.faa.gov), under the heading of "FAA Enforcement Actions" for violations 14 CFR 91.11, "Unruly Passengers," a grand total of 266 air rage incidents for year 2000 were reported. Apparently, somebody's not reporting accurate numbers to the FAA, which, in turn, is obviously not reporting accurate numbers to the flying public. It is important to note that when the FAA investigates a case of interference with flight crew, it is looking for violations of civil law, not criminal law, and will seek civil penalties, not imprisonment, against an individual. However, we believe that all instances of interference with flight crew should be treated under criminal law and then assessed a substantial penalty under civil law.

According to an analysis of law enforcement records from the twenty-five busiest airports in the United States, law enforcement officers responded to an average of 2.72 calls per week requesting assistance for unruly passengers in 2000. That's approximately 3,536 calls per year for only twenty-five airports—more than ten times the number the FAA reported for *all* flights in and out of the United States!

Clearly, somewhere in the system there exists a serious breakdown in number crunching, communication, and reporting. Maybe the guidelines for reporting instances of air rage need to be refined. As they stand now, the FAA has classified air rage offenders into three categories.

Category 1

A flight attendant requests a passenger to comply with a particular required federal regulation, and/or makes a request to the passenger to curb the disturbing behavior.

Examples of this may include instances whereby a passenger does not interfere directly with the flight attendants or the flight safety of the aircraft: an individual who verbally abuses the flight crew, intimidates other passengers, or is belligerent, loud, and obnoxious. In addition, smoking may also belong in this category, even though it could endanger the lives of other passengers and the crew.

Unfortunately, as long as the passenger eventually complies with the request to cease and desist, no further action is required by the flight attendant. In fact, flight attendants are advised that this incident need not be reported to the cockpit, the air carrier, or the FAA. In other words, even though a violation has occurred, the airline is not concerned and generally considers it a customer service issue.

Category 2

A flight attendant makes repeated requests for a passenger to comply with a particular required federal regulation, and/or makes repeated requests to the passenger to curb the disturbing behavior.

In this case, the passenger continues the disturbance, which now begins to interfere with cabin safety and the security of the flight. Examples of this include the continuation of verbal abuse or a continuing refusal to comply with federal regulations, such as failing to fasten a seat belt or operating unauthorized electronic equipment. The flight attendant is now instructed to follow company policy regarding cockpit notification.

In a category 2 interference case, the captain may at some point have to leave the cockpit in an attempt to defuse the situation. The captain, in conjunction with the flight attendants, may provide the passenger with written notification that he may be in violation of federal law and is required to behave on board the aircraft. In addition, some airlines may require that the flight crew prepare a "Trip Irregularity Report," stating that a serious situation had occurred on board the flight. Copies of these reports *may* be provided to appropriate company personnel and according to the guidelines, a report *may* be filed with the local office of the Federal Aviation Administration.

In other words, there is no requirement to report a serious category 2 incident to the FAA.

Category 3

The captain and/or flight attendant's requests, for a passenger to comply with a particular required federal regulation fails and/or the passenger continues the disturbance which interferes with the crew member duties, even after receiving verbal/written notification from the crew.

An example of a category 3 incident may include an instance when a fellow passenger or crew member is injured or subjected to a credible threat of injury, or handcuffs or restraints are used to subdue the passengers. Further, if an aircraft makes an unscheduled landing to remove a passenger, that may also be categorized as a category 3.

According to FAA guidelines, the suggested requirement is to have the flight crew identify the passenger and notify the local law enforcement to meet the flight upon arrival.

* * *

These guidelines, which the FAA provides to airlines for handling cases of interference with flight crew, are only guidelines. The FAA suggests that the information be reviewed by each airline's legal department, to ensure that it accurately states the airline's policies and legal duties and further protects the rights of the airline and personnel when addressing these very serious cases.

It is obvious that the guidelines provided by the Federal Aviation Administration are not conducive to accurate reporting of instances of air rage. It gives the airlines complete discretion whether or not to report these instances at all. In category 3, since the only suggested requirement is to notify law enforcement personnel, the FAA doesn't even have to be notified—because it is not a law enforcement agency, but a regulatory one. As a result, more instances go unreported.

This is exacerbated further because the FAA is divided by who does what within the agency. The FAA is broken up into nine regions across the country. For the past three years, air rage cases have been handled by the FAA Civil Aviation Security Division in two of the nine regions—essentially the East and West Coasts. In the other seven regions of the United States, the FAA Flight Standards District Office handles the cases. Assigning two different factions of the FAA to cover the same incident breeds confusion and discontent among the ranks.

The FAA Civil Aviation Security Office deals with security-related issues—bombings, hijackings, and airport/air carrier security—whereas the FAA Flight Standards District Office is concerned with safety issues—aircraft maintenance, pilot issues, and crew training. Furthermore, in addition to having two different factions of the FAA cover air rage instances, each of the nine regions operates relatively independently and institutes its own regionwide procedures when dealing with air rage incidents.

Even more disconcerting, FAA personnel have the discretion to initiate a case or not. If an FAA employee does not receive accurate information from the police reports or the police chose not to respond, the air rage incident, as far as the FAA is concerned, never happened.

The information FAA Headquarters in Washington reports to the American public is only as good as the information it receives from the field. And when it comes to air rage, the numbers are far from accurate.

THE FBI AND THE REPORTING OF AIR RAGE

The Federal Bureau of Investigation may be called to investigate an onboard disturbance, but only during a category 3 incident. However, due to the small number of agents who are in proximity to an airport, handling an interference with flight crew case is generally low on the FBI's priority list. In the case of a terrorist attack, the FBI would be there. Critical investigations and national security issues take priority before the FBI responds to an air rage incident at the airport. The FBI is required to report violations of criminal law to the U.S. Attorney's Office.

If the U.S. Attorney believes that it may be a high-profile case, she will direct an FBI agent to make an arrest. Similarly, if the U.S. Attorney believes the case will make her look good, then, and only then, will the FBI take a case. The rest of the cases are generally not investigated and are often referred back to the FAA for a possible civil penalty or termination of the case. Criminal referrals to the FBI are few and far between. Less then 5 percent of the actual number of air rage incidents reported to the FBI will ever become a criminal case.

WHAT CAN BE DONE TO IMPROVE REPORTING?

Airlines must take the responsibility to ensure that all employees are clear on what actions should be taken when an incident occurs. It is imperative that airlines develop a structured reporting program using those employees who are most familiar with the security aspects of the airline, including crew members.

The reporting program should encourage employees to promptly report all cases of interference on standardized incident reports. The written reports should contain at a minimum the date, time, flight number, origin/destination of the flight, and the names, addresses, and phone numbers of the crew members. In addition, it is crucial to obtain statements from the crew or passengers—or both—in order to provide law enforcement officials with objective and impartial information. The most important information for an air rage incident is the name, address, and physical description of the offending passenger.

The methods used could be as simple as matching the seat assignment number with the passenger, or obtaining the name and address from luggage tags. Using a frequent flier number is the easiest way to identify a passenger. Invariably, the name and address will be correct. Even a seasoned air rage offender will keep his address and phone number updated with the airline, to ensure that his frequent flyer mileage has been credited to his account.

The reporting program should also provide information about which airline officials should be contacted when an incident occurs. The local FAA office should be informed immediately by the airline when an incident takes place. Information should also be provided to the crew members on how they may directly contact the Federal Aviation Administration and law enforcement offices from the air, which may circumvent any attempt by the airline to cover up an incident.

It is imperative that airline security employees keep a copy of the written report and follow up with the appropriate authorities for a proper resolution to the incident. In addition, copies of the report should be provided to local law enforcement personnel, the airline's corporate security department, the FAA, and the FBI.

Finally, the reporting program should also provide information regarding the filing of complaints against passengers. The process of pursuing violations requires an ongoing commitment and should not be taken lightly. Airline employees must get involved and may even be required to testify during informal hearings or subsequent court proceedings. Airline employees must have the support of the airline, and not be afraid to take a stand against air rage offenders.

Clearly, no one wants to turn the airline industry into Big Brother. But, incidents that threaten the physical safety of other passengers and the crew need to be reported.

Air carriers must also provide training for crew members and other responsible personnel in handling passengers who interfere with the performance of crew member duties. The training should acknowledge that it is not desirable to have cockpit crew members leave the cockpit, especially in cases where there are only two cockpit members. The training should also recognize the authority of the captain and that the decision to have a crew member leave the cockpit is solely at the discretion of captain.

Airlines should conduct training for all airline crew members on how to deal with passenger misconduct in addition to dealing with hijacking and other unusual circumstances. This specific training should include information that will help the crew members recognize those situations that may, when combined with the traits of some passengers, create stress, or situations that may escalate into serious disturbances.

When responding to imminent danger posed by a passenger, crew members may need to solicit help from other crew members, employees, or passengers in order to help restrain an individual. Usually the other person will be another flight attendant. However, the remaining flight attendants have other passengers to attend to and safety-related duties that may preclude them from assisting during the incident.

It is important to note that on commercial aircraft operating with nineteen to forty-six seats, there is only one flight attendant; therefore passengers may need to get involved. In addition, commuter planes with nineteen seats or fewer are not required to have flight attendants. Passengers may again need to be prepared to get involved in order to protect themselves, the flight crew, and their lives. However, this does not mean passengers should themselves turn into an angry, violent mob.

Finally, crew members need to be trained to fill out the incident reports that the air carrier has developed for the purpose of handling passengers who commit an incident of air rage. When law enforcement officers are called to meet the flight, crew members need to be informed that significant delays may occur and additional written statements may be required. Crew members must be assured that the airline fully supports their cooperation with the authorities, regardless of the impending delays and/or monetary costs.

The bottom line is that airlines must be held accountable for reporting these instances to local law enforcement officials and the FAA as they occur, to facilitate the integrity of the reporting structure and ensure proper guidance and assistance in handling these situations.

LOCAL LAW ENFORCEMENT AND THE REPORTING OF AIR RAGE

For the most part, local law enforcement authorities are not overly concerned with reporting incidents of air rage. Crimes that are committed on board an aircraft fall under federal jurisdiction, not local or state law. Outside of detaining a passenger and writing a brief synopsis, local authorities are rarely able or willing to get involved.

Incidents of interference with crew members could be a serious violation of federal aviation regulations and may initially warrant a response from local law enforcement agencies or the FBI. In most of these cases, the initial response will be provided by a local law enforcement agency. In some smaller airports around the country, there may be no resident law enforcement unit at the airport, so the responsibility to respond would fall on the agency or department that has territorial jurisdiction for the airport. Significant delays may occur before law enforcement assistance arrives on the scene.

When an incident of interference with flight crew occurs on board an aircraft the captain should immediately notify the airline's dispatch office and the air traffic control tower. The captain must make the request for law enforcement personnel to meet the aircraft. However, in order for law enforcement to take action, there must be a legal basis for intervention. For instance, physically assaulting a crew member or another passenger would certainly warrant law enforcement action. Not only is this a violation of federal law it is also a violation of state law, otherwise known as simple battery. In this case, local law enforcement agencies have the authority to detain and arrest the perpetrator. However, if the incident involves an individual who smokes in the lavatory, starts a small fire in the trash bin, which sets off the smoke detectors and causes a panic onboard the aircraft, there is no legal basis for criminal action from local law enforcement agencies. Therefore, local law enforcement agencies are not required to report this to anyone. Certainly the airline does not want to create an issue, and if no one calls the FAA, no one will ever know. Unfortunately, the lives of innocent passengers will be put at risk again and again if the individual is allowed to go free without consequences.

The confusion over jurisdiction and authority regarding air rage incidents is a great concern for any local law enforcement officer in his response. Because of this uncertainty, arrests more than likely do not occur. Any action taken must be clearly and undeniably within the scope of the authority for the law enforcement officer. Yet the lack of clarity that exists in explaining who is to investigate air rage makes it difficult for local law enforcement officials to act.

To further alienate local law enforcement, if an arrest is made, or if the case is referred to the FBI, local prosecution of the case is undermined by federal law. So in essence, the actions of local law enforcement becomes a big waste of time. According to the federal aviation regulations, the prosecution of air rage cases rests with the appropriate office of the U.S. Attorney's Office, not local judges and juries.

Since there is no mandated requirement for local law enforcement agencies to report incidents of air rage, the responsibility must fall back on the airlines. The airline must inform all members of the cabin crew that full cooperation is necessary in reporting an incident in a timely manner and the necessity of providing statements, if requested by local law enforcement, on behalf of the FBI and the FAA. Only when notification is made to the federal agencies can action be taken against an individual by the government for violation of a criminal statute or for violation of civil law under the specific federal aviation regulations.

Reports that are forwarded to the FAA may result in joint investigation with the FBI. Cases in which the FBI declines to investigate may still be handled by the FAA and could result in a civil penalty for the passenger involved in interfering with the crew member.

It is important to note that these same conflicts for reporting air rage arise on international flights. Local law enforcement will still respond, and as long as the aircraft is a U.S. carrier or a foreign carrier within the special jurisdiction of the United States, the federal agencies need to be contacted in order for an air rage incident to be handled properly.

Local law enforcement departments should be encouraged to report all—even minor—instances of air rage to the FAA and the FBI immediately upon notification from the crew members that there is a problem on board the aircraft. In addition, local law enforcement agencies should be encouraged to submit written reports regarding their involvement with the incident, and be responsible for obtaining copies of the incident reports from crew members. Having accurate records is the only way to address the problem.

AIRLINE PASSENGERS AND THE REPORTING OF AIR RAGE

Today, passengers who complain and report incidents of air rage are often sent a letter of apology from the airline and given a travel voucher for their next flight. The letter is almost always the same and will often resemble something like the following:

Dear Mr. / Mrs. / Ms. Valued Customer:

There is no excuse for the unsatisfactory service you received when you traveled with us recently to Horrorville. We should have been more responsive to your needs and I am sorry our employees were not more successful in lessening the inconvenience of the flight disturbance. I can imagine how frustrating it must have been especially when another passenger threw that bottle at your head. Please accept my sincere apology for all that occurred.

I would like to assure you that your comments will be used as a focus of discussion on how to better serve our customers in the future. You have provided good insight and the opportunity to improve, and we will do our best to do just that!

As a more tangible evidence of our concern and regret for your disappointing experience, a $100.00 transportation voucher is enclosed. It is valid for twelve months and may be used toward the purchase of another ticket on the airline of your choice. Please note that the voucher may not be used for travel during those numerous blackout dates.

Mr. / Mrs. / Ms. Valued Customer, it is clear from your comments that we both share a belief in the importance of quality service. We want your travel on our airline to be pleasant and trouble free, and appreciate being told when it is not. I hope this one near-death experience does not cause you to lose confidence in us. We value you as a customer and are eager to demonstrate our ability to provide the level of service you expect from us.

Sincerely,
(The secretary of some Customer Service Manager)

Most seasoned travelers have received a letter like this at one time or another. Unfortunately, the $100 travel voucher often deters the general public from reporting instances of air rage or providing voluntary statements to the authorities when requested.

Nevertheless, the traveling public also has an obligation to report incidents of air rage just as they would if they had witnessed a bank robbery. It will only be through checks and balances and numerous reporting avenues that air rage incidents will finally be addressed, and the serious and repeat perpetrators jailed.

When an incident of air rage does occur we have a tendency to forget about the passengers who were victimized, who had no choice except to witness the abominable behavior of some sociopathic swine. Take a good look at an airline's "Contract of Carriage." This document contains the conditions for travel on a particular air carrier and what can reasonably be expected. Generally, it will cover the following topics:

- Limits on liability for personal injury or death
- Rights of the air carrier and limits on liability for delay or failure to perform service, including schedule changes, substitution of alternate air carriers and/or aircraft, and rerouting procedures
- Limits on liability for baggage including fragile or perishable goods and availability of excess valuation coverage
- Claims/restrictions, including the time periods in which a passenger must file a claim or bring an action against the air carrier
- Rules of the air carrier to change the terms of the contract at its discretion
- Rules on reconfirmation of reservation and check-in times

Buried deep within most "Contracts of Carriage" is a statement stating that "the airline may refuse to transport any passenger for the following reasons":

1. The passenger's conduct is abusive/disorderly or the individual appears to be under the influence of drugs/alcohol.
2. The passenger exhibits behavior that is abnormal and/or that might jeopardize the safety of the aircraft or its occupants.
3. The passenger's mental or physical condition is such that it is determined that the passenger cannot safely complete the trip.

Therefore, an air carrier is under contract with any individual who purchases a ticket to ensure that the safety/security of the flight is not compromised. Every passenger has the responsibility to notify the airline when a potentially dangerous situation is about to occur, especially before the aircraft leaves the gate.

Today, that decision to deny a passenger boarding is often left up to an eighteen-year-old gate agent whose sole responsibility is to board all the passengers and get the aircraft out on time. Further, if the aircraft does leave the gate, it is in the passenger's best interest to discretely report irrational behavior on board the aircraft as soon as possible to the flight crew, to prevent a further escalation of an air rage incident. Don't be afraid to get involved. To turn a phrase, "the life you save may be your own."

So who's responsible for reporting incidents of air rage? It's not a difficult answer: all of the above. Every person who flies, every government employee, every government agency, and, most importantly, the airlines have a responsibility to report incidents of air rage to ensure proper reporting and swift justice for the perpetrator.

7
THE LACK OF CONSEQUENCES

In the rare instance where an air rage case is reported *and* prosecuted in the United States, it is more often than not settled with a civil penalty, a slap on the wrist, or nothing at all.

On a flight from Philadelphia, a woman returning to her seat from the lavatory began spraying perfume on her fellow passengers while she complained about the bad odor in the cabin. When one of the newly sprayed passengers raised an objection to the woman's behavior, the perfume-toting woman called her "white trash" and told her to sit down. When the woman finally returned to her seat, she found that the elderly passenger directly in front her had placed her seat in the reclined position. The enraged woman gave the seat a "mule kick" which broke the chair's back and sandwiched the senior citizen against the seat in front of her. When the husband of the elderly woman confronted the instigator, she told him, "I'll kill you and I'll sue your family so bad you'll be living in the street." In spite of the assault, the woman was not prosecuted since it was determined the incident was merely "an altercation between passengers."

A British man on a flight from Orlando to Manchester, England, was arrested after the operators of a charter flight said he threatened to punch out an airplane window, shouting, "You will all get sucked out and die."

The flight was diverted to Bangor, Maine, and the passenger was placed in custody by local police. Reports claimed that the man put his foot through a video monitor and then made a statement about punching out a window so everyone would get sucked out and die. Many of the 204 people on board the plane reportedly started screaming. After the passenger's

115

release the next day from the Bangor jail, the carrier, Airtours, announced that he had been banned from its flights for life.[1]

A crazed passenger on a flight from Seattle to Minneapolis was detained and fined after allegedly punching the man seated next to him several times because "he didn't like the cologne he was wearing." The incident was particularly distressing because the victim—an eighty-year-old—was sleeping when the attack occurred. Nevertheless, after investigators concluded their report, the attacker was merely fined and allowed to continue on to his destination.

Typically, in the United States, if a penalty is levied as punishment for any behavior that is deemed dangerous, it is almost always a monetary fine. Embarrassingly, the standard fine is a paltry $1,100. If the perpetrator decides to plead guilty, he simply shows up, writes a check, and walks out as if it were a speeding ticket. If he pleads guilty and claims financial hardship, he can cut a deal with the FAA to reduce the fine by 50 percent or more.

WHAT CAN LOCAL
LAW ENFORCEMENT DO?

As we briefly mentioned in the previous chapter, local authorities in the United States assigned to an airport have limited jurisdiction when an incident of air rage occurs. The local law enforcement presence at an airport is actually a requirement of Federal Aviation Regulations 107.15 and 107.17, which essentially state that airports have to have law enforcement officers on duty for the protection of the airport facility, to respond to incidents at the checkpoints and to keep the peace.

When an incident of air rage occurs, local law enforcement officers are generally always the first ones on the scene. Their response may include interviewing one or more members of the crew, other passengers who witnessed the incident, and/or the air rage offender. Action may be taken by the law enforcement agency responding, in the form of an arrest for simple battery, or a report may be taken and forwarded to the FAA and FBI, or the air rage offender may simply be held until federal authorities are notified. In all cases of air rage the FAA and FBI should be called immediately to meet the arriving aircraft. Today, the FAA and FBI are notified only for the most serious incidents such as assaults against crews, intimidation using a dangerous weapon, and the threat or actual sabotage of an aircraft.

Local authorities have the authority to arrest under state law for simple battery. This generally occurs when the FAA or FBI is not notified of an air rage incident or if they are unable to get to the airport. If an air rage offender is criminally prosecuted under state law for an act of battery, for instance, federal criminal prosecution would not likely be pursued because of the "double jeopardy" factor. However, the offender may still be prosecuted under civil law. In many jurisdictions, assault and battery is defined as a action taken toward an individual that threatens bodily harm or the infliction of physical injury. In some states abusive or suggestive language, unless used in a threatening manner, is not considered an assault. Of course, when physical contact does occur, a state or a federal official may arrest the individual for assault and battery. It's dependent upon whoever happens to show up.

In the past, physical violence between passengers was generally handled under state law, falling generally under simple assault and battery. Legislation has recently been enacted to ensure that passenger-to-passenger conflicts while aboard an aircraft are dealt with and prosecuted on the federal level. In the past, these conflicts were never dealt with properly, but now it is clear that these passenger conflicts involve the crew members; even when the confrontation is not directed at the cabin crew, it is just as deadly and dangerous.

In summation, local law enforcement agencies can do little to curb the skyrocketing incidents of air rage. Their principal duties are to support the federal agencies when and if they respond to an incident. The importance of local law enforcement agencies can not be overstated. They must gather as much information as possible and detain the perpetrator until help arrives.

CRIMINAL VERSUS CIVIL CHARGES

In the United States, air rage offenders can be charged with under civil law, criminal law, or both. As noted earlier, the two agencies primarily responsible for dealing with incidents of air rage in the United States are the Federal Aviation Administration and the Federal Bureau of Investigation. The

FAA is a reglatory agency which falls under the Department of Transportation and is not considered a law enforcement agency. Therefore, the FAA would charge an individual under civil law and propose a civil penalty. The FBI, which works under the Department of Justice, is a law enforcement agency and seeks prosecution of an air rage offender under criminal law.

WHOSE JOB IS IT, ANYWAY?

Within the FAA, two separate divisions investigate instances of air rage. As noted earlier, in the middle of the country incidents are investigated by the FAA Airways Flight Standards Division, and on the East and West Coasts they are investigated by the FAA Security Division.

The Airways Flight Standards Division is responsible for the general safety of the aircraft. Clearly, air rage affects the safety of a flight. It cannot be emphasized enough that having two separate divisions of the same government agency conduct similar yet different investigations has proven to be detrimental to the program. It breeds confusion and a lack of consistency on the number of cases written and where and when they are written. According to the cases reviewed, the majority of the cases appear to have occurred on the East and West Coasts, as opposed to the middle of the country. This may be due in part to a pilot program that was initiated by the FAA in 1997, to have the Security Division handle the air rage incidents. The Security Division has reportedly done a better job of posting the numbers, so to speak, than the Flight Standards Division, even though the Security Division is responsible for handling the incidents in only two of the nine regions of the country.

The Airways Flight Standards Division should remain focused on safety concerns rather than air rage incidents. The Flight Standards Division has enough responsibility and should concentrate on certifying the airlines and pilots, and ensuring that maintenance practices are being followed by the air carriers. The FAA Security Division should have total and complete control over these incidents, since air rage should be treated as a criminal matter. FAA security special agents are better trained and at least have some authority to follow up on and work with other law enforcement agencies to prosecute these individuals.

FAA ENFORCEMENT ACTIONS

The Federal Aviation Administration publishes a quarterly compilation of enforcement actions against those who violate federal aviation law. This compilation, located on the FAA Web site (www.faa.gov), is based on data from the agency's Enforcement Information System (EIS). The EIS is primarily used as a tracking mechanism for those within the aviation industry who hold a certificate from the FAA. Some of the entities that require certification include the air carriers, aircraft repair stations, and flight schools. In addition, foreign air carriers, pilots, and even individual members of the public who violate federal law and commit unlawful acts against civil aviation may be found in the EIS. When a case is opened against an individual for a suspected act of air rage, the individual is entered into the EIS. Once in the system, it is used for case development and is also used to determine if the individual is a repeat offender. If the individual has been convicted of a previous incident on board an aircraft, that individual could be subjected to an additional fine.

The FAA has the authority to issue a civil penalty up to $50,000 for violations of certain aviation laws and regulations. However, there is technically no ceiling for a civil penalty. For example, an air carrier is subject to a civil penalty of up to $11,000 for a single violation of the aviation law or an FAA regulation. The air carrier could have one hundred violations connected to one incident and, therefore, the civil penalty could easily reach $1 million. Under the law others, including individuals accused of committing an act of air rage, are subject to a civil penalty of $1,100 per violation.

It is interesting to note that although most cases of air rage involve multiple violations, the standard fine is usually only $1,100. This is primarily due to the fact that the FAA agent assigned to the case has the discretion to pursue all of the violations, some of the violations, or none at all, depending upon her workload. Even if an individual did commit two or three violations while on board an aircraft, the perpetrator of a violent outburst would receive only a paltry $2,200 or $3,300 fine, respectively, and a slap on the wrist.

In the spring of 2000, Congress gave the FAA the authority to raise the civil penalty for air rage violations from $1,100 to $25,000. Yet as of the spring of 2001, the $25,000 fine has not yet been invoked. Apparently no guidance has been issued to the FAA employees on how to apply this new dollar amount to their cases. This does not sound like an insurmountable problem. It would not take more than a memo to notify the agents that it is now permissible and legal to assess a $25,000 penalty. This new penalty, whenever it goes into effect, will undoubtedly be limited to certain instances and then left up to the agent's discretion. Unfortunately this act of legislation, which has been ignored, has done little or nothing to slow or deter the rapid increase in air rage incidents.

DUE PROCESS

Why does it always seem that the rights of the accused far outweigh the rights of those who have been injured? If the FAA determines that a case is warranted, the agent assigned to the case writes a letter of investigation to the individual who committed the act of air rage. The individual then has an opportunity before a case is written to give his side of the story. If the case agent believes the story of the air rage perpetrator, the case may be closed with a simple warning letter. If the case agent believes that the individual deserves the $1,100 fine, a full case will be written and sent on to the FAA Legal Department for review.

The cases that are reviewed, as a matter of public record, appear to be so detailed that they must take several days to complete. One has to question the priorities of an agent doing paperwork at her desk for several days to obtain an $1,100 fine when she should instead be at the airport, responding to other reports of air rage. But at least in those instances the individual pays something—or does he?

There is an opportunity at the beginning of most of these enforcement actions for the alleged violator to request an informal hearing with an FAA attorney. This informal hearing usually occurs after the case has been written but before a judgment can be made. The alleged violator has the opportunity to bring to the FAA attorney any information favorable to the case, such as exculpatory or mitigating evidence. During these informal hearings an enforcement action can sometimes be resolved to the mutual satisfaction of both the FAA and the alleged violator. In other words, cases are often resolved without resorting to the full litigation process, since this saves on the expense of litigation.

If an individual from New York commits an incident of air rage on his way to Los Angeles, and the aircraft lands as scheduled in Los Angeles, the FAA office in Los Angeles would open up the case against the individual. If the FAA agent assigned to the case determined that a $1,100 civil penalty was warranted, the individual from New York could request an informal hearing to discuss the incident. The hearing would be held in New York, for the convenience of the alleged violator. The U.S. government would have to pay the hotel, airfare, and meal expenses for the FAA attorney, the FAA agent who wrote the case, and any primary witnesses to the alleged incident. This could easily amount to several thousand dollars —to settle an $1,100 case! In most of these instances FAA attorneys may suggest that that the informal hearings be conducted via telephone. In appreciation of the alleged violator's participation, the settlement for air rage case may reflect a much lower civil penalty due to a compromise on both sides. Often during this process charges may be dropped against the individual and the record expunged from the EIS altogether!

If, for some reason, the alleged violator was insistent upon a face-to-face informal hearing, he and the FAA entourage would have to travel to New York, and the $1,100 fine would remain in place, but he would have several more options. The individual from New York could appeal the notice of civil penalty to an administrative law judge who is assigned to the Department of Transportation. Complicating the matter further, the administrative law judge could rule in favor of the FAA, and then the violator could appeal the case to the FAA administrator. All this for an $1,100 fine!

Throughout this entire process, if the alleged violator can at any time prove financial hardship, the FAA attorney has the authority to lower the fine based on the violator's ability to pay and/or set up a payment plan to suit the offender's needs. It would appear that the time and money spent by the FAA to investigate, write, and prosecute a case is hardly worthwhile and the cases that are prosecuted do not seem to have a deterrent effect on the growing number of incidents.

Justice in these cases should be swift for individuals accused and convicted of air rage incidents. All incidents of air rage should be made a matter of record and be considered an open case. It should not be left up to the discretion of an FAA agent. The $25,000 penalty should be strictly enforced, and no deals should be cut to reduce the fine. We must hold these individuals accountable for their actions, and the only way that this will happen is to treat this crime as a serious offense and hit the individual where it hurts: in the pocket book.

This whole scenario is based on one very important factor: the individual who is accused of an act of air rage must provide current a name, address, and phone number to the initial law enforcement agency responding to the scene. Now this information may sound like a relatively simple thing to get, but it appears that several hundred cases a year are thrown out because the individual cannot be located. A full case may even be written, but if the individual leaves no forwarding address or refuses to accept certified mail from the FAA, the air rage offender wins.

Apparently, it is not worthwhile for the government to pursue these individuals as the cost far outweighs any civil penalty that would be obtained. Once again, there appears to be a lack of consequences for those individuals who know how to use the system.

FBI INVOLVEMENT IN AIR RAGE PROSECUTION

The Federal Bureau of Investigation plays an integral part in deciding whether an air rage perpetrator is brought to justice. When, or if, the FBI is called in to handle a serious air rage incident, the U.S. Attorney will most certainly be involved. The U.S. Attorney guides and directs local FBI agents in handling reported instances of air rage. Unfortunately, it would appear that the U.S. Attorney may need some guidance on the importance of pursuing these types of cases.

The U.S. Attorney's Office is, of course, inundated with a tremendous amount of work, so it must set priorities in handling new cases. Research indicates that some U.S. Attorney's Offices across the country are more aggressive than others in pushing the FBI to pursue incidents of air rage. However, their lack of consistency breeds a tremendous amount of frustration for those looking to make air rage offenders face up to the consequences of their actions.

A PRETRIAL DIVERSION AGREEMENT

When the U.S. Attorney does decide to prosecute a reported incident, it is often settled with a pretrial diversion agreement. A pretrial diversion agreement is a document drafted by the U.S. Attorney's Office and approved by a judge. This document is an agreement between the air rage offender and the United States of America that settles the criminal aspect of the incident without incarceration. The following is a complete example of a pretrial diversion that was issued against an individual who was high on drugs and alcohol, verbally abused fellow passengers, punched a flight attendant, and attempted to break into the cockpit in an attempt to take control of the airplane.

> You have been reported to have interfered with the flight crew members which is an offense against the United States in violation of Title 49, United States Code, Section 46504. On an aircraft in the special jurisdiction of the United States, you knowingly assaulted and intimidated a flight attendant of the aircraft, interfered with the performance of the duties of the attendant, and lessened the ability of the attendant to perform those duties.
>
> Upon accepting responsibility for your behavior and by your signature on this Agreement, it appears after an investigation of the offense and your background, that the interests of the United States and your own interests and the interests of justice will be served by the following procedures, on the authority of the Attorney General of the United States, and the United States Attorney who is assigned to this district. The prosecution in this district for these offenses shall be deferred for a period of 6 months from this date, provided you abide by the following conditions and the requirements of this Agreement.
>
> Should you violate the conditions of this Agreement, the United States Attorney may revoke or modify any conditions of this Pretrial Diversion Program or change the period of supervision. The United States Attorney may At any time within the period of your supervision initiate prosecution for these offenses should you violate the conditions of this Agreement. In such an event your statement accepting responsibility may be used against you. In this case you will be issued a notice specifying the conditions of the Agreement which you have violated.
>
> After you successfully complete your Pretrial Diversion Program and

fulfill all the terms and conditions of the Agreement, no prosecution for the offenses will be instituted in this District, and the charges against you will be dismissed.

General provisions

1. You shall not violate any law, including federal, state, or local. You shall immediately contact your Pretrial Diversion Supervisor if you are arrested or questioned by any law enforcement officer.

2. You shall continue to live in this District, and if you intend to move, you shall inform your supervisor so that an appropriate transfer of the program responsibility can be made.

3. You shall report to your supervisor as directed and keep him/her informed of your whereabouts.

4. You shall follow the program and the special conditions that follow.

Special Conditions

A. You shall not fly on any commercial flights unless you receive prior approval from your supervisor.

B. You are to refrain from any use of alcohol and any use or unlawful possession of a narcotic drug and other controlled substances. You shall submit to drug and/or alcohol testing at the discretion of your supervisor.

C. In lieu of community service, you shall write a letter of apology to the flight attendant and include the rules and regulations which you broke, the consequences which could occur when passengers fail to abide by these rules. The letter must be submitted to your supervisor prior to your hearing before the Magistrate Judge.

Acknowledgment

I certify that I am aware of the Sixth Amendment to the Constitution of the United States which provides that in all criminal prosecutions the accused shall have the right to a speedy and public trial. I am also aware that Rule 48(b) of the Federal Rules of Criminal Procedures provides that the Court may dismiss an indictment, information, complaint for unnecessary delay in presenting a charge to the Grand Jury in bringing a defendant to trial. I request that the United States Attorney for this District defer such prosecution. I agree and consent that any delay from the date of this Agreement to the date of initiation of prosecution, as provided for in these terms and shall be deemed a necessary delay at my request. I waive any defense to such prosecution on the ground that such delay operated to deny my rights under Rule 48 (b) of the Federal Rules of Criminal Prosecution.

I hereby state that the above has been read and explained to me. I understand the conditions of my Pretrial Diversion Program and agree that I will comply with all the provisions of this Agreement.

Signed, air rage Offender

Once again, the time and money spent to prosecute this individual is not commensurate with the crime. This individual should have been jailed and assessed a stiff civil penalty. Instead, the individual is allowed to go free and may be sitting next to you on your next flight.

Was justice really served with this pretrial diversion, or has the money, time, and energy gone to waste? Even brief jail sentences would send the message to would-be air rage offenders that such behavior will not be tolerated.

The FAA is the principal agency governing the air transportation system in the United States. In most countries around the world there is an FAA equivalent organization that oversees the air transportation system of that country. The FAA is by far the world's largest aviation organization in the world, employing some fifty-five thousand people worldwide.

The rest of the world turns to the United States for leadership and training, and often requests assistance from the many talented professionals employed here. What kind of role model do we make on this front? Since 40 percent of all commercial flights in the world take place in the United States, you can make the quantum leap that more cases of the air rage occur here than in any other country in the world. Since we have not handled the problem well, it may be time for the United States to ask for assistance in dealing with this issue. Input from the rest of the world may be critical in an attempt to deal with this issue consistently here and on a worldwide basis.

This is an issue of global proportions and an issue that needs to be addressed on a larger scale through the assistance of the International Civil Aviation Organization (ICAO). The lack of consequence for air rage in many countries around the world could be curtailed by addressing the air rage issue on a global scale.

PROSECUTION OF AIR RAGE OUTSIDE OF THE UNITED STATES

In the international arena, countries around the world have developed laws that combine the United States civil and criminal codes together. Recently, an individual in England was sentenced to one year in jail and ordered to pay a $3,000 fine for failing to stop using his cell phone while on board a flight. Foreign countries, in some ways, are way ahead of the United States in pursuing the criminal aspect of air rage.

Bluntly put, the only way to curb this global crisis is to jail those individuals who are responsible for putting others in danger. The monetary fines that are imposed by the FAA are often inconsequential compared to the standard of living in the United States. Worldwide, and especially in the United States, all instances of air rage should be dealt with in a criminal court, not just a civil court.

THE ROLE OF THE INTERNATIONAL CIVIL AVIATION ORGANIZATION

The ICAO is located in Montreal. The aims and objectives of the ICAO are to develop the principles and techniques of international air navigation and foster the planning and development of international air transport so as to (1) ensure the safe and orderly growth of international civil aviation throughout the world; (2) encourage of aircraft design and operation for peaceful purposes; (3) encourage the development of airways, airports, and air navigation facilities for international civil aviation; (4) meet the needs of the peoples of the world for safe, regular, efficient, and economical air transport; (5) prevent economic waste caused by unreasonable competition;

(6) ensure that the rights of the contracting states are fully respected and that every contracting state has a fair opportunity to operate international airlines; (7) avoid discrimination between contracting states; (8) promote safety of flight in international air navigation; and (9) promote generally the development of all aspects of international civil aeronautics.[2]

The ICAO has a sovereign body, the assembly, and a governing body, the council. The assembly meets at least once every three years and is convened by the council. Each contracting state is entitled to one vote. Decisions of the assembly are taken by a majority of the votes cast, except when otherwise provided in the convention. At these sessions the work of the organization in its technical, economic, and legal aspects is reviewed. It provides guidance to other bodies of the ICAO for their future work.

The council is a permanent body responsible to the assembly and is composed of thirty-three contracting states elected by the assembly for a three-year term. In the election, adequate representation is given to states of chief importance in air transport. Other states not otherwise included, which make large contributions to civil aviation, and states not otherwise included whose designation ensures representation of the major geographic areas of the world are also represented on the council.

The council, the Air Navigation Commission, the Air Transport Committee, the Legal Committee, the Committee on Joint Support of Air Navigation Services, the Finance Committee, the Committee on Unlawful Interference, the Personnel Committee, and the Technical Cooperation Committee provide the continuing direction of the work of the organization. One of the major duties of the council is to adopt "International Standards and Recommended Practices" and to incorporate these as annexes to the Convention on International Civil Aviation. The council may act as arbiter between contracting states on matters concerning aviation and implementation of the convention, it may investigate any situation that presents avoidable obstacles to the development of international air navigation, and it may take whatever steps are necessary to maintain the safety and regularity of operation of international air transport.

The Committee on Unlawful Interference needs to be assigned the task of tackling air rage and must take the lead in educating the contracting states on how to deal consistently with these on a worldwide basis.

Air rage should be treated as any other act of unlawful interference, such as hijacking. When a hijacking occurs, all law-abiding countries are concerned and pledge to give their support and follow the procedures that were established at the various ICAO conventions. Air rage is no exception. Whenever an incident occurs in the world it should be put in a database available to all governments so the international community can learn how to better deal with these incidents.

8

AIR RAGE VERSUS AIR TERRORISM

In the past fifteen years, there have been over 325 documented incidents of airline disasters around in the world. In approximately 62 percent of those incidents, there is a reasonable explanation for the disaster: for instance, weather, mechanical failure, and even runway collisions. The other 38 percent have an explanation or a "likely cause of the crash" that will never really be confirmed.

For example, we know for a fact that there have been fifteen incidents of a bomb or explosion destroying an aircraft, which may seem like a relatively small number over the past fifteen years. But there have been four incidents that have never been categorized, in addition to ten incidents of aircraft crashing into the sea and thirty-seven incidents of commercial aircraft crashing into mountains. Now, we could blame the pilots for their lack of skill or even the flight plan for inherent flaws, but it is also possible that air rage or an act of air terrorism may have played a role.

AIR RAGE AND AIR TERRORISM

At its core, air rage is generally more personal and spontaneous, whereas air terrorism is usually more planned and political. Nevertheless, they are separate but equally dangerous threats.

Air rage can be a precursor to air terrorism. Air rage can lead to an incident of air terrorism quickly and without warning. There is, however, a fundamental difference between the two categories. Air rage perpetrators are generally dissatisfied and distraught with an aspect of the airline experience. Whether it's an issue with the airline or through drugs, alcohol, or mental illness, an act of air rage may be the result. The individual reacts, insisting on taking matters into his own hands. This is a spontaneous and sometimes deadly form of aggression.

An act of air terrorism is generally committed by individuals for political, economic, or social reasons and is generally planned in advance. Individuals who commit air terrorism may be on a what they believe is a mission from a higher authority or they may feel that life has no meaning.

AIR TERRORISM AND AVIATION SECURITY

According to the final report of the White House Commission on Aviation Security to President Clinton in 1997, improved security for air travelers is a major concern that must be confronted.

The FBI, the CIA, and other intelligence sources have been warning that the threat of terrorism is changing in two important ways. First, it is no longer merely an overseas threat from foreign terrorists. People and places in the United States have joined the lists of targets, and Americans have joined the ranks of terrorists. The bombings of the World Trade Center in New York and the Murrah Federal Building in Oklahoma City are clear examples of the shift.

The second change is that in addition to well-known, established terrorist groups, it is becoming more common to find terrorists working alone or in ad hoc groups, some of whom are not afraid to die carrying out their designs.

Although the threat of terrorism is increasing, the danger of an individual becoming a victim of a terrorist attack, let a lone an aircraft bombing, will doubtless remain very small. But terrorism isn't merely a matter of statistics. We fear a plane crash far more than we fear something like a car accident. One might survive a car accident, but there's no chance in a plane that crashes from thirty thousand feet above the earth. This fear is one of the reasons terrorists see airplanes as attractive targets. Moreover, they know that airlines are often seen as national symbols. When terrorists attack a U.S. air carrier, they are in essence attacking the United States. Terrorists have so little respect for decent values and innocent lives that they have no compunction destroying children, women, and men at random.

This cannot be tolerated or allowed to intimidate free societies. There must be a concerted national effort to fight terrorism. There must be a willingness to apply sustained economic, political, and commercial pressure on countries sponsoring terrorists. There must be an unwavering commitment to pursuing terrorists and bringing them to justice. There must be the resolve to punish those who would violate sanctions imposed against terrorist states.

Today's aviation security is based in part on the defenses erected in the 1970s against hijackers and on recommendations made by the Commission on Aviation Security and Terrorism, which was formed in the wake of the bombing of PanAm 103 over Lockerbie, Scotland, on December 21, 1988. In that case, 259 passengers and 11 people on the ground were killed when the flight from Heathrow to New York blew up thirty-eight minutes after takeoff. Improvements in aviation security have been complicated because government and industry often found themselves at odds, unable to resolve disputes over financing, effectiveness, technology, and potential impacts on operations and passengers.

Airline passengers should not have to choose between enhanced security and efficient and affordable air travel. Both goals are achievable if the federal government, airlines, airports, aviation employees, local law enforcement agencies, and passengers work together to achieve them. Accordingly, the commission recommends a new partnership that will marshal resources more effectively and focus all parties on achieving the ultimate goal: enhancing the security of air travel for the flying public.

The commission considered the question of whether or not the FAA is the appropriate government agency to have the primary responsibility for regulating aviation security. The commission believes that, because of its extensive interactions with airlines and airports, the FAA is the appropriate agency, with the following qualifications: first, that the FAA must improve the way it carries out its mission; and second, that the roles of intelligence and law enforcement agencies in supporting the FAA must be more clearly defined and coordinated. The commission's recommendations address those conditions.

NEW TERRORIST THREATS

The terrorist threat is changing and growing. Therefore, it is important to improve security not just for familiar threats, such as explosives in checked baggage, but also to explore means of assessing and countering emerging threats, such as the use of biological or chemical agents or the use of missiles. While these do not present significant threats at present, it would be shortsighted not to plan for their possible use and take prudent steps to counter them for the not-so-distant future.

The commission believes that aviation security should be composed of system that are layered, integrated, and working together to produce the highest possible levels of protection. Each of the commission's recommendations should be looked upon not in isolation, but as a part of a whole.

The following are excerpts of the commission's recommendations:

3.1. The federal government should consider aviation security as a national security issue, and provide substantial funding for capital improvements. The Commission believes that terrorist attacks on civil aviation are directed at the United States, and that there should be an ongoing federal commitment to reducing the threats that they pose.

3.2. The FAA should establish federally mandated standards for security enhancements. These enhancements should include standards for use of Explosive Detection Systems (EDS) machines, training programs for security personnel, use of automated bag match technology, development of profiling programs (manual and automated), and deployment of explosive detection canine teams.

3.3. The Postal Service should advise customers that all packages weighing over 16 ounces will be subject to examination for explosives and other threat objects in order to move by air.

3.5. The FAA should implement a comprehensive plan to address the threat of explosives and other threat objects in cargo and work with industry to develop new initiatives in this area.

3.6. The FAA should establish a security system that will provide a high level of protection for all aviation information systems. In addition to improving the physical security of the traveling public, information systems critical to aircraft, air traffic control and airports should also be protected. The National Security Agency must play a role in coordinating information security measures, setting standards and providing oversight of system security to ensure protection against outside interference, disruption and corruption.

3.8. Submit a proposed resolution, through the U.S. Representative, that the International Civil Aviation Organization begin a program to verify and improve compliance with international security standards. Although 185 nations have ratified the International Civil Aviation Organization convention, and the security standards contained in it, compliance is not uniform. This creates the potential for security vulnerabilities on connecting flights throughout the world. To help raise levels of security throughout the world, the International Civil Aviation Organization needs greater authority to determine whether nations are in compliance. Strong U.S. sponsorship for adding verification and compliance capabilities to the International Civil Aviation Organization could lead to enhanced worldwide aviation security.

3.11. Access to airport controlled areas must be secured and the physical security of aircraft must be ensured. Air Carriers and airport authorities, working with FAA, must develop comprehensive and effective means by which to secure aircraft and other controlled areas from unauthorized access and intrusion. Use of radio frequency transponders to track the location of people and objects in airport controlled areas, including aircraft, offers significant advantages over the current security measures commonly used today. Where adequate airport controlled area and aircraft security are not assured by other means, this technology should be considered for use at both international and domestic airports.

3.12. Establish consortia at all commercial airports to implement enhancements to aviation safety and security. The FAA should direct its officials responsible for oversight of security procedures at the nation's 450 commercial airports to convene relevant aviation and law enforcement entities for the purpose of implementing the Commission's recommendations and further improving aviation safety and security. At each airport, these partners will: (1) immediately conduct a vulnerability assessment; and (2) based on that assessment, develop an action plan that includes the deployment of new technology and processes to enhance aviation safety and security.

3.24. Begin implementation of full bag-passenger match. Matching bags to passengers ensures that the baggage of anyone who does not board the plane is removed. Full bag match ensures that no unaccompanied bag remains onboard a flight.

3.27. Significantly increase the number of FBI agents assigned to counter-terrorism investigations, to improve intelligence, and to crisis response.

3.28. Provide anti-terrorism assistance in the form of airport security training to countries where there are airports served by airlines flying to the U.S.

THE ROLE OF THE FAA

The FAA maintains records of aircraft hijackings, bombing attacks, and other significant criminal acts against civil and general aviation interests worldwide. This information is used to compile a report which is found in the Criminal Acts against Civil Aviation at the FAA Web site (www.faa.gov).

ACTS OF AIR TERRORISM

The following stories are classified as incidents of air terrorism and have been treated as such by the governments involved.

A plan to hijack an airplane may have been foiled by a security checkpoint in Fort Lauderdale, Florida. A gun was discovered in a carry-on bag that had been placed on the X-ray belt at the screening checkpoint. Initially no one claimed the bag and the Fort Lauderdale Police Department was immediately notified of the incident. When the bag was opened there was a note inside that said, "Warning, this is a hijacking, I am a revolutionary and willful martyr, I am prepared to die, are you?" The individual who placed the bag on the belt was never positively identified; however, a few hours later an individual attempted to claim a similar bag at the airport's lost-and-found center. The police department was contacted again and the individual was detained for questioning.

The individual refused to identify himself, but claimed he was a member of a "Muslim faction" who had been sent by his organization to pick up a bag that was supposed to contain church documents.

The Fort Lauderdale police did an exceptional job of identifying the individual and found that he had a series of prior arrests. The individual was, in fact, a convicted felon who was charged in a first degree murder in New Mexico, but had fled while he was out on bail. The individual was taken into custody and extradited back to New Mexico, where he faces additional federal charges.

A flight attendant hijacked an Iranian passenger flight from Tehran to the Persian Gulf island of Kish. Reportedly, the flight attendant had an altercation with a passenger over the food service and became fed up with his job. The flight attendant dropped a serving tray in the aisle, removed his flight bag from an overhead compartment, and pulled out a gun. The flight attendant entered the flight deck, and fired a shot over the head of the captain, and ordered him to head west. The captain requested permission to land in Saudi Arabia and Jordan but permission was denied. The captain pleaded with Israel to allow him to land, as the aircraft was now dangerously low on fuel. The Israelis eventually allowed the plane to land at Avda Airbase, which is located in a sparsely populated section of the desert.

The flight attendant released the passengers and crew and surrendered to Israeli authorities. The flight attendant was reportedly "disgruntled," and decided that he needed a change. His long-term goal was to seek political asylum in Europe or the United States and according to him there was no time like the present to fulfill his dream. The aircraft was refueled and returned to Iran with all passengers and crew members on board.

An Avianca aircraft on a domestic flight between Bucaramanga and Bogota was hijacked by at least five armed members of the National Liberation Army (ELN) terrorist/insurgent organization. Most of the hijackers, who sat in various sections of the aircraft, were dressed as businessmen and one wore the collar of a Catholic priest. The hijacker who entered the cockpit issued specific flight instructions to the pilots and demonstrated a clear knowledge of aeronautical matters. Avianca flight 9463, a twin-engine turboprop Fokker 50 aircraft carrying approximately thirty-six passengers and five crew members, was diverted north to a clandestine dirt airstrip near the town of Simiti in the department of Southern Bolivar. Simiti is located approximately eighty miles northwest of Bucaramanga.

After the aircraft landed safely, the tires were punctured so that the plane could not be moved, and an estimated fifty to one hundred armed guerrillas herded the passengers into nearby boats on the Magdalena River. The guerrillas then took their hostages into the remote jungle area. The ELN hijacked the plane to pressure the Colombian government into treating it, the smaller of two Colombian guerrilla groups, as an equal partner in peace negotiations and to demonstrate their capability to conduct a well-planned and sophisticated operation. Colombian guerrillas have carried out hijackings in the past, but the subsequent kidnapping of all passengers and crew from a plane is unprecedented in Colombia and throughout most of the world.

A maintenance employee at Logan International Airport in Boston, Massachusetts, found suspicious materials in a bag located in a rest room. The employee contacted police after finding materials and components associated with an explosive device. The carry-on bag included a blasting cap, wires, black powder, safety flares, pellets, a battery, and even a small hand grenade.

Fortunately, the materials were unassembled and were safely removed by members of the Explosive Detection Unit of the Massachusetts State Police. The FBI immediately took over the case and within a few days determined the identity of the suspect and issued a warrant for his arrest.

The day before the explosives showed up at the airport, an individual robbed a bank in Salem, Massachusetts. During the robbery, a teller was shown a bag and was told it contained a bomb. It was allegedly the exact same bag that was found in the rest room at Logan Airport. The suspect was captured within hours of this discovery and was indicted by a federal grand jury on three counts: armed robbery, carrying an explosive device during the commission of a felony, and bringing an explosive device onto airport property.

A Lufthansa commuter jet was hijacked while en route from Prague, Czech Republic, to Düsseldorf, Germany. The Canadair Regional jet carried nineteen passengers and four crew. About fifteen minutes before the scheduled landing, a passenger walked up to the front of the plane and asked whether the plane was in German air space. Claiming to have a gun and a trigger mechanism for an explosive device, the man then demanded to be taken to the United Kingdom. When informed that there was insufficient fuel to reach the UK, the hijacker allowed the plane to land in Düsseldorf. The passengers were probably not aware of the incident and deplaned normally. The hijacker deplaned after all of the other passengers and then surrendered to police. No weapons or explosives were found.

A knife-wielding passenger tried to force Xiamen Airlines flight 8502, en route from Shanghai to Xiamen, to fly to Taiwan. The hijacker, a hospital worker from Shanghai who had recently been laid off, was subdued by in-flight security. The plane, a Boeing 737 with sixty-eight passengers and seven crew members, landed safely at Xiamen International Airport, and the hijacker was taken into custody. There were no injuries to passengers in the incident, but the hijacker was slightly injured in the scuffle.

An unemployed janitor was arrested in Roanoke, Virginia, for broadcasting phony transmissions to pilots of commercial and private aircraft. Air traffic control transmissions are restricted; however, the janitor broke into the system and gave instructions to pilots to abort takeoffs and landings and even change altitudes. At one point the janitor argued with legitimate air traffic controllers, confusing the pilots and causing havoc over a six-week period. In addition, the janitor transmitted false distress signals, causing a twenty-four-hour state of alert for the crash, fire, and rescue crews stationed at the airport. Eventually, authorities traced the signals to a mobile transmitter on the outskirts of the Roanoke Regional Airport. The janitor was charged with communicating false information over a restricted frequency, endangering the safety of aircraft in flight, and using obscene language over radio frequencies. Fortunately, the janitor will be in jail for many years and radio frequency systems have been revamped, making a recurrence of this type of incident almost impossible.

On December 24, 1999, Indian Airlines flight 844 was hijacked while en route to New Delhi, India, from Kathmandu, Nepal. The Airbus A-300 aircraft carried 174 passengers and 15 crew members. Approximately thirty minutes after takeoff, an armed, masked person stood up to announce the hijacking. At about the same time, four other hijackers wearing red masks took up positions throughout the plane. The hijackers demanded to be flown to Lahore, Pakistan, but Pakistani officials refused permission to land and the plane was flown to Amritsar, India. The plane was not refueled, although passengers were threatened; it left, only to make an emergency landing in Lahore. Here, food, water, and fuel were provided. The plane took off again and landed in Dubai on December 25, where twenty-seven passengers were released in exchange for food and fuel. The plane then departed for Kandahar, Afghanistan, where it remained until the incident ended on December 31.

In Afghanistan, the hijackers demanded the release from an Indian jail of a leader of the Kashmiri separatist group Harakat-ul-Mujahidin. Other demands were made but eventually dropped. On December 29, the Indian government agreed to exchange three jailed Muslim militants for the safe return of the plane and passengers. The passengers and crew were released on December 31 and returned to India, while the five hijackers were given ten hours to depart Afghanistan. One passenger was killed in Amritsar for refusing to follow the instructions of the hijackers.

A Korea-bound airliner came within five minutes of dumping fuel into the Pacific Ocean after receiving a bomb threat. A St. Louis man was charged with phoning in the bomb threat, which almost caused the airliner to return to San Francisco International Airport. According to FBI reports, the man called the airline from St. Louis several times, urging Korean Airlines to hold the flight to Seoul so that his girlfriend would have time to make the connection from St. Louis. The airline politely told the man that they would be unable to hold the aircraft for one person.

The man at this point decided to take matters into his own hands. He allegedly phoned the Korean Airlines again and stated that "while he was in line at the ticket counter he had overheard two men saying that there would be an explosion on board the Seoul flight this evening." During his big moment, however, the man provided the wrong flight number, which only added to the confusion.

Korean Airlines, like all air carriers, takes bomb threats very seriously and the appropriate authorities were immediately notified. All Korean Airlines aircraft on the ground were searched and cleared before they were allowed to take off. The flight that the girlfriend was supposed to be on had already departed on time. This was the aircraft which almost had to dump fuel into the Pacific Ocean and return to San Francisco.

Airlines are not stupid, however, and this sort of thing has happened before. When the girlfriend arrived in San Francisco she was met by the authorities, and asked for her cooperation. She was shocked and outraged, but she confirmed that it was her boyfriend's voice on the recording of the phone call. San Francisco police officials then called the boyfriend, who confirmed that he did in fact make the threat against Korean Airlines.

Within hours of the boyfriend's admission, FBI agents were on his doorstep and placed him under arrest. The boyfriend now faces up to ten years in prison for making a false report of a terrorist threat.

A Chinese man claiming to possess an explosive device attempted to hijack a Chinese airliner on a domestic flight from Shanghai to Guangzhou. Just after the hijacker emerged from the rear lavatory, he blew a whistle and announced to the passengers that he was now in command of the airplane. The hijacker, who was wearing only one shoe, clutched an unidentified item in a newspaper, claimed he had a bomb and ordered the passengers in the rear of the aircraft to move forward, so he could keep an eye on them. The hijacker told the flight attendants to tell the captain to divert the aircraft to Taiwan. Since the hijacker had moved all the passengers forward, he was uncomfortable going to the cockpit to ensure that his demands had been met. The captain, now fully aware that the hijacker had essentially backed himself into a corner, ignored the hijackers demands to go to Taiwan and diverted the aircraft to the nearest available airport, in Hangzhou, Zhejiang Province. As the flight was landing, two security guards on board the aircraft took advantage of the opportunity and overpowered the hijacker, who was caught off guard. When the flight arrived in Hangzhou the hijacker was arrested, and taken into custody without further incident. None of the passengers or crew were injured in the incident. The unidentified item in the newspaper turned out to be the hijacker's left shoe.

A passenger on board a British Airways flight from London's Heathrow to Hong Kong found a note in the rear lavatory claiming that there was a bomb on board the aircraft. Passengers and crew feared that the plane was going to explode at any moment. The pilot of the British Airways Boeing 747 declared an emergency and diverted the jumbo jet to Berlin's Tegel Airport, which does not ordinarily handle that size aircraft.

Passengers were evacuated and an extensive search began of the aircraft, including the passenger compartments, cargo holds, and all of the baggage and freight. No explosive or incendiary device was found. But according to a Berlin Police Department spokesman, they identified a suspect through fingerprint analysis of the note. It was a member of the crew who apparently was frustrated at his failure to receive a promotion at his last employee review.

A Sudan Airways jet was hijacked during a domestic flight between Khartoum and Merowe, Sudan. Two hijackers, a man and a woman, demanded to be taken to Cairo, Egypt. The male hijacker was apparently armed with a small handgun and the female hijacker was armed with an umbrella. The pilot, realizing this was a rather unique situation, informed the duo that the aircraft would need to be refueled in Port, Sudan. Sudanese authorities immediately began to negotiate with the hijackers and soon all the passengers and crew were released unharmed. Shortly thereafter, the hijackers surrendered peacefully and were taken into custody. According to media reports the hijackers were newlyweds who wanted to travel to Cairo on their honeymoon, but could not afford the airfare. In an interview the couple stated that hijacking the plane was their only chance for a once-in-a-lifetime trip.

A Bosnian male passenger took over an Austrian Airlines flight from Berlin, Germany, to Vienna, Austria. The man, who was seated in the front of the plane, gained access to the cockpit while carrying a small wooden stick and a three-inch steak knife. The man demanded that the aircraft return to Berlin immediately. During the short flight the man drank approximately three bottles of wine, and other assorted liquors. After the aircraft landed safely at Berlin's Tegel Airport, the aircraft was moved to an isolated location. While the authorities negotiated with the perpetrator in the front of the aircraft, German police boarded the aircraft from the rear and placed him under arrest. According to the police report, the man later claimed he was simply bored with his life and was looking for some action.

In Hawaii, just after takeoff, an Aloha Airlines flight attendant discovered what appeared to be an explosive device in a brown paper bag. The Boeing 737 aircraft was en route from Honolulu International Airport to Maui, Hawaii. The flight attendant stated that the bag had fallen into the aisle from an overhead compartment. The device was a cylinder attached to a travel alarm clock with an attached 9-volt battery. The captain declared an emergency and immediately returned to Honolulu International Airport. Passengers and crew were evacuated and an explosive ordinance team was dispatched to the aircraft. After the suspect device was removed from the aircraft, it was determined to be a can of hair spray; fortunately, there was no evidence of explosives, wires, or blasting caps.

Upon further investigation by the authorities in Hawaii, it was determined that the flight attendant who found the device was responsible for the entire incident. He was accused of constructing the device, and then placing it on board the aircraft just before departure. It is unknown the real cause for his actions but apparently, the flight attendant was looking for attention, and wanted to be a "hero."

The flight attendant was sentenced to five years probation, ordered to be confined to a halfway house and participate in a work release program for six months, and ordered to pay restitution to the airline.

A hoax device was found at the Federal Express facility in Anchorage, Alaska. A package that was apparently found by an employee near an outbound cargo container contained three cylinders taped together, wires, and a battery. The employee immediately contacted the authorities and evacuated the area. Shortly after the device was located, a phone call was received at the Federal Express facility. The unidentified male caller said, "You found the first bomb, but you'll never find the second one. . . . "

Fortunately, the device did not contain explosives, even though it appeared to be authentic. Although the facility was searched for several hours, the second device was never found. The perpetrator was never identified, and Federal Express lost tens of thousands of dollars and incurred multiple delays.

A Kenyan Airlines plane was robbed of some of its cargo while on the runway at Murtala Mohamed International Airport in Lagos. The Boeing 737 aircraft, carrying 104 passengers, arrived in Lagos from Nairobi, Kenya, shortly before midnight and taxied through an ill-lit section of the airport. While taxiing to the terminal, the pilot found the taxiway blocked by several large pieces of wood. Unable to maneuver around the obstacles, the pilot radioed the control tower for emergency assistance. While this conversation was occurring, approximately a dozen men ran to the plane, forced open the cargo hold, and removed as much luggage as possible. The thieves were able to escape undetected before an army unit responded some thirty minutes later. It is unknown whether the perpetrators were ever caught.

A man being deported from Turkey to Egypt hijacked an EgyptAir Boeing 737-500 aircraft shortly after departure from Istanbul, Turkey. Because the cockpit door was inadvertently left open during the flight, the hijacker was able to enter the flight deck unobstructed. He threatened the flight crew with what was initially believed to be a knife but was almost certainly a ballpoint pen. He alternately demanded that the flight be diverted to London or Germany. The flight crew convinced the hijacker to allow the plane to land at Fuhlsbuettel Airport in Hamburg, Germany. After landing, all passengers were released and German police apprehended the hijacker. The second officer suffered a minor cut on his neck during the flight, but it is undetermined what caused the injury. There were no other injuries or damage to the aircraft.

Recently, an explosive device detonated in a hangar at Ghisonaccia Airport on Corsica. The twenty-kiogram device destroyed or damaged five planes, three gliders, and the hangar. The damage was estimated at several million French francs. Although no one took credit for the attack, police believe professionals were responsible.

A male passenger on board a Southwest Airlines flight from Oakland, California, to Austin, Texas, attempted to hijack the aircraft to Cuba via New York. The passenger handed a note to a flight attendant demanding a ransom of $13 million in cash, stating that he had "nitro" in his hand and a bomb in his luggage. The passenger, who allegedly remained seated throughout the entire incident, received word from the cockpit that the aircraft did not have enough fuel to make it to New York.

The passenger first became distraught, and then advised the flight attendant that he was only joking. The aircraft, which was scheduled to make a stop in San Diego, arrived on time and without further incident. The passenger, who was very cooperative through the remainder of the flight, was arrested without incident by the authorities in San Diego. The passenger had purchased a one-way ticket, had no luggage, and admitted to writing the note the day before his trip. The passenger was charged with attempted air piracy and interference with flight crew.

Offenses such as these represent serious threats to aviation safety and security, and in those incidents involving U.S. air carriers or facilities outside the United States are often intended as symbolic attacks against the United States. Hijackings and commandeering incidents are viewed within the context of the U.S. federal criminal statute (49 USC 1472 [I]), which defines air piracy as any seizure or exercise of control, by force or violence or threat of force or violence, or by any other for of intimidation, and with wrongful intent, of any aircraft.

Fortunately, there appears to be a slight decline in the United States and abroad in instances of air terrorism against the United States, due to three very successful programs: the International Aviation Safety Assessment Program, the Foreign Airport/Air Carrier Assessment Program, and the Federal Air Marshal Program.

The International Aviation Safety Assessment Program focuses on a specific country's particular civil aviation authority and its ability to adhere to international standards and recommended practices (SARPs) established by the Chicago Convention in 1944 and overseen by the ICAO. Every ICAO member country agrees to uphold the international standards established by ICAO. According to the FAA, the assessment includes:

- Aviation law
- Aviation regulations

- Regulatory organization infrastructure
- Adequate, technically qualified personnel
- Inspector guidance material
- Documents and records of certification
- Records of continuing inspections and surveillance

Under the Chicago Convention, the FAA has the authority to assess those carriers conducting scheduled service into the United States. Once an assessment has been completed the FAA will classify each country according to the findings as either meeting the ICAO standards or not. The countries will then be placed in one of two categories.

Category I (Acceptable). The particular airline complies with the ICAO licensing and air carrier oversight standards, and may enter the United States.

Category II (Unacceptable). The air carrier does not comply with ICAO standards, and the foreign air carrier is subjected to heightened FAA operations inspections and surveillance. An air carrier without service to the United States at the time of the assessment is banned until it meets the requirements in Category I.

All aircraft, regardless of registry, must follow all applicable operating rules and regulations when conducting flight operations within the United States. Currently, the FAA oversees 150 U.S. air carriers and a staggering 600 foreign air carriers that are authorized to provide commercial air service to the United States.

The FAA performs ramp check inspections of these foreign air carriers to ensure that the crew members have valid, appropriate pilot certificates in their possession for the type of operation they are conducting and the aircraft is certified and safe to operate within the airspace of the United States.

The second major program has its roots in the International Aviation Development Act of 1985. This act of Congress mandates that the FAA assess the effectiveness of security procedures at foreign airports an with the foreign carriers that serve the United States. This program assesses airports and air carriers on the basis of security measures, which must also comply with ICAO standards and recommended practices. In this program, special agents from the FAA conduct security assessments to verify that the international standards are being met. Upon completion of the security assessment, feedback is provided to the host government and, upon request, assistance will be provided in order to improve security measures with the air carrier and the airport. The host government is generally grateful for the input and complies as a matter of economics. It is in the best interest of the host country to comply with the recommendations of the United States if air service is to continue uninterrupted.

The FAA, despite the criticism it receives, is still recognized as the world leader in implementing safety and security standards for civil aviation.

The third program the United States has in place to combat terrorism is the Federal Air Marshal Program. This program is actually an expansion of the Sky Marshal Program from the 1970s. It was designed primarily to deter hijackings to and from Cuba. Federal air marshals are special agents who fly on selected high-risk routes for the purpose of deterring hijacking attempts and other criminal acts and to ensure the safety of passengers and crew members. The International Security and Development Act of 1985 established the statutory basis for the FAA's Federal Air Marshal Program and gave authority to the Secretary of Transportation to authorize those individuals to carry firearms and make arrests.

Federal air marshals travel in teams and are carried aboard aircraft on a priority basis, without charge, and are seated according to a predetermined, strategic operational plan. No one on board a flight will ever know when an air marshal is present, except for the pilots and flight attendants. Federal air marshals are subjected to an initial screening process which includes physiological evaluation, stringent physical fitness standards, and, of course, firearms training. It is interesting to note that the firearms standards for the air marshals are the highest standard in use by any other government agency. This distinguished armed security force is capable of rapid deployment and next-flight availability anywhere in the world.

The air marshal training facility and operational headquarters is located near Atlantic City, New Jersey. The facility includes outdoor firing ranges with moving targets, mock-ups of narrow- and wide-body aircraft equipped with computer-activated targets, and an observation platform. In addition, the indoor facilities include a firing range that utilizes laser technology to accurately identify targets, a defensive training room, modern classrooms, and, of course, a state-of-the-art physical fitness center.

Federal air marshals fly every day of the year on U.S. carriers throughout the world. They are dispatched into areas where terrorist activities indicate the highest probability of attack. The limited public information about the air marshal program is what makes the program so successful. This full-time dedicated force takes a very proactive approach in deterring would-be terrorist organizations around the world. Although it's difficult to measure success as a deterrent, these individuals are on our side protecting the interests of the United States, its property, and, most importantly, its citizens.

9

ACTIONS TO REDUCE AIR RAGE

As the number of nasty passengers keeps growing, Bangor, Maine, has become the drop-off point for many unsuspecting, violent air rage offenders. Every year dozens of international flights divert to Bangor to drop off unruly passengers. The airport embraces its role of taking menacing passengers out of the sky. Its geographical location provides the first and last opportunity to get rid of unwanted passengers inbound to the United States and outbound to Europe.

In addition, the Bangor Airport Authority estimates that 25 percent of landings at the airport are by airliners that never intended to land there. The most common reasons an airliner diverts to Bangor is for mechanical malfunctions, passenger illness/medical problems, fueling emergencies, and, of course, the newest crisis on the horizon, air rage incidents. The airport is located on the site of a former air force base and has a runway over 11,400 feet long—enough to accommodate the space shuttle, if necessary.

For Bangor, air rage has become big business. For everyone else it's a real mess. There is a tremendous amount of inconvenience and expense shared by all individuals involved in an air rage incident. International passengers are delayed and may miss connecting flights; vacations and business trips are interrupted; the flight, which is now off schedule, will cost the airline tens of thousands of dollars to reaccommodate passengers at downline cities; and additional fuel and flight crew costs also add to the tally. The only one happy about an incident of air rage is the city of Bangor, which reportedly gets between $5,000 and $7,500 for each flight diversion.

Statistics compiled from incidents of air rage diverting into Bangor,

Maine, indicate a variety of reasons for the unruly behavior. Twenty-seven percent of air rage incidents involve alcohol; 22 percent involve perceived mental illness or passenger instability; 19 percent involve passenger disputes; 12 percent involve smokers who just can't do without a fix; 9 percent involve safety issues, such as refusing to fasten a seat belt or stow baggage when required; 6 percent of the incidents are attributed to customer service issues and/or personality conflicts; and 3 percent are attributed to food and beverage complaints.

Bangor has become very efficient in handling instances of air rage and everyone in this city seems to be on the same page, so to speak, in working together to solve this issue as a group. The U.S. Attorney's office is involved and willing to take on cases. FBI agents are very responsive and respond twenty-four hours a day without hesitation. The FAA's New England Regional Office provides support and clarification on laws and regulations. And, of course, the first responders—the state, county, and local police officials—handle the incidents with an exceptional degree of professionalism. Finally, the Bangor Airport Authority does an excellent job of orchestrating all the parties involved. It appears that almost every incident of air rage at Bangor has been handled with efficiently and a great deal of expertise.

Once we recognize and understand what causes people to commit air rage, then we can move forward to solve the problem. However, this is much easier said than done. The sheer scope of the airline industry makes it so. One and one-half billion passengers transported each year to all of the world's two hundred–plus nations, with the help of millions of aviation-related employees, make the implementation of any changes within the industry formidable, to say the least. Getting agreement from all the entities involved in the air travel industry on anything seems nearly impossible.

Nevertheless, changes within the industry on a global scale do take place. For example, although air terrorism still remains a threat, it is diminishing compared to twenty or thirty years ago. As discussed, the number of hijackings has fallen in recent years due to the global acceptance of standards and procedures that deal directly with the issue.

The same needs to happen when it comes to handling air rage. That is, governments, law enforcement agencies, airlines, and regulatory authorities need to come together to formulate effective, common solutions to a common problem. As of this writing, however, no collective solutions exist.

Instead, one finds the implementation of divergent, and sometimes conflicting, attempts to resolve the air rage crisis. A study of the subject reveals that each entity often attempts to formulate and execute its own solutions, while others may be very well trying their own. The end result is a cacophony of ideas. Although some may appear on the surface to be viable, there has not been enough research and investigation to determine which, if any, will provide the long-term solutions we need. With the hope of sparking more discussion and analysis on the subject, this chapter will detail a few of the more widespread attempts to curb the rise of air rage. It will recommend and detail some actions governments, law enforcement agencies, regulatory authorities, and the airline industry can take to address air rage head-on.

GOVERNMENTAL ACTIONS

Governments the world over are grappling with ways to write laws that reduce the number of air rage incidents. Two routes governments can take to implement such laws can be through the signing of international treaties and legislation on the part of individual nations.

International treaties can create law for a large number of countries at the same time. The drawback is that the sheer number of governments negotiating a treaty can make the process arduously slow. Enforcement of such agreements is also difficult to implement.

A quicker and more efficient path to real government action on air rage is most likely to occur at the national level. Several countries have already taken action to combat air rage.

Any country trying to write laws dealing with air rage usually considers which specific offenses can be prosecuted under existing laws, whether the offenses should be criminal or civil offenses, how jurisdiction should be extended to appropriate law enforcement agencies, and how prosecution of foreign nationals should be addressed.

The British government has been taking the lead on implementing policies designed to reduce air rage incidents. Effective September 1, 1999, any passenger "acting in a disruptive manner" could face a prison sentence of up to two years. The revision to the original law broadens the scope of disruptive passenger behavior. The new Air Navigation Order covers threatening or abusive language toward a crew member, behaving in a threatening or abusive manner toward a crew member, and interfering with the duties of a crew member.

LAW ENFORCEMENT ACTIONS

Once governments write laws to deal with air rage, law enforcement officials will need a clear understanding of their roles and responsibilities. Moreover, law enforcement officials will need to know how to interface with airport personnel and flight crews so as to best assess a given situation so as to act accordingly.

In Darlington, England, police and airport officials have put together a protocol with security managers and airlines traveling in and out of Teeside Airport to ensure the fastest, safest procedures are in place. The new policy means that any report of air rage will be treated as an emergency by police. In other words, anyone disruptive at the airport or on flights leaving, landing, or being diverted to Teeside will be immediately arrested and prosecuted. Officers will take statements from passengers on the aircraft and members of the crew, even if it causes flights to be delayed or means new crews have to be brought in. Moreover, airport staff and officers are to be given additional training on air rage. Sergeant Adrian Greene of the Darlington police says, "Disruptive behavior poses such a safety hazard, it has to be regarded as an emergency and offenders will be treated accordingly. Posters will be going up around the airport warning members of the public."[1]

REGULATORY AGENCY ATTEMPTS

The responsibility of regulatory agencies is to monitor passenger safety and to take the initiative to combat many of the root causes of air rage. Regulatory agencies need to be at the forefront of the battle against air rage because the problem is growing and, as mentioned, is the greatest threat to the safety and security of the flying public. Regulatory agencies have the responsibility to bridge the gap between national laws and the airline industry. They must serve at the center of any action taken to curb the increase in air rage.

A new system designed to improve the flow of air traffic in severe weather and, therefore, reduce delays was implemented by the FAA during March 2000. The spring-summer 2000 initiative launched a cooperative effort by the FAA, airlines, and airports to find ways to reduce the growing number of delays for air travelers. The new program brings FAA officials and airline managers together twice a week via conference calls to discuss weather and other problems affecting schedules and to work out ways to deal with them.

This program was developed by the FAA and airlines in response to the delays caused over previous summers, many of which were caused by weather. For the first time, the FAA and the airlines are using the same weather forecasts, making it easier to determine how to best handle storms.

The program improves communication with pilots so they will know sooner when they will be able to depart and can relay the information to passengers. It also uses lower-level airspace to enable the air traffic control system to absorb more volume at peak times and permits the use of military airspace off the East Coast in severe weather, allowing alternatives to north-south routings.

Although the system has begun to show promise, it is still too early to measure its effects on delays.

AIRLINE INDUSTRY ATTEMPTS

Along with regulatory agencies, airlines must play a pivotal role in addressing the causes of air rage. The IATA, the global organization representing the airline industry, has taken several initiatives to crack down on air rage. Airlines could develop zero tolerance policies toward air rage, similar to the ones instituted for hijacking, that would be a deterrent for those likely to commit air rage.

Airlines could accomplish this task by fully integrating all of their employees into the process. Staff should be informed of the scope of the law protecting them if they are forced to respond to an air rage incident.

Staff should also be trained on how to monitor alcohol consumption and intervene if necessary. Communication channels that detail drunk passengers need to be maintained. And in the event an intoxicated passenger should try to board an aircraft, staff should have at their disposal the complete support of the airline in denying that passenger from boarding.

The French, always known for their love of nicotine, have been trying to deal with the smoking ban that was recently announced on their national carrier, Air France. As a result, the airline announced that flight attendants will be handing out nicotine substitute tablets to help passengers suffering through the flight.

The airline has decided to extend its ban on smoking along Asian, African, South American, and Middle Eastern routes. The airline already enforces a smoking ban on long-haul flights to North American, Caribbean, and Indian Ocean destinations.

There will also be a doctor specializing in smoking disorders available to help passengers in the airline's main Paris terminal.

In recent months, German pilots have urged their employers to help avert air rage attacks by offering nicotine to smoke-starved passengers.

Cabin baggage standards would also ease the stress of flying, making it easier and faster to board and deplane an aircraft.

Other airline actions could involve the use of restraints and the employment of specialists whose sole responsibility is to confront air rage offenders.

Beginning January 1, 2001, Switzerland's national airline began cracking down hard on passengers who misbehave. When faced with the growing number of air rage cases, Swissair decided to train its staff in the use of plastic ties, to be used against those passengers who are behaving in an unruly or aggressive manner. Swissair spokesman Jean Claude Donzel says the carrier made the decision after the number of cases of air rage doubled over the previous year.

"Air rage and all disturbances are not slowing," he said. "We have an increase in cases, and it does not look as if it will calm down, so we had to offer another solution."[2]

Delta Airlines has hired Mike Brooks, a former hostage negotiator for the Washington Metropolitan Police, to battle air rage. As manager of air rage and workplace violence cases, the six-foot-seven-inch, 255-pound Brooks teaches flight attendants, gate agents, and pilots how to interact with abusive passengers, with the goal of preventing the incidents before they occur.

The growth in air rage incidents on Delta flights prompted the airline to create Brooks's position. In fact, Brooks might be the first manager at a carrier dedicated solely to preventing air rage and confronting the passengers causing incidents. Brooks often telephones passengers who were abusive on previous flights to "chat" about their past behavior. He even meets some of them in person before they board their next flight.[3]

The German carrier Lufthansa has permitted the carrying of handcuffs on board its flights with which to restrain passengers who become violent. According to airline spokesman Michael Lamberty, the airline saw no legal reason not to issue the handcuffs, as the Tokyo Convention gives it the right to take necessary security measures. And although rival German airlines use plastic handcuffs, Lufthansa ordered aluminum sets.[4]

Several European airlines have expressed an interest in a new weapon that is intended to subdue air rage perpetrators. A lasso harness, the brain-child of a former police officer, is designed to be thrown around the head and shoulders of the offender, instantly disabling the passenger by pinning down the arms. Then, staff can move in with a second harness to fasten the legs.

The use of other passengers to help subdue air rage offenders is gaining support as a possible solution to curb air rage. Steven Luckey, chairman of the security committee for the Airline Pilots Association, says that although the recruitment of passengers to help in cases of air rage raises liability and privacy concerns, passengers provide a great resource to flight crews looking to restrain an air rage offender. Luckey compares the idea with a "Good Samaritan law."[5]

An aviation industry panel organized by the ICAO wants closed-circuit television cameras placed inside cabins to deter air rage incidents. The recommendations come as planes are increasingly becoming equipped with video cameras. Already, some airlines use the cameras to let passengers see passing terrain or to give pilots an extra eye on runways.[6]

The ICAO, which is part of the United Nations and helps develop international aviation standards, calls for placing the cameras inside the cabin in order to help the crew keep tabs on passengers. Milton Hill Jr.—secretary on the panel organized by the ICAO—says safety outweighs privacy concerns. "An aircraft is not a private place, so don't expect privacy on the airplane," Hill says.[7]

AFTERWORD

Passengers who commit air rage fall into every category of air traveler: male and female; young and old; first class, business class, and economy class. As discussed in the earlier chapters, the root causes for the global rise in the scope and magnitude of air rage incidents are numerous and varied. They include the lack of a realistic definition of air rage; the broken air transport system; the abuse of alcohol; the use and transport of illegal drugs; the inability of smokers to get their nicotine fix; the effects of mental illness; the advent of cattle class; the confusion caused by carry-on baggage; the use of the airlines to deport illegal immigrants; the failure to accurately and consistently report air rage cases; and the lack of consequences for the vast majority of air rage offenders.

The study of human nature is by far the most complex ever undertaken by our species. To provide all of the reasons why people do things is impossible. We recognize this reality. Although the causes discussed in this book probably represent 90 to 95 percent of the reasons why people commit air rage, there are quite possibly other contributing factors that we have failed to discuss.

Nevertheless, our purpose in undertaking this project has and remains the same: to educate the public about the scope and magnitude of the air rage problem and to open up debate about how to best solve this emerging crisis in the skies.

It is our sincere wish that this book inspires more hard-hitting investigation and dialogue concerning the air rage problem. If anything is clear, it is that air rage will not simply fall off the radar screen. It is incumbent upon everyone involved in the air transport industry—including passengers—to pressure decision makers to explore viable and real-world solutions that best protect the safety and security of the flying public from would-be air rage offenders. We hope the publication of this book makes that process easier.

NOTES

1. THE PHENOMENON OF AIR RAGE

1. Gallup News Service, September 13, 1999, press release.

2. Ibid.

3. Pauline Arrillaga and Sharon Crenson, "Truth Proves Elusive in Airline Death," Associated Press, September 30, 2000.

4. Angie Cannon, "The Mystery of a Midair Homicide," *U.S. News & World Report*, October 2, 2000, p. 42.

5. *Air Rage: The Prevention and Management of Disruptive Passenger Behavior* (London: International Transport Workers' Federation, 2000), p. 5

6. Ibid.

7. The statute is detailed under Chapter 465 of the U.S. Revised Code, Section 46504, labeled "Interference with flight crew members and attendants."

8. Jeffrey Gold, "Man Who Put Airline Worker in Hospital Sues Continental," Associated Press State and Local Wire, July 31, 1999.

9. "Pilot, Police Intervene in Kournikova Dispute with Flight Crew," Associated Press State and Local Wire, March 27, 2000.

10. "FBI Investigating Whether Passengers Endangered Flight's Safety," Associated Press State and Local Wire, October 6, 2000.

11. "How 747 Pilot Knocked Out Drunken Pop Star," *South China Morning Post*, February 23, 2000, p. 1.

2. THE BROKEN SYSTEM

1. "Airline Head Warns of Crowded Skies," *Point Cast Network*, December 7, 1999.

2. Frank James, "Aviation Leaders Urge New Flight Restrictions," *Chicago Tribune*, September 29, 2000, p. B4.

3. Ibid.

4. Ibid.

3. ALCOHOL AND DRUGS

1. "Pennsylvania Man Indicted for Causing Disturbance on US Airways Flight," Associated Press State and Local Wire, March 8, 2000.

2. Dylan Dronfield, "Passenger Who Hates Flying Jailed," PR Newswire, Europe Press, August 14, 2000.

3. Ralph Riegel, "Soldier the Height of Heroism," *Irish Independent*, September 27, 2000, p. A6.

4. Mitchel Maddux, "Newark Passengers Detained After Complaints of Air Rage," *Bergen County (NJ) Record*, May 3, 2000, p. A3.

5. Tom Godfrey, "Edmonton Woman Removed from Plane," *Edmonton Sun*, February 22, 2000, p. 4.

6. "Flight Grounded After Passengers Become Unruly," Associated Press State and Local Wire, December 1, 2000.

7. "Drunken Passenger Arrested after London-Johannesburg Flight," Agence France Presse, January 14, 2001.

8. Adam Miler, "Bombed on Board," *New York Post*, February 21, 2000, p. 19.

9. "Woman Pleads Guilty to Unruly Behavior on Jetliner," Associated Press, September 27, 2000.

10. "Drunk Guilty of Assaulting Flight Attendant Deported," *Calgary Sun*, July 28, 1999.

11. "Passenger's Behavior Forces Emergency Landing," Associated Press State and Local Wire, November 25, 1999.

12. Bob Mitchell, "Woman Gets Jail Sentence for Air Rage," *Toronto Star*, October 4, 2000.

13. "Couple Fined for Fondling on Flight," Associated Press State and Local Wire, April 5, 2000.

14. "Air France Passenger Strips Off During Flight," Agence France Presse, September 6, 1999.

15. Ibid.

16. "Drunken Passenger Forces Trans-Pacific Flight to Land in Alaska," Deutsche Presse-Agentur, January 10, 2001.

17. "Two Lost Drinkers Flew to Moscow," *Irish Times*, November 23, 2000.

18. "Air Rage Man Jailed in Australian First," Agence France Presse, April 5, 2000.

19. "Cocaine-Filled Condom Bursts in Man's Belly," *Edmonton Sun*, October 6, 2000, p. 26

20. Samantha Lyster, "101 Cocaine Packages in Stomach," *Birmingham Post*, May 23, 2000, p. 3.

21. "Heroin Wraps Detected in Gennan Man's Stomach, Intestine," Deutsche Presse-Agentur, July 6, 1999.

22. "Man Arrested with Cocaine in His Luggage," *St. Petersburg Times*, July 6, 1999, p. 3B.

23. Tom Godfrey, "Customs Wigs Out Over Cocaine," *Edmonton Sun*, July 6, 1999, p. 44.

24. "Police Raid Strikes Smugglers," *Toronto Star*, November 30, 2000.

25. "K-9s Find Cocaine in Airline Food Tray," *Tampa Sun-Sentinel*, January 17, 2001, p. 3B.

26. John Holland, "17 Indicted in Drug Smuggling Ring," *Tampa Sun-Sentinel*, November 3, 2000, p. 3B.

27. "Woman Who Bit Flight Attendant Ordered Deported to Middle East," Associated Press State and Local Wire, November 4, 2000.

28. "Stewardess Tells of Her Attack Ordeal," *Irish News*, November 14, 1999, p. 17.

4. MENTAL ILLNESS

1. Recognized mental illnesses are described and categorized in the book *Diagnosis and Statistical Manual of Mental Disorders*, 6th ed. (New York: APA, 2000). The book is compiled by the American Psychiatric Association.

2. Dr. R. Reid Wilson, "Achieving Comfortable Fight," Anxieties.com [online], www.anxieties.com/7Flying/fear_of_flying_summary.htm.

3. Ibid.

4. Carri Geer, "Man Sentenced for Disrupting Flight," *Las Vegas Review Journal*, January 22, 2000. p. 14.

5. Vanessa Allen, "Italian Convicted of Drugging Businessman on Plane," PR Newswire Europe, May 3, 2000.

6. "Air Rage Interrupts America West Flight," Associated Press Local and State Wire, July 13, 2000.

7. Matthew Stennard, "Woman Restrained on Sydney-to-S.F. Trip," *San Francisco Chronicle*, September 21, 2000, p. A22.

8. Kiley Russell, "Southwest Flight Diverted to Las Vegas," Associated Press State and Local Wire, June 14, 1999.

9. Paul Gallagher, "Legal Victory by Girl Groped on KLM Flight," *London Daily Express*, December 15, 2000, p. C17.

10. Nicky Burridge, "Men Admits Threatening to Kill Over Aircraft Noise," PR Newswire Europe, February 25, 2000.

11. "Ohio Man Sentenced for Assaulting Child," Associated Press State and Local Wire, May 17, 2000.

5. THE ADVENT OF CATTLE CLASS

1. *Chicago Tribune*, January 10, 2001, p. D5.

2. Ibid.

3. Gail Cox, "Restroom Case Yields Sanctions," *National Law Journal*, May 15, 1989, p. 3.

4. "Flight Should Carry Health Warnings," *BBC News*, November 22, 2000.

5. Stanley Mohler, "Blood Clotting Presents Serious Medial Problems for Passengers and Crews," *Human Factors and Aviation Medicine* 44, no. 4 (1987): 2

6. David Derbyshire, "Long Flight Cost Lives Every Year," *London Telegraph*, January 10, 2001.

7. Leo Rozmaryn, "Sporting Goods, Oddly Shaped Items have the Highest Injury Rates," *Human Factors and Aviation Medicine* 43, no. 3 (1998): 1.

8. *The Prevention and Management of Disruptive Passenger Behavior*, (London: International Transport Workers' Federation, 2000), p.10.

9. Rozmaryn, "Sporting Goods," p.1

10. *USA Today*, July 27, 1998, p. A4.

11. Ibid.

12. *Boston Globe*, January 10, 2001, p. A4.

13. Excerpted from International Air Transport Association, "Carriage of Passengers with Infectious Diseases," *IATA Passenger Services Conference Resolution Manual*, Recommendations PSC (19) 1798, June 1, 1998.

14. Ibid.

15. Ibid.

16. Nancy Keates, "Something's in the Air," *Chicago Tribune*, July 30, 2000, p. 7.

17. Steven Luckey, Chairman, National Security Committee, Airline Pilots Association, testimony before the Committee on Transportation and Infrastructure, U.S. House of Representatives, June 11, 1998.

18. Flight Safety Foundation, "Guidelines Enable Health Authorities to Access Risk of Tuberculosis Aboard Aircraft," *Cabin Crew Safety* 33, no. 4 (1998): 1.

19. Ibid.

20. Excerpted from International Air Transport Association, "Carriage of Passengers with Infectious Diseases."

21. Alan Sipress, "Officers at BWI Find No Bomb, Just Cozy Snakes," *Washington Post*, May 24, 2000, p. B2.

7. THE LACK OF CONSEQUENCES

1. "Man Arrested After Plane Crew Says He Threatened to Break Window," AP Worldstream, May 4, 1999.

2. To learn more about IACO procedures, visit its Web site at www.icao.int/index.html.

9. ACTIONS TO REDUCE AIR RAGE

1. Karen Smith, "Air Rage Menace Leads to Airport's Get Tough Stance," *BBC World News*, May 15, 2000.

2. Claire Doole, "Swiss Airline Gets Tough on Air Rage," *BBC World News*, January 1, 2001.

3. "Former Hostage Negotiator Battles Air Rage," Cox News Service, November 27, 2000.

4. "German Airline to Carry Cuffs to Restrain Violent Passengers," Agence France Presse, April 2, 2000.

5. Blake Morrison, "Security Expert Suggests Air Passenger Skills List," *USA Today*, January 8, 2001, p. 4A.

6. Chris Woodyard, "Panel Wants Cameras in Plane Cabins," *USA Today*, September 28, 2000, p. 1B.

7. Ibid.

APPENDIX A

NOTICE OF U.S. FEDERAL REGULATION VIOLATION

The "Notice of U.S. Federal Regulation Violation" sheet is a sample provided to the airlines by the FAA to use for unruly passengers, or can be used a as a guide in creating their own, in conjunction with their own airline policies.

NOTICE OF U.S. FEDERAL REGULATION VIOLATION

Your behavior appears to be in violation of Federal law. It you fail to control your actions, federal authorities will be notified and requested to meet this flight.

THIS IS A WARNING THAT FEDERAL LAW PROHIBITS THE FOLLOWING:

- Assaults, threats, intimidation or interference with a crewmember in performance of the crewmember's duties aboard an aircraft being operated. **14 CFR 91.11**
- Disruptive behavior due to alcohol consumption. **14 CFR 121.575**
  - > Alcohol-related disturbance created by passenger
  - > Consumption of alcoholic beverage unless served by a crewmember
  - > Alcohol service to a passenger who appears to be intoxicated
- Failure to follow instructions given by a crewmember regarding compliance with passenger safety regulations such as the following:

14 CFR 121.317

> No smoking in lavatories at any time
> No smoking when "NO SMOKING" sign is illuminated
> Tampering with, disabling or destroying smoke detector installed in any airplane lavatory
> Requirement to keep seat belt fastened while the "FASTEN SEAT BELT" sign is lighted
> Operation of an electronic device when prohibited

An incident report may be filed with the appropriate federal agency if you do not refrain from this behavior. The Federal Aviation Act provides for fines of up to $10,000. In the case of interference with a crewmember in the performance of crewmember duties, imprisonment for up to twenty years may be imposed in addition to the fine.

APPENDIX B

FAA ADVISORY CIRCULAR 120-65

Advisory Circular 120-65 was issued to the air carriers, flight crew members, and law enforcement officials in October 1996. The advisory provides information and guidance that may be used to manage and reduce instances of passenger interference with crew members.

ADVISORY CIRCULAR

Date: 10/18/96   AC No: 120-65
Initiated by: AFS-200   Change:

Subject:
INTERFERENCE WITH CREWMEMBERS
IN THE PERFORMANCE OF THEIR DUTIES

1. PURPOSE. This advisory circular (AC) provides information to air carriers, crewmembers, law enforcement officers, and the general public regarding methods which may be used to manage and reduce the instances of passenger interference with crewmembers. This AC provides general information about the types of subjects which could be included in an operator's program. In addition, examples of this type of information are provided in Appendices 1, 2, 3, 4, 5, and 6. These examples are based on material provided by the airline industry. Airlines wishing to adapt these samples for their own use should carefully read the legal disclaimer at the top of each sample.

2. <u>RELATED CFR SECTIONS</u>. Title 14 of the Code of Federal Regulations (14 CFR) sections 91.11, 108.10, 108.11, 108.19, 121.317, 121.575, 135.121, and 135.127.

3. <u>DISCUSSION</u>. It is important that both the traveling public and crewmembers have a safe environment when on board an aircraft. Pertinent regulation says that no person may assault, threaten, intimidate, or interfere with a crewmember in the performance of the crewmember's duties aboard an aircraft. The majority of passenger violations are filed under this rule. Additional regulations prohibit the boarding of passengers or serving alcohol to passengers who appear to be intoxicated. Passengers must also obey passenger information signs such as the no smoking and seatbelt sign. In addition, they must obey the instructions of the crewmembers regarding compliance with these signs.

a. Crewmembers, airlines, and Federal Aviation Administration (FAA) personnel have concerns about the increase and nature of occurrences where passengers intimidate, threaten, and/or interfere with crewmembers. In addition, passengers have complained to the FAA and the airlines about being intimidated and uncomfortable because of some of the actions of fellow passengers. Therefore, this document has been prepared to provide guidance about the type of programs that are designed to reduce the number of problems and the stress caused by these incidents.

b. In order to properly discuss this matter, it is necessary to make some attempt to define the types of occurrences. For purposes of this AC, the FAA has divided the types of events into broad catagories which are contained in the chart in Appendix 1. This chart provides one means of categorizing passenger misconduct. Additional examples of defining passenger misconduct are contained in the various appendices to this document. Any of these examples is acceptable. In addition, these are not the only means of categorizing passenger misconduct; an air carrier can develop its own methods of defining these occurrences.

4. <u>POLICY OF THE OPERATOR</u>. One of the most important aspects of any program dedicated to the reduction of violence in the workplace is the commitment of each individual, including those with management responsibilities. Therefore, partnerships which include employees with differing

responsibilities, and appropriate goverment personnel should be formed to develop procedures, handle violence, and provide assistance to individuals who are involved in passenger disturbances.

a. Airlines should make it clear to all employees what actions should be taken when an incident occurs that meets any of the broad categories found in Appendix 1. The operator's program should involve all personnel who have direct contact with passengers. The emphasis of the program should be on keeping dangerous passengers off the airplanes. There should be clear lines of responsibility regarding the handling of these events. These responsibilities should include offering and/or providing counseling for those who are involved in or who witness the events. Employee assistance groups can also play an important role in providing this assistance.

b. Operators should establish policies which define the operator's philosophy concerning zero tolerance. Appendices 2, 3, 4, and 5 contain programs which have worked well and provide examples of policy statements where air carriers have provided information about their zero tolerance philosophies.

c. It is important that the operator provide the public with the appropriate information and thereby provide a safe environment for crewmembers and for the traveling public. The operator should provide material to passengers regarding the seriousness of inappropriate behavior on an airplane, including failure to follow instructions from crewmembers. Further, the material should contain information to the passengers about the consequences of their actions including possible fines and incarceration. Public awareness information can be in the form of pamphlets passed out at airport gates, included in ticket envelopes, articles in onboard magazines, posters in gate areas, public address announcements, information given in video tapes, or any other method that management believes will convey the message to the public. A sample of the information that could be disseminated is included in Appendix 6.

5. <u>WRITTEN PROGRAMS</u>. Operators should make it clear to all employees what actions should be taken when an incident occurs and involves a crewmember. This program should be included in crewmember, security personnel, and other appropriate manuals. The written information should be disseminated to all employees of the air carrier who could have the responsibility for handling a situation with a dangerous passenger. A sample

form carried on board the flights by crewmembers giving information about one method of handling onboard incidents in provided in Appendix 5.

a. It is important that written programs be developed with employees who are familiar with the security aspect of the airline, including crewmembers. These are the people who have the most experience with and are familiar with the local law enforcement jurisdictions and will be the most likely to help educate their staff about passenger interference with crewmembers.

b. The written program should encourage employees to promptly report cases of interference on reporting forms such as the sample provided in Appendix 5. The written report should contain at least the names of the crewmembers, the date, flight number, seat number, origin/destination of flight, the name, address, and description of the offending passengers, and the names and addresses of witnesses. If positive identification is not established by the crewmembers, then the written program should provide guidance on securing identification through appropriate airline personnel, law enforcement, or other methods as appropriate.

c. The written program should also provide information about personnel in the company who should contact law enforcement and the FAA. Information should also be provided regarding how crewmembers may directly contact the FAA and law enforcement on their own.

d. In addition, the written program should include information regarding filing complaints against passengers. The process of pursuing violations requires an ongoing commitment and should not be taken lightly. The employee may be required to testify in any subsequent court proceedings.

6. <u>TRAINING</u>. Air carriers should provide training for crewmembers and other responsible personnel for handling passengers who interfere in the performance of crewmember duties. The training should acknowledge that it is not desirable to have cockpit crewmembers leave their stations, especially in cases where there are two cockpit crewmembers. Nevertheless, the training should also acknowledqe the authority of the captain and that the decision to leave the cockpit is the responsibility of the captain. Airlines may want to include training on passenger misconduct in the required training during crew resource management, hijacking, and other unusual situations. Regardless of how the training is provided, it should include information which will help the crewmember recognize those situations which may, when combined

with traits of some passengers, create stress. The training should include information about how to manage conflict situations such as:

a. *Responding to Imminent Danger.* If the passenger becomes abusive, solicit help from other crewmembers, other employees, or passengers to help restrain the individual. Usually the other person will be another flight attendant; however, at times it may be wise to involve passengers. This is especially true when the flight is operating with one flight attendant. Cockpit crewmembers should be kept well-informed. The decision to have a crewmember leave the cockpit is the responsibility of the captain. Flight attendants should provide as much information as possible to the cockpit crew. The captain should be given the passenger's name (if possible), description and the name and description of traveling companions, seat number, and if medical attention is needed. Inform the captain if you wish. authorities to meet the inbound flight.

b. *Reporting the Information.* Flight attendants should be informed on the use of the forms which the air carrier has developed for the purpose of handling passengers who cause disturbances. When law enforcement officials are called to meet the flight, crewmembers need to be informed that written statements will be taken upon arrival and that they may be called to testify in court.

7. LAW ENFORCEMENT AND FAA RESPONSE. Incidents of interference with crewmembers could be a serious violation of regulations and may warrant a response from local law enforcement or the Federal Bureau of Investigation (FBI). In most cases, the initial response will be provided by the airport law enforcement department or, if there is no resident law enforcement unit at the airport, the department having overall responsibility for law enforcement support to the airport.

a. When the incident of interference is sufficient to warrant a response from law enforcement, the captain should notify dispatch/flight following and request a law enforcement representative and an air carrier representative meet the airplane upon arrival at the gate.

b. Law enforcement response may involve interviewing one or more members of the crew, other passengers who witnessed the incident, and the subject passenger(s). Action may be taken by the law enforcement department responding or a report may be forwarded by the local law enforcement to the FBI and FAA. In some cases, the FBI and FAA may be called to meet the arriving airplane. This will usually happen for the more serious incidents such as assault, intimidation using a dangerous weapon, threat or actual attempted sabotage or hijacking.

c. It should be noted that every incident of interference will not warrant a response from law enforcement personnel. A crewmember must ask a law enforcement representative to meet the aircraft. In order to take action, there must be a legal basis for an officer to do so. For example, physically assaulting a crewmember would warrant law enforcement action. However, for example, if the incident involves failure to fasten a seatbelt, there may not be a legal basis for criminal action from the local law enforcement unit. This does not imply that a formal complaint needs to be filed by a member of the crew for action to be taken. If there is a serious incident, the action may be taken by the government for violation of a criminal statute or for violation of specific regulations.

d. The airline should inform all members of the crew that full cooperation is necessary in reporting an incident in a timely manner and providing statements if requested by local law enforcement, the FBI, or the FAA.

e. Jurisdiction and authority for action is a consideration for any law enforcement officer's response and an arrest may not be the result in every case. Any action taken must be within the scope of authority for the law enforcement officer. If an arrest is made by the airport law enforcement unit or, if a case is referred to the FBI for investigation, prosecution still rests with the appropriate office of the prosecuting attorney.

f. Reports forwarded to the FAA may result in joint investigative efforts by the FAA and FBI. Cases where the FBI declines to investigate may still be worked by the FAA and could result in a civil penalty for the passenger involved in interfering with the crewmember.

g. The FAA has asked its principal inspectors and managers to emphasize review of incidents involving interference, with crewmembers. A partnership effort between the FAA, FBI, local law enforcement, and the industry which emphasizes communication and cooperation should lessen the number of incidents of interference.

The same procedures should he followed for international flights and the law enforcement response will be those, of the destination government.

Thomas C. Accardi
Director, Flight Standards Service

*   *   *

This sample airline information should be reviewed by each airline's legal department to assure that it accurately states the airline's policies and the legal duties, responsibilities, and rights of the airline and airline personnel. The FAA does not provide legal advice about the specifics of tort and criminal law.

APPENDIX 1

CATEGORY ONE. Flight attendant requests passenger to comply. (These are actions which do not interfere with cabin or flight safety such as minor verbal abuse.)	Passenger complies with request.	There is no further action required by the flight attendant. (Such an incident need not be reported to the cockpit, the carrier, or the FAA.)
CATEGORY TWO. Flight attendant requests passenger to comply.	Passenger continues disturbance which interferes with cabin safety such as continuation of verbal abuse or continuing refusal to comply with federal regulations (such as failure to fasten seatbelt when sign is illuminated, operation of unauthorized electronic equipment). In addition, the crewmember should follow company procedures regarding cockpit notification.	After attempting to defuse the situation, the captain and the flight attendant will coordinate on the issuance of the Airline Passenger In-flight Disturbance Report or other appropriate actions. The flight attendant completes the report. Completed report is given to appropriate company personnel upon arrival. In turn, company personnel may file the incident report with the FAA.
CATEGORY THREE.	Examples: (1) when crewmember duties are disrupted due to continuing interference, (2) when a passenger or crewmember is injured or subjected to a credible threat of injury, (3) when an unscheduled landing is made and/or restraints such as handcuffs are used, and (4) if operator has program for written notification and passenger continues disturbance after receiving written notification.	Advise cockpit, identify passenger, then cockpit requests the appropriate law enforcement office to meet the flight upon its arrival.

APPENDIX 2. SAMPLE AIRLINE POLICY BULLETIN—ASSAULTS ON EMPLOYEES

Although rare, assaults on employees by customers do occur. In many cases, the assault occurs simultaneously with other actions which interfere with the duties of a crewmember. Until today, the Company has handled these cases on an individual basis with the employees involved. This policy is being adopted in an effort to help employees at all levels better understand their rights and responsibilities in the event of an assault.

In many jurisdictions, an assault is defined as an action taken toward an individual that creates a threat of bodily harm, or the apprehension of physical injury. In some jurisdictions, abusive or suggestive language, unless used in a manner that creates the threat of violence or harm, is not considered an assault. If physical contact occurs, the incident is usually defined as battery. Often, an event involving an assault or battery is generally referred to as an assault.

Special Protection for Crewmembers

Crew interference is governed by federal regulation (Title 14 of the Code of Federal Regulations [14 CFR] section 91.11). Crew interference is defined as an incident where a passenger assaults, threatens, intimidates or interferes with a crewmember while in performance of crew duties on board an aircraft. THIS AIRLINE WILL NOT TOLERATE ASSAULT, THREATS, INTIMIDATION, AND INTERFERENCE. ANY EMPLOYEE WHO IS SUBJECTED TO ASSAULT WHILE AT WORK WILL RECEIVE COMPANY SUPPORT (INCLUDING LEGAL ADVICE . . . PAID ABSENCE TO APPEAR IN COURT DURING A CRIMINAL PROCEEDING).

The decision to press charges requires an ongoing commitment by the employee and should not be taken lightly. The employee may file a complaint or be required to testify in any subsequent court proceedings.

The Company will provide legal counsel and supervisory assistance in pursuing appropriate action to any employee who is subjected to abuse, physical violence, or intimidation on the job.

An employee may also pursue a civil action against a party who has committed an assault or battery. A civil action is brought for the purpose of recovering money damages.

In addition, support is available to any employee who is the victim of an assault through the airline's Employee Assistance Program at (*phone number*). The Company, jointly with the union, also provides a critical incident stress debriefing team which is available to flight attendants in certain circumstances.

It is important that employees report assaults immediately to the Company. All reports will receive follow-up by the appropriate department. All reports of crew interference are filed with the FAA for recording and possible civil enforcement action. Additional reports obtained for the FBI or local police are attached to the crew reports to assist the FAA in their investigation and assignment of appropriate penalty.

It is important to obtain as much information about the offender as possible. A name and address, as well as witness statements, are valuable. At a minimum, a description of the attacker, including physical characteristics, will be important when pursuing legal action. In an aircraft situation, the passenger's assigned seat designation often allows the Company to obtain information through its reservations records.

As always, employees are expected to be understanding in trying to resolve the frustrations of our customers. However, no one can be expected to tolerate physical abuse of any kind.

APPENDIX 3. SAMPLE AIRLINE INFORMATION BULLETIN

AIRLINE SECURITY INFORMATION BULLETIN

TO: ALL PUBLIC-CONTACT, FLIGHT OPERATIONS, IN-FLIGHT, AND ASSOCIATED MANAGEMENT PERSONNEL

SUBJECT: ASSAULTS ON EMPLOYEES

Just as any of us would take action if a family member needed help, each of us may feel an obligation to respond when a fellow employee needs help. Our corporate values clearly support this by asking us to show respect for each other as individuals and demonstrating integrity in everything we do.

When a fellow employee is in distress, for any reason, we should immediately and effectively assist that person. This certainly applies in cases of assault. Not coming to the aid of an employee in distress as a result of a customer's actions constitutes a clear failure to adhere to our corporate values. If serious physical assaults are ignored by pilots or managers, for example, basic safety and security may be compromised—and an individual's dignity violated. When a coworker or crewmember ignores an assaulted employee, that employee most likely will feel ignored and abandoned by the airline as well.

It is very important to be aware that authorities should be called for assistance with unruly customers or instances of out-and-out battery. Furthermore, flight officers have an obligation to follow-up on an assault which occurs on an aircraft by requesting that authorities meet the trip and by filing a "Captain's Report of Crewmember Interference."

The following are questions and answers which will provide you with more information about the issue of assault in the workplace.

Q. What does "ASSAULT" actually mean?

A. Many jurisdictions define assault as an action taken toward an individual that creates a threat of bodily harm or the apprehension of physical injury. Abusive or suggestive language, if it is not utilized in a manner that creates the threat of violence or harm, is not considered an assault in some jurisdictions. Generally speaking, if physical contact should occur, the incident is defined as battery. Often, any event involving an assault or battery is referred to as an assault.

Q. What is the company's policy regarding assault?

A. At (airline), assault will not be tolerated. Any employee who is subjected to assault while at work will receive company support, including legal assistance and paid absence to appear in court during a related criminal proceeding.

Q. Will the company provide me with a lawyer?

A. The company will provide legal assistance and supervisory assistance in pursuing appropriate criminal remedial action to any employee who is subjected to abuser physical violence, or intimidation on the job. The airline, however, will provide legal advice throughout the proceedings.

Q. What if I want to file a civil suit?

A. The decision to pursue a civil action against a party who has committed an assault or battery belongs to the employee. A civil action is brought for the purpose of recovering monetary damages. The company will, however, support the employee, counsel him or her as to their rights, and even assist in finding or retaining an attorney.

Assault in the workplace is a very serious issue. By lending a helping hand when necessary, we can support each other.

APPENDIX 4. SAMPLE PROCEDURES DEALING WITH FLIGHT ATTENDANT ASSAULT

POLICY: Title 14 of the Code of Federal Regulations (14 CFR) section 91.11 states, "No person may assault, threaten, intimidate, or interfere with a crewmember in the performance of the crewmembers' duties aboard an aircraft being operated."

PROCEDURES:

During Boarding, at the Gate, or Taxi-Out:
- If the boarding flight attendant or agent identifies a passenger exhibiting inappropriate behavior, they should confer and prior to the passenger boarding, notify the captain and the lead agent. An example of inappropriate behavior could be a passenger who appears to be intoxicated, or has questionable medical problem that could be an immediate threat to other customers or themselves.
- If the passenger is on board the aircraft, the lead flight attendant will notify the captain of the passenger's name, seat number, and the nature of the problem.
- Reports of this nature can be reported during the sterile cockpit period if necessary.

After Takeoff/En Route:
- The captain will be notified by the lead flight attendant if any passenger displays disruptive behavior, appears to be intoxicated, or is smoking on a nonsmoking flight.
- After attempting to defuse the situation, the captain and the lead flight attendant will coordinate on the issuance of the Airline Passenger In-flight Disturbance Report to the passenger.
- It may not be safe for a cockpit crewmember to leave the cockpit. If the passenger becomes abusive, solicit help from other cabin crewmembers, other company employees, or passengers to help restrain the individual.
- Upon arrival, the captain will make a Public Address System Announcement (PA) requesting all passengers remain seated.
- The lead flight attendant will coordinate with the captain to identify passengers involved to the authorities.

Postflight:
- All flight attendants will complete a flight attendant report. Verify the name and address, if possible, of the passenger engaging in misconduct, and of any witnesses.
- Flight attendants need to be prepared to make a verbal and written statement to the local authorities upon landing. Flight attendants will retain a copy of any written report.
- The captain will facilitate any meetings with local authorities and/or appropriate airline personnel.
- Followup assistance, such as legal counseling, medical assistance, or personnel counseling will be provided by the flight attendant department or other appropriate departments.

APPENDIX 5. SAMPLE REPORTING FORM

AIRLINE PASSENGER IN-FLIGHT DISTURBANCE REPORT

Date: _____

Flight # _____ Departure City: _____

Arrival City: _____

Passenger Information: Name: _____

Seat #: _____

Address: _____

Description of Incident: _____

_____

_____

Witness Name:_____ Seat #: _____

Address: _____

Phone #: _____

F/A Name: _____

Employee #: _____ Base: _____

F/A Signature: _____

Captain Name: _____

Employee #: _____ Base: _____

Captain Signature: _____

NOTICE: Your behavior may be in violation of Federal law. You should immediately cease if you wish to avoid prosecution and your removal from this aircraft at the next point of arrival.

This is a formal warning that Federal law prohibits the following (reference Title 14 of the Code of Federal Regulations (14 CFR) parts 91 and 121):

- Threatening, intimidating, or interfering with a crewmember (section 91.11)
- Smoking on a nonsmoking flight or in the lavatory (section 121.317)
- Drinking any alcoholic beverages not served by a crewmember or creating an alcohol-related disturbance (section 121.575)

An incident report will be filed with the FAA. If you do not refrain from these activities you will be prosecuted. The Federal Aviation Act provides for civil monetary fines and, in some cases, imprisonment.

APPENDIX 6. POSSIBLE LANGUAGE FOR IN-FLIGHT MAGAZINE AND/OR TICKET WALLETS

TITLE 14 OF THE CODE OF FEDERAL REGULATIONS
(14 CFR) SECTION 91.11

Please be advised that interference with crewmembers'
(including flight attendants) duties is a violation of Federal law.

An incident report may be filed with the
Federal Aviation Administration regarding a passenger's behavior.

Under Federal law, no person may assault, threaten, intimidate,
or interfere with crewmembers (including flight attendants) in the
performance of their duties aboard an aircraft under operation.

Federal law permits penalties for crew interference to include
substantial fines, imprisonment, or both.

APPENDIX C

FEDERAL AVIATION REGULATION (FAR) PART 108—AIRPLANE OPERATOR SECURITY

This regulation governs domestic air carrier security, and requires each U.S. air carrier to adopt and carry out an FAA-approved security program. This program is called the Air Carrier Standard Security Program (ACSSP). Each provision of the program has the force of the regulation itself. The ACSSP is a restricted document, designed to provide a secure operating environment, and prevent or deter aircraft hijacking, sabotage, and related criminal acts.

Note: This document contains FAR Part 108 including Amendment 108-17 as published in the Federal Register on September 24, 1998.

PART 108-AIRPLANE OPERATOR SECURITY

Authority: 49 U.S.C. 106(g), 5103, 40113, 40119, 44701–44702, 44705, 44901–44905, 44907, 44913–44914, 44932, 44935–44936, 46105.

Source: Docket No. 108, 46 FR 3786, Jan. 15, 1981, unless otherwise noted.

Sec. 108.1 Applicability.

a. This part prescribes aviation security rules governing—
   1. The operations of holders of FAA air carrier operating certificates or operating certificates engaging in scheduled passenger operations or public charter passenger operations;
   2. Each person aboard an airplane operated by a certificate holder described in paragraph (a)(1)of this section;
   3. Each person on an airport at which the operations described in paragraph (a)(1) of this section are conducted;
   4. Each certificate holder who receives a Security Directive or Information Circular and each person who receives information from a Security Directive or an Information Circular issued by the Director of Civil Aviation Security; and
   5. Each person who files an application or makes entries into any record or report that is kept, made or used to show compliance under this part, or to exercise any privileges under this part.
b. This part does not apply to helicopter or to all-cargo operations.

[Doc. No. 24883, Amdt. 108-4, 51 FR 1352, Jan. 10, 1986, as amended bu Amdt. 108-6, 54 FR 28984, July 10, 1989; Amdt. 107-9, 61 FR 64244, Dec. 3, 1996]

Sec. 108.3 Definitions.

The following are definitions of terms used in this part:

a. "Certificate holder" means a person holding an FAA operating certificate when that person engages in scheduled passenger or public charter passenger operations or both.

b. "Passenger seating configuration" means the total number of seats for which the aircraft is type certificated that can be made available for passenger use aboard a flight and includes that seat in certain airplanes which may be used by a representative of the Administrator to conduct flight checks but is available for revenue purposes on other occasions.

c. "Private charter" means any charter for which the charterer engages the total capacity of an airplane for the carriage of:
  1. Passengers in civil or military air movements conducted under contract with the Government of the United States of the Government of a foreign country; or
  2. Passengers invited by the charterer, the cost of which is borne entirely by the charterer and not directly or indirectly by the individual passengers.

d. "Public charter" means any charter that is not a "private charter."

e. "Scheduled passenger operations" means holding out to the public of air transportation service for passengers from identified air terminals at a set time announced by timetable or schedule published in a newspaper, magazine, or other advertising medium.

f. "Sterile area" means an area to which access is controlled by the inspection of persons and property in accordance with an approved security program or a security program used in accordance with Sec. 129.25.

Sec. 103.4 Falsification.

No person may make, or cause to be made, any of the following:

a. Any fraudulent or intentionally false statement in any application for any security program, access medium, or identification medium, or any amendment thereto, under this part.
b. Any fraudulent or intentionally false entry in any record or report that is kept, made, or used to show compliance with this part, or to exercise any privileges under this part.
c. Any reproduction or alteration, for fraudulent purpose, of any report, record, security program, access medium, or indentification medium issued under this part

[Amdt. 107-9, 61 FR 64244, Dec. 3, 1996]

Sec. 108.5 Security program: Adoption and implementation.

a. Each certificate holder shall adopt and carry out a security program that meets the requirements of Sec. 108.7 for each of the following scheduled or public charter passenger operations:
   1. Each operation with an airplane having a passenger seating configuration of more than 60 seats.
   2. Each operation that provides deplaned passengers access, that is not otherwise controlled by a certificate holder using an approved security program or a foreign air carrier using a security program required by Sec. 129.25, to a sterile area.
   3. Each operation with an airplane having a passenger seating configuration of more than 30 but less than 61 seats; except that those parts of the program effecting compliance with the requirements listed in Sec. 108.7(b)(1), (2), and (4) need only be implemented when the Director of Civil Aviation Security or a designate of the Director notifies the certificate holder in writing that a security threat exists with respect to the operation.
b. Each certificate holder that has obtained FAA approval for a secu-

rity program for operations not listed in paragraph (a) of this section shall carry out the provisions of that program.

Sec. 108.7 Security program: Form, content, and availability.

a. Each security program required by Sec. 108.5 shall—
1. Provide for the safety of persons and property traveling in air transportation and intrastate air transportation against acts of criminal violence and air piracy;
2. Be in writing and signed by the certificate holder or any person delegated authority in this matter;
3. Include the items listed in paragraph (b) of this section, as required by Sec. 108.5; and
4. Be approved by the Administrator.
b. Each security program required by Sec. 108.5 must include the following, as required by that section:
1. The procedures and a description of the facilities and equipment used to perform the screening functions specified in Sec. 108.9.
2. The procedures and a description of the facilities and equipment used to perform the airplane and facilities control functions specified in Sec. 108.13.
3. The procedures used to comply with the applicable requirements of Sec. 108.15 regarding law enforcement officers.
4. The procedures used to comply with the requirements of Sec. 108.17 regarding the use of X-ray systems.
5. The procedures used to comply with the requirements of Sec. 108.19 regarding bomb and air piracy threats.
6. The procedures used to comply with the applicable requirements of Sec. 108.10.
7. The curriculum used to accomplish the training required by Sec. 108.23.
8. The procedures and a description of the facilities and equipment used to comply with the requirements of Sec. 108.20 regarding explosives detection systems.

c. Each certificate holder having an approved security program shall—

1. Maintain at least one complete copy of the approved security program at its principal business office;

2. Maintain a complete copy or the pertinent portions of its approved security program or appropriate implementing instructions at each airport where security screening is being conducted;

3. Make these documents available for inspection upon request of any Civil Aviation Security Inspector;

4. Restrict the distribution, disclosure, and availability of sensitive security information, as defined in part 191 of this chapter, to persons with a need-to-know; and

5. Refer requests for sensitive security information by other persons to the Assistant Administrator for Civil Aviation Security.

[Doc. No. 108, 46 FR 3786, Jan. 15, 198 1, as amended by Amdt. 108-3, 50 FR 28893, July 16, 1985; Amdt. 108-7, 54 FR 36946, Sept. 5, 1989; Amdt. 108-15, 62 FR 13744, Mar. 21, 1997]

Sec. 108.9 Screening of passengers and property.

a. Each certificate holder required to conduct screening under a security program shall use the procedures included, and the facilities and equipment described, in its approved security program to prevent or deter the carriage aboard airplanes of any explosive, incendiary, or a deadly or dangerous weapon on or about each individual's person or accessible property. and the carriage of any explosive or incendiary in checked baggage.

b. Each certificate holder required to conduct screening under a security program shall refuse to transport—

1. Any person who does not consent to a search of his or her person in accordance with the screening system prescribed in paragraph (a) of this section; and

2. Any property of any person who does not consent to a search or inspection of that property in accordance with the screening system prescribed by paragraph (a) of this section.

c. Except as provided by its approved security program each certificate holder required to conduct screening under a security program shall use the procedures included, and the facilities and equipment described, in its approved security program for detecting explosives, incendiaries, and deadly or dangerous weapons to inspect each person entering a sterile area at each preboarding screening checkpoint in the United States for which it is responsible, and to inspect all accessible property under that person's control.

d. Each certificate holder shall staff its security screening checkpoints with supervisory and nonsupervisory personnel in accordance with the standards specified in its security program.

[Doc. No. 108, 46 FR 3786, Jan. 15, 1981, as amended by Amdt. 108-4, 51 FR 1352, Jan. 10, 1986; Amdt. 108-5, 52 FR 48509, Dec. 22, 1987; Doc. No. 26422, Amdt. Nos. 107-6 and 10810, 56 FR 26522, Aug. 20, 1991]

Sec. 108.10 Prevention and management of hijackings and sabotage attempts.

a. Each certificate holder shall—
   1. Provide and use a Security Coordinator on the ground and in flight for each international and domestic flight, as required by its approved security program; and
   2. Designate the pilot in command as the inflight Security Coordinator for each flight, as required by its approved security program.
b. Ground Security Coordinator. Each ground Security Coordinator shall carry out the ground Security Coordinator duties specified in the certificate holder's approved security program.
c. Inflight Security Coordinator. The pilot in command of each flight shall carry out the inflight Security Coordinator duties specified in the certificate holder's approved security program.

[Doc. No. 24719, 50 FR 28891, July 16, 1985]

Sec. 108.11 Carriage of weapons.

a. No certificate holder required to conduct screening under a security program may permit any person to have, nor may any person have, on or about his or her person or property, a deadly or dangerous weapon, either concealed or unconcealed, accessible to him or her while aboard an airplane for which screening is required unless:

    1. The person having the weapon is—

        i. An official or employee of the United States, or a State or political subdivision of a State, or of a municipality who is authorized by his or her agency to have the weapon; or

        ii. Authorized to have the weapon by the certificate holder and the Administrator and has successfully completed a course of training in the use of firearms acceptable to the Administrator.

    2. The person having the weapon needs to have the weapon accessible in connection with the performance of his or her duty from the time he or she would otherwise check it in accordance with paragraph (d) of this section until the time it would be returned after deplaning.

    3. The certificate holder is notified—

        i. Of the flight on which the armed person intends to have the weapon accessible to him or her at least 1 hour, or in an emergency as soon as practicable, before departure; and

        ii. When the armed person is other than an employee or official of the United States, that there is a need for the weapon to be accessible to the armed person in connection with the performance of that person's duty from the time he or she would otherwise check it in accordance with paragraph (d) of this section until the time it would be returned to him or her after deplanning.

    4. The armed person identifies himself or herself to the certificate holder by presenting credentials that include his or her clear, full-face picture, his or her signnature, and the signature of the authorizing official of his or her service or the official seal of his or her service. A badge, shield, or similar may not be used as the sole means of identification.

5. The certificate holder—

6. Ensures that the armed person is familiar with its procedures for carrying a deadly or dangerous weapon aboard its airplane before the time the person boards the airplane;

7. Ensures that the identity of the armed person is known to each law enforcement officer and each employee of the certificate holder responsible for security during the boarding of the airplane; and

8. Notifies the pilot in command, other appropriate crewmembers, and any other person authorized to have a weapon accessible to him or her aboard the airplane of the location of each authorized armed person aboard the airplane.

b. No person may, while on board an airplane operated by a certificate holder for which screening is not conducted, carry on or about that person a deadly or dangerous weapon, either concealed or unconcealed. This paragraph does not apply to—

1. Offcials or employees of a municipality or a State, or of the United States, who are authorized to carry arms; or

2. Crewmembers and other persons authorized by the certificate holder to carry arms.

c. No certificate holder may knowingly permit any person to transport, nor may any person transport or tender for transport, any explosive, incendiary or a loaded firearm in checked baggage aboard an airplane. For the purpose of this section, a loaded firearm means a firearm which has a live round of ammunition, cartridge, detonator, or powder in the chamber or in a clip, magazine, or cylinder inserted in it.

d. No certificate holder may knowingly permit any person to transport, nor may any person transport or tender for transport, any unloaded firearm in checked baggage aboard an airplane unless—

1. The passenger declares to the certificate holder, either orally or in writing before checking the baggage, that any firearm carried in the baggage is unloaded;

2. The firearm is carried in a container the certificate holder considers appropriate for air transportation;

3. When the firearm is other than a shotgun, rifle, or other firearm

normally fired from the shoulder position, the baggage in which it is carried is locked, and only the passenger checking the baggage retains the key or combination; and

4. The baggage containing the firearm is carried in an area, other than the flightcrew compartment, that is inaccessible to passengers.

e. No certificate holder may serve any alcoholic beverage to a person having a deadly or dangerous weapon accessible to him or her nor may such person drink any alcoholic beverage while aboard an airplane operated by the certificate holder.

f. Paragraphs (a), (b), and (d) of this section do not apply to the carriage of firearms aboard air carrier flights conducted for the military forces of the Government of the United States when the total cabin load of the airplane is under exclusive use by those military forces if the following conditions are met:

1. No firearm is loaded and all bolts to such firearms are locked in the open position; and

2. The certificate holder is notified by the unit commander or officer in charge of the flight before boarding that weapons will be carried aboard the aircraft.

[Doc. No. 108, 46 FR 3786, Jan. 15, 1981, as amended by Amdt. 108-4, 51 FR 1352, Jan. 10, 1986]

Sec. 108.13 Security of airplanes and facilities.

Each certificate holder required to conduct screening under a security program shall use the procedures included, and the facilities and equipment described, in its approved security program to perform the following control functions with respect to each airplane operation for which screening is required:

a. Prohibit unauthorized access to the airplane.

b. Ensure that baggage carried in the airplane is checked in by a responsible agent and that identification is obtained from persons, other than known shippers, shipping goods or cargo aboard the airplane.

c. Ensure that cargo and checked baggage carried aboard the airplane is handled in a manner that prohibits unauthorized access.

d. Conduct a security inspection of the airplane before placing it in service and after it has been left unattended.

Sec. 108.14 Transportation of Federal Air Marshals.

a. Each certificate holder shall carry Federal Air Marshalls, in the number and manner specified by the Administrator, on each scheduled and public charter passenger operation designated by the Administrator.

b. Each Federal Air Marshal shall be carried on a first priority basis and without charge while on official duty, including repositioning flights.

c. Each certificate holder shall assign the specific seat requested by a Federal Air Marshal who is on official duty.

[Doc. No. 24714, 50 FR 27925, July 8, 1985]

Sec. 108.15 Law enforcement officers.

a. At airports within the United States not governed by Part 107 of this chapter, each certificate holder engaging in scheduled passenger or public charter passenger operations shall—

1. If security screening is required for a public charter operation by Sec. 108.5(a), or for a scheduled passenger operation by Sec. 108.5(b) provide for law enforcement officers meeting the qualifications and standards, and in the number and manner specified, in Part 107; and

2. When using airplanes with a passenger seating configuration of 31 through 60 seats in a public charter operation for which screening is not required, arrange for law enforcement officers meeting the qualifications and standards specified in Part 107 to be available to respond to an incident, and provide to its employees, including crewmembers, as appropriate, current information with respect to procedures for obtaining law enforcement assistance at that airport.

b. At airports governed by Part 107 of this chapter, each certificate holder engaging in scheduled or public charter passenger operations, when using airplanes with a passenger seating configuration of 31 through 60 seats for which screening is not required, shall arrange for law enforcement officers meeting the qualifications and standards specified in Part 107 to be available to respond to an incident and provide its employees, including crewmembers, as appropriate, current information with respect to procedures for obtaining this law enforcement assistance at that airport.

Sec. 108.17 Use of X-ray systems.

a. No certificate holder may use an X-ray system within the United States to inspect carry-on or checked articles unless specifically authorized under a security program required by Sec. 108.5 of this part or use such a system contrary to its approved security program. The Administrator authorizes certificate holders to use X-ray systems for inspecting carry-on or checked articles under an approved security program if the certificate holder shows that—

1. For a system manufactured before April 25, 1974, it meets either the guidelines issued by the Food and Drug Administration (FDA), Department of Health, Education, and Welfare (HEW) and published in the Federal Register (38 FR 21442, August 8, 1973); or the performance standards for cabinet X-ray systems designed primarily for the inspection of carry-on baggage issued by the FDA and published in 21 CFR 1020.40 (39 FR 12985, April 10, 1974);

2. For a system manufactured after April 24, 1974, it meets the standards for cabinet X-ray systems designed primarily for the inspection of carry-on baggage issued by the FDA and published in 21 CFR 1020.40 (39 FR 12985, April 10, 1974);

3. A program for initial and recurrent training of operators of the system is established, which includes training in radiation safety, the efficient use of X-ray systems, and the identification of weapons and other dangerous articles;

4. Procedures are established to ensure that each operator of the

system is provided with an individual personnel dosimeter (such as a film badge or themoluminescent dosimeter). Each dosimeter used shall be evaluated at the end of each calendar month, and records of operator duty time and the results of dosimeter evaluations shall be maintained by the certificate holder; and

5. The system meets the imaging requirements set forth in an approved Air Carrier Security Program using the step wedge specified in American Society for Testing and Materials Standard F792-82.

b. No certificate bolder may use an X-ray system within the United States unless within the preceding 12 calendar months a radiation survey has been conducted which shows that the system meets the applicable performance standards in 21 CFR 1020.40 or guidelines published by the FDA in the Federal Register of August 8, 1973 (38 FR 21442).

c. No certificate holder may use an X-ray system after the system is initially installed or after it has been moved from one location to another, unless a radiation survey is conducted which shows that the system meets the applicable performance standards in 21 CFR 1020.40 or guidelines published by the FDA in the Federal Register of August 8, 1973 (38 FR 21442) except that a radiation survey is not required for an X-ray system that is moved to another location if the certificate holder shows that the system is so designed that it can be moved without altering its performance.

d. No certificate holder may use an X-ray system that is not in full compliance with any defect notice or modification order issued for that system by the FDA, unless that Administration has advised the FAA that the defect or failure to comply does not create a significant risk or injury, including genetic injury, to any person.

e. No certificate holder may use an X-ray system to inspect carry-on or checked articles unless a sign is posted in a conspicuous place at the screening station and on the X-ray system, which notifies passengers that such items are being inspected by an X-ray and advises them to remove all X-ray, scientific, and high-speed film from carry-on and checked articles before inspection. This sign shall also advise passengers that they may request that an inspection be made of their photographic equipment and film packages without exposure to an X-ray system. If the X-ray system exposes any carry-on or checked articles to more than 1 milliroentgen during the inspection, the certificate holder shall post a sign which advises passengers to remove film of all kinds from their articles before inspection. If requested by passengers, their photographic equipment and film packages shall be inspected without exposure to an X-ray system.

f. Each certificate holder shall maintain at least one copy of the results of the most recent radiation survey conducted under paragraph (b) or (c) of this section and shall make it available for inspection upon request by the Administrator at each of the following locations:

　　1. The certificate holder's principal business office; and

　　2. The place where the X-ray system is in operation.

g. The American Society for Testing and Materials Standard F792-82, "Design and Use of Ionizing Radiation Equipment for the Detection of Items Prohibited in Controlled Access Areas," described in this section is incorporated by reference herein and made a part hereof pursuant to 5 U.S.C. 552(a)(1). All persons affected by these amendments may obtain copies of the standard from the American Society for Testing and Materials, 1916 Race Street, Philadelphia, PA 19103. In addition, a copy of the standard may be examined at the FAA Rules Docket, Docket No. 24115, 800 Independence Avenue, SW, Washington, DC, weekdays, except Federal holidays, between 8:30 A.M. and 5 P.M.

h. Each certificate holder shall comply with X-ray operator duty time limitations specified in its security program.

[Doc. No. 108, 46 FR 3796, Jan. 15,1981, as amended by Amdt. 108-1, 50 FR 25656, June 20, 1985; Doc. No. 26522, Amdt. Nos. 107-6 and 108-10, 56 FR 41425, Aug. 20,1991; Doc. No. 26268, Amdt. No. 108-11, 56 FR 48373, Sept. 24, 1991]

Sec. 108.18 Security Directives and Information Circulars.

a. Each certificate holder required to have an approved security program for passenger operations shall comply with each Security Directive issued to the certificate holder by the Director of Civil Aviation Security, or by any person to whom the Director has delegated the authority to issue Security Directives, within the time prescribed in the Security Directive for compliance.

b. Each certificate holder who receives a Security Directive shall—

1. Not later than 24 hours after delivery by the FAA or within the time prescribed in the Security Directive, acknowledge receipt of the Security Directive;

2. Not later than 72 hours after delivery by the FAA or within the time prescribed in the Security Directive, specify the method by which the certificate holder has implemented the measures in the Security Directive; and

3. Ensure that information regarding the Security Directive and measures implemented in response to the Security Directive are distributed to specified personnel as prescribed in the Security Directive and to other personnel with an operational need to know.

c. In the event that the certificate holder is unable to implement the measures contained in the Security Directive, the certificate holder shall submit proposed alternative measures, and the basis for submitting the alternative measures, to the Director of Civil Aviation Security for approval. The certificate holder shall submit proposed alternative measures within the time prescribed in the Security Directive. The certificate holder shall implement any alternative measures approved by the Director of Civil Aviation Security.

d. Each certificate holder who receives a Security Directive or Information Circular and each person who receives information from a Security Directive or Information Circular shall—

1. Restrict the availability of the Security Directive or Information, Circular and information contained in the Security Directive or the Information Circular to those persons with an operational need to know; and

2. Refuse to release the Security Directive or Information Circular and information regarding the Security Directive or Information Circular to persons other than those with an operational need to know without the prior written consent of the Director of Civil Aviation Security.

(Approved by the Office of Management and Budget under control number 2120-0098)

[Doc. No. 25953, 54 FR 28984, July 10, 1989]

Sec. 108.19 Security threats and procedures.

a. Upon receipt of a specific and credible threat to the security of a flight, the certificate holder shall—
   1. Immediately notify the ground and in-flight security coordinators of the threat, any evaluation thereof, and any countermeasures to be applied; and
   2. Ensure that the in-flight security coordinator notifies the flight and cabin crewmembers of the threat, any evaluation thereof, and any countermeasures to be applied.
b. Upon receipt of a bomb threat against a specific airplane, each certificate holder shall attempt to determine whether or not any explosive or incendiary is aboard the airplane involved by doing the following:
   1. Conducting a security inspection on the ground before the next flight or, if the airplane is in flight, immediately after its next landing.
   2. If the airplane is being operated on the ground, advising the pilot in command to immediately submit the airplane for a security inspection.
   3. If the airplane is in flight, immediately advising the pilot in command of all pertinent information available so that necessary emergency action can be taken.
c. Immediately upon receiving information that an act or suspected act of air piracy has been committed, the certificate holder shall notify

the Administrator. If the airplane is in airspace under other than United States jurisdiction, the certificate holder shall also notify the appropriate authorities of the State in whose territory the airplane is located and, if the airplane is in flight, the appropriate authorities of the State in whose territory the airplane is to land. Notification of the appropriate air traffic controlling authority is sufficient action to meet this requirement.

[Doc. No. 109, 46 FR 3786, Jan. 15, 1981, as amended by Amdt. 108-4, 51 FR 1352, Jan. 10, 1986; Amdt. 108-9, 56 FR 27869, June 17, 1991]

Sec. 108.20 Use of Explosives Detection Systems.

When the Administrator shall require by amendment under Sec. 108.25, each certificate holder required to conduct screening under a security program shall use an explosive detection system that has been approved by the Administrator to screen checked baggage on international flights in accordance with the certificate holder's security program.

[Doc. No. 25956, 54 FR 36946, Sept. 5, 1989]

Sec. 108.21 Carriage of passengers under the control of armed law enforcement escorts.

a. Except as provided in paragraph (e) of this section, no certificate holder required to conduct screening under a security program may carry a passenger in the custody of an armed law enforcement escort aboard an airplane for which screening is required unless—
   1. The armed law enforcement escort is an official or employee of the United States, of a State or political subdivision of a State, or a municipality who is required by appropriate authority to maintain custody and control over an individual aboard an airplane;
   2. The certificate holder is notified by the responsible government entity at least 1 hour, or in case of emergency as soon as possible, before departure—

  i. Of the identity of the passenger to be carried and the flight
     on which it is proposed to carry the passenger; and
 ii. Whether or not the passenger is considered to be in a max-
     imum risk category;
3. If the passenger is considered to be in a maximum risk category,
   that the passenger is under the control of at least two armed law
   enforcement escorts and no other passengers are under the control of those two law enforcement escorts;
4. No more than one passenger who the certificate holder has been
   notified is in a maximum risk category is carried on the airplane;
5. If the passenger is not considered to be in a maximum risk category, the passenger is under the control of at least one armed
   law enforcement escort, and no more than two of these persons
   are carried under the control of any one law enforcement escort;
6. The certificate holder is assured prior to departure, by each law
   enforcement escort that—
  i. The officer is equipped with adequate restraining devices
     to be used in the event restraint of any passenger under the
     control of the escort becomes necessary; and
 ii. Each passenger under the control of the escort has been
     searched and does not have on or about his or her person or
     property anything that can be used as a deadly or dan-
     gerous weapon;
7. Each passenger under the control of a law enforcement escort
   is—
  i. Boarded before any other passengers when boarding at the
     airport where the flight originates and deplaned at the des-
     tination after all other deplaning passengers have
     deplaned;
 ii. Seated in the rear-most passenger seat when boarding at
     the airport where the flight originates; and
iii. Seated in a seat that is neither located in any lounge area
     nor located next to or directly across from any exit; and
8. A law enforcement escort having control of a passenger is
   seated between the passenger and any aisle.

b. No certificate holder operating an airplane under paragraph (a) of this section may—

1. Serve food beverage or provide metal eating utensils to a passenger under the control of a law enforcement escort while aboard the airplane unless authorized to do so by the law enforcement escort.

2. Serve a law enforcement escort or the passenger under the control of the escort any alcoholic beverages while aboard the airplane.

c. Each law enforcement escort carried under the provisions of paragraph (a) of this section shall, at all times, accompany the passenger under the control of the escort and keep the passenger under surveillance while aboard the airplane.

d. No law enforcement escort carried under paragraph (b) of this section or any passenger under the control of the escort may drink alcoholic beverages while aboard the airplane.

e. This section does not apply to the carriage of passengers under voluntary protective escort.

Sec. 108.23 Training.

a. No certificate holder may use any person as a Security Coordinator unless, within the preceding 12 calendar months, that person has satisfactorily completed the security training as specified in the certificate holder's approved security program.

b. No certificate holder may use any person as a crewmember on any domestic or international flight unless within, the preceding 12 calendar months or within the time period specified in an Advanced Qualification Program approved under SFAR 58 that person has satisfactorily completed the security training required by Sec. 121.417(b)(3)(v) or Sec. 135.331(b)(3)(v) of this chapter and as specified in the certificate holder's approved security program. With respect to training conducted under Sec. 121.417 or Sec. 135.331, whenever a crewmember who is required to take recurrent training completes the training in the calendar month before or the calendar month after the calendar month in which that training is required, he is considered to have completed the training in the calendar month in which it was required.

[Doc. No. 24719, 50 FR 28893, July 16, 1985, as amended by Amdt. 108-8, 55 FR 40275, Oct. 2, 1990]

Sec. 108.25 Approval of security programs and amendments.

a. Unless otherwise authorized by the Administrator, each certificate holder required to have a security program for a passenger operation shall submit its proposed security program to the Administrator for approval at least 90 days before the date of the intended passenger operations. Within 30 days after receiving the program, the Administrator either approves the program or notifies the certificate holder to modify the program to comply with the applicable requirements of this part. The certificate holder may petition the Administrator to reconsider the notice to modify within 30 days after receiving the notice, and, except in the case of an emergency requiring immediate action in the interest of safety, the filing of the petition stays the notice pending a decision by the Administrator.

b. The Administrator may amend an approved security program if it is determined that safety and the public interest require the amendment, as follows:

1. The Administrator notifies the certificate holder, in writing, of the proposed amendment, fixing a period of not less than 30 days within which it may submit written information, views, and arguments on the amendment.

2. After considering all relevant material, the Administrator notifies the certificate holder of any amendment adopted or rescinds the notice. The amendment becomes effective not less than 30 days after the certificate holder receives the notice, unless the certificate holder petitions the Administrator to reconsider the amendment, in which case the effective date is stayed by the Administrator.

3. If the Administrator finds that there is an emergency requiring

immediate action with respect to safety in air transportation or in air commerce that makes the procedure in this paragraph impracticable or contrary to the public interest, the Administrator may issue an amendment, effective without stay, on the date the certificate holder receives notice of it. In such a case, the Administrator incorporates the findings, and a brief statement of the reasons for it, in the notice of the amendment to be adopted.

c. A certificate holder may submit a request to the Administrator to amend its program. The application must be filed with the Administrator at least 30 days before the date it proposes for the amendment to become effective, unless a shorter period is allowed by the Administrator. Within 15 days after receiving a proposed amendment, the Administrator either approves or denies the request. Within 30 days after receiving from the Administrator a notice of refusal to approve the application for amendment, the applicant may petition the Administrator to reconsider the refusal to amend.

Sec. 108.27 Evidence of compliance.

On request of the Administrator, each certificate holder shall provide evidence of compliance with this part and its approved security program.

[Doc. 24719, 50 FR 28894, July 16, 1985; 50 FR 35535, Aug. 30, 1985; 51 FR 44875, Dec. 12, 1986]

Sec. 108.29 Standards for security oversight.

a. Each certificate holder shall ensure that:
  1. Each person performing a security-related function for the certificate holder has knowledge of the provisions of this part 108, applicable Security Directives and Information Circulars promulgated pursuant to Sec. 108.18, and the certificate holder's security program to the extent that the performance of the function imposes a need to know.
  2. Daily, a Ground Security Coordinator at each airport:

      i. Reviews all security-related functions for effectiveness and compliance with this part, the certificate holder's security program, and applicable Security Directives; and

     ii. Immediately initiates corrective action for each instance of noncompliance with this part, the certificate holder's security program, and applicable Security Directives.

b. The requirements prescribed in paragraph (a) of this section apply to all security-related functions performed for the certificate holder whether by a direct employee or a contractor employee.

[Doc. No. 26522, Amdt. Nos. 107-6 and 108-10, 56 FR 41425, Aug. 20, 1991]

Sec. 108.31 Employment standards for screening personnel.

a. No certificate holder shall use any person to perform any screening function, unless that person has:

  1. A high school diploma, a General Equivalency Diploma, or a combination of education and experience which the certificate holder has determined to have equipped the person to perform the duties of the position;

  2. Basic aptitudes and physical abilities including color perception, visual and aural acuity, physical coordination, and motor skills to the following standards:

      i. Screeners operating X-ray equipment must be able to distinguish on the X-ray monitor the appropriate imaging standard specified in the certificate holder's security program. Wherever the X-ray system displays colors, the operator must be able to perceive each color;

     ii. Screeners operating any screening equipment must be able to distinguish each color displayed on every type of screening equipment and explain what each color signifies;

    iii. Screeners must be able to hear and respond to the spoken voice and to audible alarms generated by screening equipment in an active checkpoint environment;

    iv. Screeners performing physical searches or other related operations must be able to efficiently and thoroughly manipulate and handle such baggage, containers, and other objects subjects to security processing; and

   v. Screeners who perform pat-downs or hand-held metal detector searches of persons must have sufficient dexterity and capability to conduct those procedures on all parts of the persons' bodies.

  3. The ability to read, speak, and write English well enough to:

    i. Carry out written and oral instructions regarding the proper performance of screening duties;

   ii. Read English language identification media, credentials, airline tickets, and labels on items normally encountered in the screening process;

  iii. Provide direction to and understand and answer questions from English-speaking persons undergoing screening; and

  iv. Write incident reports and statements and log entries into security records in the English language.

  4. Satisfactorily completed all initial, recurrent, and appropriate specialized training required by the certificate holder's security program.

b. Notwithstanding the provisions of paragraph (a)(4) of this section, the certificate holder may use a person during the on-the-job portion of training to perform security functions provided that the person is closely supervised and does not make independent judgments as to whether persons or property may enter a sterile area or aircraft without further inspection.

c. No certificate holder shall use a person to perform a screening function after that person has failed an operational test related to that function until that person has successfully completed the remedial training specified in the certificate holder's security program.

d. Each certificate holder shall ensure that a Ground Security Coordinator conducts and documents an annual evaluation of each person assigned screening duties and, may continue that person's employment in a screening capacity only upon the determination by that Ground Security Coordinator that the person:

  1. Has not suffered a significant dimunition of any physical ability required to perform a screening function since the last evaluation of those abilities;

2. Has a satisfactory record of performance and attention to duty; and

3. Demonstrates the current knowledge and skills necessary to courteously, vigilantly, and effectively perform screening functions.

e. Paragraphs (a) through (d) of this section do not apply to those screening functions conducted outside the United States over which the certificate holder does not have operational control.

f. At locations outside the United States where the certificate holder has operational control over a screening function, the certificate holder may use screeners who do not meet the requirements of paragraph (a)(3) of this section, provided that at least one representative of the certificate holder who has the ability to functionally read and speak English is present while the certificate holder's passengers are undergoing security processing.

[Doc. No. 26522, Amdt. Nos. 107-8 and 108-10, 56 FR 41425, Aug. 20, 1991]

Sec. 108.33 Employment history, verification and criminal history records checks.

a. Scope. The following persons are within the scope of this section:

1. Each employee or contractor employee covered under a certification made to an airport operator, pursuant to Sec. 107.31 (n) of this chapter, made on or after November 23, 1998.

2. Each individual issued air carrier identification media that one or more airports accepts as airport approved media for unescorted access within a security identification display area (SIDA) as described in Sec. 107.25 of this chapter.

3. Each individual assigned, after November 23, 1998, to perform the following functions:

   i. Screen passengers or property that will be carried in a cabin of an aircraft of an air carrier required to screen passengers under this part.

   ii. Serve as an immediate supervisor (checkpoint security

supervisor [CSS]), or the next supervisory level (shift or site supervisor), to those individuals described in paragraph (a)(3)(i) of this section.

b. Employment history investigations required. Each air carrier must ensure that, for each individual described in paragraph (a) of this section, the following requirements are met:

1. The individual has satisfactorily undergone Part 1 of an employment history investigation. Part 1 consists of a review of the previous 10 years of employment history and verifications of the 5 employment years preceding the date the employment history investigation is initiated as provided in paragraph (c) of this section; and

2. If required by paragraph (c)(5) of this section, the individual has satisfied Part 2 of the employment history investigation. Part 2 is the process to determine if the individual has a criminal record. To satisfy Part 2 of the investigation the criminal records check must not disclose that the individual has been convicted or found not guilty by reason of insanity, in any jurisdiction, during the 10 years ending on the date of such investigation, of any of the crimes listed below:

   i. Forgery of certificates, false marking of aircraft, and other aircraft registration violation, 49 U.S.C. 46306;

   ii. Interference with air navigation, 49 U.S.C. 46308;

   iii. Improper transportation of a hazardous material, 49 U.S.C. 46312;

   iv. Aircraft piracy, 49 U.S.C. 46502;

   v. Interference with flightcrew members or flight attendants, 49 U.S.C. 46504;

   vi. Commission of certain crimes aboard aircraft in flight, 49 U.S.C. 46506;

   vii. Carrying a weapon or explosive aboard aircraft, 49 U.S.C. 46505;

   viii. Conveying false information and threats, 49 U.S.C. 46507;

   ix. Aircraft piracy outside the special aircraft jurisdiction of the United States, 49 U.S.C. 46502(b);

    x. Lighting violations involving transporting controlled substances, 49 U.S.C. 46315;

    xi. Unlawful entry into an aircraft or airport area that serves air carriers or foreign air carriers contrary to established security requirements, 49 U.S.C. 46314;

    xii. Destruction of an aircraft or aircraft facility, 18 U.S.C. 32;

    xiii. Murder;

    xiv. Assault with intent to murder;

    xv. Espionage;

    xvi. Sedition;

    xvii. Kidnapping or hostage taking;

    xviii. Treason;

    xix. Rape or aggravated sexual abuse;

    xx. Unlawful possession, use, sale, distribution, or manufacture of an explosive or weapon;

    xxi. Extortion;

    xxii. Armed robbery;

    xxiii. Distribution of, or intent to distribute, a controlled substance;

    xxiv. Felony arson; or

    xxv. Conspiracy or attempt to commit any of the aforementioned criminal acts.

c. Investigative steps. Part I of the employment history investigations must be completed on all persons described in paragraph (a) of this section. If required by paragraph (c)(5) of this section, Part 2 of the employment history investigation must also be completed on all persons listed in paragraph (a) of this section.

    1. The individual must provide the following information on an application:

        i. The individual's full name, including any aliases or nicknames;

        ii. The dates, names, phone numbers, and addresses of previous employers, with explanations for any gaps in employment of more than 12 consecutive months, during the previous 10-year period;

    iii. Any convictions during the previous 10-year period of the crimes listed in paragraph (b)(2) of this section.

2. The air carrier must include on the application form a notification that the individual will be subject to an employment history verification and possibly a criminal records check.
3. The air carrier must verify the identity of the individual through the presentation of two forms of identification, one of which must bear the individual's photograph.
4. The air carrier must verify the information on the most recent 5 years of employment history required under paragraph (c)(1)(ii) of this section. Information must be verified in writing, by documentation, by telephone, or in person.
5. If one or more of the conditions (triggers) listed in Sec. 108.33(c)(5)

    1. through (iv) exist, the employment history investigation must not be considered complete unless Part 2 is accomplished. Only the air carrier may initiate Part 2. Part 2 consists of a comparison of the individual's fingerprints against the fingerprint files of known criminals maintained by the Federal Bureau of Investigation (FBI). The comparison of the individual's fingerprints must be processed through the FAA. The air carrier may request a check of the individual's fingerprint-based criminal record only if one or more of the following conditions exist:

        i. The individual does not satisfactorily account for a period of unemployment of 12 consecutive months or more during the previous 10-year period.

        ii. The individual is unable to support statements made on the application form.

        iii. There are significant inconsistencies in the information provided on the application.

        iv. Information becomes available to the air carrier during the investigation indicating a possible conviction for one of the crimes listed in paragraph (b.) (2) of this section.

d. Individual notification. Prior to commencing the criminal records check, the air carrier must notify the affected individuals and identify a point of contact for follow-up. An individual who chooses not to submit fingerprints may not be granted unescorted access privilege and may not be allowed to hold screener or screener supervisory positions.

e. Fingerprint processing. If a fingerprint comparison is necessary under paragraph (c)(5) of this section to complete the employment history investigation the air carrier must collect and process fingerprints in the following manner:

1. One set of legible and classifiable fingerprints must be recorded on fingerprint cards approved by the FBI and distributed by the FAA for this purpose.

2. The fingerprints must be obtained from the individual under direct observation by the air carrier or a law enforcement officer. Individuals submitting their fingerprints must not take possession of their fingerprint card after they have been fingerprinted.

3. The identity of the individual must be verified at the time fingerprints are obtained. The individual must present two forms of identification, one of which must bear the individual's photograph.

4. The fingerprint card must be forwarded to FAA at the location specified by the Administrator.

5. Fees for the processing of the criminal records checks are due upon application. Air carriers must submit payment through corporate check, cashier's check, or money order made payable to "U.S. FAA," at the designated rate for each fingerprint card. Combined payment for multiple applications is acceptable. The designated rate for processing the fingerprint cards is available from the local FAA security office.

f. Determination of arrest status. In conducting the criminal record checks required by this section, the air carrier must not consider the employment history investigation complete unless it investigates arrest information for the crimes listed in paragraph (b)(2) of this section for which no disposition has been recorded and makes a determination that the arrest did not result in a disqualifying conviction.

g. Availability and correction of FBI records and notification of disqualification.

  1. At the time Part 2 is initiated and the fingerprints are collected, the air carrier must notify the individual that a copy of the criminal record received from the FBI will be made available to the individual if requested in writing. When requested in writing, the air carrier must make available to the individual a copy of any criminal record received from the FBI.

  2. Prior to making a final decision to deny authorization to an individual described in paragraph (a) of this section, the air carrier must advise the individual that the FBI criminal record discloses information that would disqualify him/her from positions covered under this rule and provide him/her with a copy of their FBI record if requested.

  3. The air carrier must notify an individual that a final decision has been made to forward or not forward a letter of certification for unescorted access to the airport operator, or to grant or deny the individual authority to perform screening functions listed under paragraph (a)(3) of this section.

h. Corrective action by the individual. The individual may contact the local jurisdiction responsible for the information and the FBI to complete or correct the information contained in his/her record before the air carrier makes any decision to withhold his/her name from a certification, or not grant authorization to perform screening functions subject to the following conditions:

  1. Within 30 days after being advised that the criminal record received from the FBI discloses disqualifying information, the individual must notify the air carrier, in writing, of his/her intent to correct any information believed to be inaccurate.

  2. Upon notification by an individual that the record has been corrected, the air carrier must obtain a copy of the revised FBI record prior to making a final determination.

  3. If no notification is received within 30 days, the air carrier may make a final determination.

i. Limits on dissemination of results. Criminal record information provided by the FBI must be used solely for the purposes of this section, and no person may disseminate the results of a criminal record check to anyone other than:

1. The individual to whom the record pertains or that individual's authorized representative;
2. Air carrier officials with a need to know; and
3. Others designated by the Administrator.

j. Employment status while awaiting criminal record checks. Individuals who have submitted their fingerprints and are awaiting FBI results may perform work details under the following conditions:

1. Those seeking unescorted access to the SIDA must be escorted by someone who has unescorted SIDA access privileges;
2. Those applicants seeking positions covered under paragraphs (a)(3) and (d)(4) of this section, may not exercise any independent judgments regarding those functions.

k. Recordkeeping.

1. The air carrier must physically maintain and control Part 1 employment history investigation file until 180 days after the termination of the individual's authority for unescorted access or termination from positions covered under paragraph (a)(3) of this section. Part 1 of the employment history investigation, completed on screening personnel must be maintained at the airport where they perform screening functions. Part 1 of the employment history investigation file must consist of the following:

   i. The application;
   ii. The employment verification information obtained by the employer;
   iii. the names of those from whom the employment verification information was obtained;
   iv. The date and the method of how the contact was made; and
   v. Any other information as required by the Administrator.

2. The air carrier must physically maintain, control and when appropriate destroy Part 2, the criminal record file, for each individual for whom a fingerprint comparison has been made. Part 2 must be maintained for 180 days after the termination of

the individual's authority for unescorted access or after the individual ceases to perform screening functions. Only direct air carrier employees may carry out Part 2 responsibilities. Part 2 must consist of the following:

  i. The results of the record check; or

  ii. Certification from the air carrier that the check was completed and did not uncover a disqualifying conviction.

3. The files required by this paragraph must be maintained in a manner that is acceptable to the Administrator and in a manner that protects the confidentiality of the individual.

l. Continuing responsibilities.

1. Any individual authorized to have unescorted access privilege to the SIDA or who performs functions covered under paragraph (a)(3) of this section, who is subsequently convicted of any of the crimes listed in paragraph (b)(2) of this section must, within 24 hours, report the conviction to the air carrier and surrender the SIDA access medium or any employment related identification medium to the issuer.

2. If information becomes available to the air carrier indicating that an individual has a possible conviction for one of the disqualifying crimes in paragraph (b)(2) of this section, the air carrier must determine the status of the conviction and, if the conviction is confirmed:

  i. Immediately revoke access authorization for unescorted access to the SIDA; or

  ii. Immediately remove the individual from screening functions covered under paragraph (a)(3) of this section.

m. Air carrier responsibility. The air carrier must:

1. Designate an individual(s), in the security program, to be responsible for maintaining and controlling the employment history investigation for those whom the air carrier has made a certification to an airport operator under Sec. 107.31 (n)(1) of this chapter and for destroying the criminal record files when their maintenance is no longer required by paragraph (k)(2) of this section.

2. Designate individual(s), in the security program, to maintain

and control Part 1 of the employment history investigations of screeners whose files must be maintained at the location or station where the screener is performing his or her duties.

3. Designate individual(s), in the security program, to serve as the contact to receive notification from an individual applying for either unescorted access or those seeking to perform screening functions of his or her intent to seek correction of his or her criminal record with the FBI.

4. Designate an individual(s), in the security program, to maintain and control Part 2 of the employment history investigation file for all employees, contractors, or others who undergo a fingerprint comparison at the request of the air carrier.

5. Audit the employment history investigations performed in accordance with this section. The audit process must be set forth in the air carrier approved security program

[Amdt. 108-17, 63 FR 51220, Sept. 24, 1998]

APPENDIX D

FEDERAL AVIATION REGULATION (FAR) PART 129—FOREIGN AIR CARRIER SECURITY

This regulation requires each foreign air carrier to adopt and carry out a FAA-approved security program for operations into and out of the United States. This security program is called the Foreign Air Carrier Model Security Program (FACMSP). Each provision of the program has the force of the regulation itself. The FACMSP is a restricted document, designed to provide a secure operating environment, and prevent or deter aircraft hijacking, sabotage, and related criminal acts.

Note: This document contains FAR Part 129 including Amendment 129-27 as published in the Federal Register July 17, 1997 (effective August 18, 1997).

PART 129—OPERATIONS: FOREIGN AIR CARRIERS AND FOREIGN OPERATORS OF U.S.-REGISTERED AIRCRAFT ENGAGED IN COMMON CARRIAGE

Special Federal Aviation Regulation No. 38-2

Authority: 49 U.S.C. 106(g), 40104–40105, 40113, 40119, 44701–44702, 44712, 44716–44717, 44722, 44901–44904, 44906.

Source: Docket No. 1994, 29 FR 1720, Feb. 5, 1964, unless otherwise noted.

EDITORIAL NOTE: For the text of SFAR No. 38-2, see Part 121 of this chapter..

Sec. 129.1 Applicability.

a. Except as provided in paragraph (b) of this section, this part prescribes rules governing the operation within the United States of each foreign air carrier holding a permit issued by the Civil Aeronautics Board or the Department of Transportation under section 402 of the Federal Aviation Act of 1958 (49 U.S.C. 1372) Or other appropriate economic or exemption authority issued by the Civil Aeronautics Board or the Department of Transportation.

b. Sections 129.14 and 129.20 also apply to U.S.-registered aircraft operated in common carriage by a foreign person or foreign air carrier solely outside the United States. For the purpose of this part, a foreign person is any person, not a citizen for the United States, who operates a U.S.registered aircraft in common carriage solely outside the United States.

[Doc. No. 24856, Amdt. 129-14, 52 FR 20029, May 28, 1987, as amended by Amdt. 129-27, 62 FR 3 8396, July 17, 1997]

Sec. 129.25 Airplane security.

a. The following are definitions of terms used in this section:
1. "Approved security program" means a security program required by Part 108 of this title approved by the Administrator.
2. "Certificate holder" means a person holding an FAA air carrier operating certificate or operating certificate when that person engages in scheduled passenger or public charter operations, or both.
3. "Passenger seating configuration" means the total number of seats for which the aircraft is type certificated that can be made available for passenger use aboard a flight and includes that seat in certain airplanes which may be used by a representative of the Administrator to conduct flight checks but is available for revenue purposes on other occasions.
4. "Private charter" means any charter for which the charterer engages the total capacity of an airplane for the carriage only of:
   i. Passengers in civil or military air movements conducted under contract with the Government of the United States or the Government of a foreign country; or
   ii. Passengers invited by the charterer, the cost of which is borne entirely by the charterer and not directly or indirectly by the individual passengers.
5. "Public charter" means any charter that is not a "private charter."
6. "Scheduled passenger operations" means holding out to the public of air transportation service for passengers from identified air terminals at a set time announced by timetable or schedule published in a newspaper, magazine, or other advertising medium.

7. "Sterile area" means an area to which access is controlled by the inspection of persons and property in accordance with an approved security program or a security program, used in accordance with Sec. 129.25.

b. Each foreign air carrier landing or taking off in the United States shall adopt and use a security program for each scheduled and public charter passenger operation, that meets the requirements of—

1. Paragraph (c) of this section for each operation with an airplane having a passenger seating configuration of more than 60 seats;

2. Paragraph (c) of this section for each operation that will provide deplaned passengers, access, that is not controlled by a certificate holder using an approved security program or a foreign air carrier using a security program required by this section, to a sterile area;

3. Paragraph (c) of this section for each operation with an airplane having a passenger seating configuration of more than 30 seats but less than 61 seats for which the FAA has notified the foreign air carrier that a threat exists; and

4. Paragraph (d) of this section for each operation with an airplane having a passenger seating configuration of more than 30 seats but less than 61 seats, when the the Director of Civil Aviation Security or a designate of the Director has not notified the foreign air carrier in writing that a threat exists with respect to that operation.

c. Each security program required by paragraph (b)(1), (2), or (3) of this section shall be designed to—

1. Prevent or deter the carriage aboard airplanes of any explosive, incendiary device or a deadly or dangerous weapon on or about each individual's person or accessible property, except as provided in Sec. 129.27 of this part, through screening by weapon-detecting procedures or facilities;

2. Prohibit unauthorized access to airplanes;

3. Ensure that baggage is accepted by a responsible agent of the foreign air carrier; and

4. Prevent cargo and checked baggage from being loaded aboard

its airplanes unless handled in, accordance with the foreign air carriers security procedures.

d. Each security program required by paragraph (b)(4) of this section shall include the procedures used to comply with the applicable requirements of paragraphs (h)(2) and (i) of this section regarding law enforcement officers.

e. Each foreign air carrier required to adopt and use a security program pursuant to paragraph (b) of this section shall have a security program acceptable to the Administrator. A foreign air carrier's security program is acceptable only if the Administrator finds that the security program provides passengers a level of protection similar to the level of protection provided by U.S. air carriers serving the same airports. Foreign air carriers shall employ procedures equivalent to those required of U.S. air carriers serving the same airport if the Administrator determines that such procedures are necessary to provide passengers a similar level of protection. The following procedures apply for acceptance of a security program by the Administrator:

1. Unless otherwise authorized by the Administrator, each foreign air carrier required to have a security program by paragraph (b) of this section shall submit its program to the Administrator at least 90 days before the intended date of passenger operations. The proposed security program must be in English unless the Administrator requests that the proposed program be submitted in the official language of the foreign air carrier's country. The Administrator will notify the foreign air carrier of the security program's acceptability, or the need to modify the proposed security program for it to be acceptable under this part, within 30 days after receiving the proposed security program. The foreign air carrier may petition the Administrator to reconsider the notice to modify the security program within 30 days after receiving a notice to, modify.

2. In the case of a security program previously found to be acceptable pursuant to this section, the Administrator may subsequently amend the security program in the interest of safety in air transportation or in air commerce and in the public interest

within a specified period of time. In making such an amendment, the following procedures apply:

    i. The Administrutor notifies the foreign air carrier, in writing, of a proposed amendment, fixing a period of not less than 45 days within which the foreign air carrier may submit written information, views, and arguments on the proposed amendment.

    ii. At the end of the comment period, after considering all relevant material, the Administrator notifies the foreign air carrier of any amendment to be adopted and the effective date, or rescinds the notice of proposed amendment. The foreign air carrier may petition the Administrator to reconsider the amendment, in which case the effective date of the amendment is stayed until the Administrator reconsiders the matter.

3. If the Administrator finds that there is an emergency requiring immediate action with respect to safety in air transportation or in air commerce that makes the procedures in public interest paragraph (e)(2) of this section impractical or contrary to the public interest, the Administrator may issue an amendment to the foreign air carrier security program, effective without stay on the date the foreign air carrier receives notice of it. In such a case, the Administrator incorporates in the notice of amendment the finding and a brief statement of the reasons for the amendment.

4. (4) A foreign air carrier may submit a request to the Administrator to amend its security program. The requested amendment must be filed with the Administrator at least 45 days before the date the foreign carrier proposes that the amendment would become effective, unless a shorter period is allowed by the Administrator. Within 30 days after receiving the requested amendment, the Administrator will notify the foreign air carrier whether the amendment is acceptable. The foreign air carrier may petition the Administrator to reconsider a notice of unacceptability of the requested amendment within 45 days after receiving notice of unacceptability.

5. Each foreign air carrier required to use a security program by paragraph (b) of this section shall, upon request of the Administrator and in accordance with the applicable law, provide information regarding the implementation and operation of its security program.

f. No foreign air carrier may land or take off an airplane in the United States, in passenger operations, after receiving a bomb or air piracy threat against that airplane, unless the following actions are taken:

1. If the airplane is on the ground when a bomb threat is received and the next scheduled flight of the threatened airplane is to or from a place in the United States, the foreign air carrier ensures that the pilot in command is advised to submit the airplane immediately for a security inspection and an inspection of the airplane is conducted before the next flight.

2. If the airplane is in flight to a place in the United States when a bomb threat is received, the foreign air carrier ensures that the pilot in command is advised immediately to take the emergency action necessary under the circumstances and a security inspection of the airplane is conducted immediately after the next landing.

3. If information is received of a bomb or air piracy threat against an airplane engaged in an operation specified in paragraph (f)(1) or (f)(2) of this section, the foreign air carrier ensures that notification of the threat is given to the appropriate authorities of the State in whose territory the airplane is located or, if in flight, the appropriate authorities of the State in whose territory the airplane is to land.

g. Each foreign air carrier conducting an operation for which a security program is required by paragraph (b)(1), (2), or (3) of this section shall refuse to transport—

1. Any person who does not consent to a search of his or her person in accordance with the security program; and

2. Any property of any person who does not consent to a search or inspection of that property in accordance with the security program.

h. At airports within the United States not governed by Part 107 of this chapter, each foreign air carrier engaging in public charter passenger operations shall—

1. When using a screening system required by paragraph (b) of this section, provide for law enforcement officers meeting the qualifications and standards, and in the number and manner, specified in Part 107; and

2. When using an airplane having a passenger seating configuration of more than 30 but less than 61 seats for which a screening system is not required by paragraph (b) of this section, arrange for law enforcement officers meeting the qualifications and standards specified in Part 107 to be available to respond to an incident and provide to appropriate employees, including crewmembers, current information with respect to procedures for obtaining law enforcement assistance at that airport.

i. At airports goverened by Part 107 of this chapter, each foreign air carrier engaging in scheduled passenger operations or public charter passenger operations when using an airplane with a passenger seating configuration of more than 30 but less than 61 seats for which a screening system is not required by paragraph (b) of this section shall arrange for law enforcement officers meeting the qualifications and standards specified in Part 107 to be available to respond to an incident and provide to appropriate employees, including crewmembers, current information with respect to procedures for obtaining law enforcement assistance at that airport.

j. Unless otherwise authorized by the Administrator, each foreign air carrier required to conduct screening under this part shall use procedures, facilities, and equipment for detecting explosives, incendiaries, and deadly or dangerous weapons to inspect each person entering a sterile area at each preboarding screening checkpoint in the United States for which it is responsible, and to inspect all accessible property under that person's control.

[Amdt. 129-11, 46 FR 3790, Jan. 15, 1981; 46 FR 7936, Jan. 26, 1981, as amended by Amdt. 129-16, 52 FR 48509, Dec. 22, 1987; Amdt. 129-18, 54 FR. 11121, Mar. 16, 1989; Amdt. 129-22, 56 FR 30126, July 1, 1991]

See. 129.26 Use of X-ray system.

a. No foreign air carrier may use an X-ray system in the United States to inspect carry-on and checked articles unless:

1. For a system manufactured prior to April 25, 1974, it meets either the guidelines issued by the Food and Drug Administration (FDA), Department of Health, Education, and Welfare and published in the Federal Register (38 FR 21442, August 8, 1973); or the performance standards for cabinet X-ray systems designed primarily for the inspection of carry-on baggage issued by the FDA and published in 21 CFR 1020.40 (39 FR 12985, April 10, 1974);

2. For a system manufactured after April 24, 1974, it meets the standards for cabinet X-ray systems designed primarily for the inspection of carry-on baggage issued by the FDA and published in 21 CFR 1020.40 (39 FR 12985, April 10, 1974);

3. A program for initial and recurrent training of operators of the system has been established, which includes training in radiation safety, the efficient use of X-ray systems, and the identification of weapons and other dangerous articles;

4. Procedures have been established to ensure that such operator of the system will be provided with an individual personnel dosimeter (such as a film badge or thermoluminescent dosimeter). Each dosimeter used will be evaluated at the end of each calendar month, and records of operator duty time and the results of dosimeter evaluations will be maintained by the foreign air carrier; and

5. The system meets the imaging requirements set forth in an accepted Foreign Air Carrier Security Program using the step wedge specified in American Society for Testing and Materials Standard, F792-82.

b. No foreign air carrier may use an X-ray system as specified in paragraph (a) of this section

1. Unless within the preceding 12 calendar months a radiation survey has been conducted which shows that the system meets the applicable performance standards in 21 CFR in the Federal

1020.40 or guidelines published by the Food and Drug Administration in the Federal Register of August 8, 1973 (38 FR 21442);

2. After the system is initially installed or after it has been moved from one location to another, unless a radiation survey is conducted which shows that the system meets the applicable performance standards in 21 CFR 1020.40 or guidelines published by the Food and Drug Administration in the Federal Register on August 8, 1973 (38 FR 21442); except that a radiation survey is not required for an X-ray system that is moved to another location, if the foreign air carrier shows that the system is so designed that it can be moved without altering its performance:

3. That is not in full compliance with any defect notice or modification order issued for that system by the Food and Drug Administration, Department of Health, Education, and Welfare, unless that Administration has advised the FAA that the defect or failure to comply is not such as to create a significant risk or injury, including genetic injury, to any person; and

4. Unless a sign is posted in a conspicuous place at the screening station and on the X-ray system which notifies passengers that carry-on and checked articles are being inspected by an X-ray system and advises them to remove all X-ray, scientific, and high-speed film from their carry-on and checked articles before inspection. This sign shall also advise passengers that they may request an inspection to be made of their photographic equipment and film packages without exposure to an X-ray system. If the X-ray system exposes any carry-on or checked articles to more than 1 milliroentgen during the inspection, the foreign air carrier shall post a sign which advises passengers to remove film of all kinds from their articles before inspection. If requested by passengers, their photographic equipment and film packages shall be inspected without exposure to an X-ray system.

c. Each foreign air carrier shall maintain at least one copy of the results of the most recent radiation survey conducted under paragraph (b)(1) or (b)(2) of this section at the place where the X-ray, system is in operation and shall make it available for inspection upon request by the Administrator.

d. The American Society for Testing and Materials Standard F792-82, "Design and Use of Ionizing Radiation Equipment for the Detection of Items Prohibited in Controlled Access Areas," described in this section is incorporated by reference herein and made a part hereof pursuant to 5 U.S.C. 552(a)(1). All persons affected by these amendments may obtain copies of the standard from the American Society for Testing and Materials, 1916 Race Street, Philadelphia, PA 19103. In addition, a copy of the standard may be examined at the FAA Rules Docket, Docket No. 24115, 800 Independence Avenue SW., Washington, DC, weekdays, except Federal holidays, between 8:30 A.M. and 5 P.M.

[Doc, No. 15286, Amdt 129-6, 41 FR 30106, July 22,1976, as amended by Amdt. 129-8, 43 FR 11978 Mar. 23,1978; Amdt. 129-10, 44 FR 54467, Sept. 20,1979; Amdt. 129-13, 50 FR 25657, June 20, 1985; Doc. No. 26268, Arndt No. 129-23, 56 FR 48374, Sept. 24, 1991]

Sec. I29.27 Prohibition against carriage of weapons.

a. No person may, while on board an aircraft being operated by a foreign air carrier in the United States, carry on or about his person a deadly or dangerous weapon, either concealed or unconcealed. This paragraph does not apply to—
   1. Officials or employees of the state of registry of the aircraft who are authorized by that state to carry arms; and
   2. (2) Crewmembers and other persons authorized by the foreign air carrier to carry arms.
b. No foreign air carrier may knowingly permit any passenger to carry, nor may any passenger carry, while aboard an aircraft being operated in the United States by that carrier, in checked baggage, a deadly or dangerous weapon, unless:
   1. The passenger has notified the foreign air carrier before checking the baggage that the weapon is in the baggage; and
   2. The baggage is carried in an area inaccessible to passengers.

[Doc. No. 15286, Amdt. 129-6, 41 FR 30107, July 22, 1976]

Sec. 129.29 Prohibition against smoking.

No person may smoke and no operator shall permit smoking in the passenger cabin or lavatory during any scheduled airline flight segment in air transportation or intrastate air transportation which is:

a. Between any two points within Puerto Rico, the United States Virgin Islands, the District of Colunibia, or any State of the United States (other than Alaska or Hawaii) or between any two points in any one of the above-mentioned jurisdictions (other than Alaska or Hawaii);
b. Within the State of Alaska or within the State of Hawaii; or
c. Scheduled in the current Worldwide or North American Edition of the Official Airline Guide for 6 hours or less in duration and between any point listed in paragraph (a) of this section and any point in Alaska or Hawaii, or between any point in Alaska and any point in Hawaii.

[Doc. No. 25590, Amdt. 129-20, 55 FR 8367, Mar. 7, 1990]

129.31 Airplane security.

Each foreign air carrier required to adopt and use a security program under Sec. 129.25(b) shall—

a. Restrict the distribution, disclosure, and availability of sensitive security information, as defined in part 191 of this chapter, to persons with a need-to-know, and
b. Refer requests for sensitive security information by other persons to the Assistant Administrator for Civil Aviation Security.

[Amdt.. 129-26; 62 FR 13744, Mar. 21 19971

Federal Register Note

62 FR 13736, No.. 55, Mar. 21, 1997

SUMMARY: This final rule strengthens the existing rules protecting sensitive security information from unauthorized disclosure. Part 191 is expanded to apply to air carriers, airport operators, indirect air carriers, foreign air carriers, and individuals, and specifies in more detail what sensitive security information they must protect. Part 191 continues to describe what information is protected from disclosure by the FAA, and describes in more detail that information. This final rule also changes part 107, 108,109, and 129 to correspond with changes it makes to part 1991. This action is necessary to counter the increased sophistication of those who pose a threat to civil aviation and their ability to develop techniques to subvert current security measures. The intended effect of this action is to prevent undue disclosure of information that could compromise public if it falls into the wrong hands, while being mindful of the public's legitimate right to know and interest in aviation information.

DATES: This rule is effective April 21, 1997. FAA will comply with the provisions of this rule on March 21, 1997.

Appendix A to Part 129—Application for Operations Specifications by Foreign Air Carriers

(a) General. Each application must be executed by an authorized officer or employee of the applicant having knowledge of the matter set forth therein, and must have attached thereto two copies of the appropriate written authority issued to that officer or employee by the applicant. Negotiations for permission to use airports under U.S. military jurisdiction is effected through the respective embassy of the foreign government and the United States Department of State.

(b) Format of application. The following outline must be followed in completing the information to be submitted in the application.

Application for Foreign Air Carrier Operations Specifications

(OUTLINE)

In accordance with the Federal Aviation Act of 1958 (49 U.S.C. 1372) and Part 129 of the Federal Air Regulations, application is hereby made for the issuance of Foreign Operations Specifications.

Give exact name and full post office address of applicant. Give the name, title, and post office address (within the United States if possible) of the official or employee to whom correspondence in regard to the application is to be addressed.

Unless otherwise specified, the applicant must submit the following information only with respect to those parts of his proposed operations that will be conducted within the United States.

Section I. Operations. State whether the operation proposed is day or night, visual flight rules, instrument flight rules, or a particular combination thereof.

Section II. Operational plans. State the route by which entry will be made into the United States, and the route to be flown therein.

Section III.

A. Route. Submit a map suitable for aerial navigation upon which is indicated the exact geographical track of the proposed route from the last point of foreign departure to the United States terminal, showing the regular terminal, and alternate airports, and radio navigational facilities. This material will be indicated in a manner that will facilitate identification. The applicant may use any method that will clearly distinguish the information, such as different colors, different types of lines, etc. For example, if different colors are used, the identification will be accomplished as follows:

1. Regular route: Black.
2. Regular terminal airport: Green circle.
3. Alternate airports: Orange circle.
4. The location of radio navigational facilities which will be used in connection with the proposed operation, indicating the type of facility to be used, such as radio range ADF, VOR, etc.

B. Airports. Submit the following information with regard to each regular terminal and alternate to be used in the conduct of the proposed operation:

1. Name of airport or landing area.
2. Location (direction distance to and name of nearest city or town).

Section IV. Radio facilities: Communications. List all ground radio communication facilities to be used by the applicant in the conduct of the proposed operations within the United States and over that portion of the route between the last point of foreign departure and the United States.

Section V. Aircraft. Submit the following information in regard to each type and model aircraft to be used.

A. Aircraft.
  1. Manufacturer and model number.
  2. State of origin.
  3. Single-engine or multiengine. If multiengine, indicate number of engines.
  4. What is the maximum takeoff and landing weight to be used for each type of aircraft?
  5. Registration markings of each U.S.-registered aircraft.

B. Aircraft Radio. List aircraft radio equipment necessary for instrument operation within the United States.
C. Licensing. State name of country by whom aircraft are certificated.

Section. VI. Airmen. List the following information with respect to airmen to be employed in the proposed operation within the United States.

A. State the type and class of certificate held by each flight crewmember.
B. State whether or not pilot personnel have received training in the use of navigational facilities necessary en route operation and instrument letdowns along or adjacent to the route to be flown within the United States.
C. State whether or not personnel are familiar with those parts of the Federal Air Regulations pertaining to the conduct of foreign air carrier operations within the United States.

D. State whether pilot personnel are able to speak and understand the English language to a degree necessary to enable them to properly communicate with Airport Traffic Control Towers and Airway Radio Communication Stations using radiotelephone communications.

Section VII. Dispatchers.

A. Describe briefly the dispatch organization which you propose to set up for air carrier operations within the United States.
B. State whether or not the dispatching personnel are familiar with the rules and regulations prescribed by the Federal Air Regulations governing air carrier operations.
C. Are dispatching personnel able to read and write the English language to a degree necessary to properly dispatch flights within the United States?
D. Are dispatching personnel certificated by the country of origin?

Section VIII. Additional Data.

A. Furnish such additional information and substantiating data as may serve to expedite the issuance of the operations specifications.
B. Each application shall be concluded with a statement as follows:

I certify that the above statements are true.

Signed this _____ day of _____ 19___

(Name of Applicant)————————————————
By————————————————————————

(Name of person duly authorized to execute this application on behalf of the applicant)

[Doc. No. 1994, 29 FR 1720, Feb. 5, 1964, as amended by Amdt. 129-14, 52 FR 20029, May 28, 1987; Amdt. 129-19, 54 FR 39294, Sept. 25, 1989; 54 FR 51972, Dec. 19, 1989]

APPENDIX E

SELECTED PROVISIONS OF THE FEDERAL AVIATION REAUTHORIZATION ACT OF 1996

The Federal Aviation Reauthorization Act of 1996 provides information regarding funding for airport improvements that would ultimately decrease compounding delays.

TITLE I—AIRPORT AND AIRWAY IMPROVEMENTS

. . .

Subtitle C—Airport Improvement Program Modifications

SEC. 148. [49 U.S.C. 47101 note] Innovative Financing Techniques.

(a) IN GENERAL.—The Secretary of Transportation is authorized to carry out a demonstration program under which the Secretary may approve applications under subchapter I of chapter 471 of title 49, United States Code for not more than 10 projects for which grants received under such subchapter may be used to implement innovative financing techniques.

(b) PURPOSE.—The purpose of the demonstration program shall be to provide information on the use of innovative financing techniques for airport development projects to Congress and the National Civil Aviation Review Commission.

(c) LIMITATION.—In no case shall the implementation of an innovative financing technique under the demonstration program result in a direct or indirect guarantee of any airport debt instrument by the Federal Government.

(d) INNOVATIVE FINANCING TECHNIQUE DEFINED.—In this section, the term "innovative financing technique" shall be limited to the following:

(1) Payment of interest.

(2) Commercial bond insurance and other credit enhancement associated with airport bonds for eligible airport development.

(3) Flexible non-Federal matching requirements.

(e) EXPIRATION OF AUTHORITY.—The authority of the Secretary to carry out the demonstration program shall expire on September 30, 1998.

. . .

TITLE II—FAA REFORM

. . .

Subtitle C—System To Fund Certain Federal Aviation Administration Functions

. . .

Sec. 274. [49 U.S.C. 40101 note] Independent Assessment of FAA Financial Requirements; Establishment of National Civil Aviation Review Commission.

(a) INDEPENDENT ASSESSMENT.—

(1) INITIATION.—Not later than 30 days after the date of the enactment of this Act, the Administrator shall contract with an entity independent of the Administration and the Department of Transportation to conduct a complete independent assessment of the financial requirements of the Administration through the year 2002.

(2) ASSESSMENT CRITERIA.—The Administrator shall provide to the independent entity estimates of the financial requirements of the Administration for the period described in paragraph (1), using as a

base the fiscal year 1997 appropriation levels established by Congress. The independent assessment shall be based on an objective analysis of agency funding needs.

(3) CERTAIN FACTORS TO BE TAKEN INTO ACCOUNT.—The independent assessment shall take into account all relevant factors, including—

(A) anticipated air traffic forecasts;

(B) other workload measures;

(C) estimated productivity gains, if any, which contribute to budgetary requirements;

(D) the need for programs; and

(E) the need to provide for continued improvements in all facets of aviation safety, along with operational improvements in air traffic control.

(4) COST ALLOCATION.—The independent assessment shall also assess the costs to the Administration occasioned by the provision of services to each segment of the aviation system.

(5) DEADLINE.—The independent assessment shall be completed no later than 90 days after the contract is awarded, and shall be submitted to the Commission established under subsection (b), the Secretary, the Secretary of the Treasury, the Committee on Commerce, Science, and Transportation and the Committee on Finance of the Senate and Committee on Transportation and Infrastructure and the Committee on Ways and Means of the House of Representatives.

(b) NATIONAL CIVIL AVIATION REVIEW COMMISSION—

(1) ESTABLISHMENT.—There is established a commission to he known as the National Civil Aviation Review Commission (hereinafter in this section referred to as the "Commission").

(2) MEMBERSHIP.—The Commission shall consist of 21 members to be appointed as follows:

(A) 13 members to be appointed by the Secretary, in consultation with the Secretary of the Treasury, from among individuals who have expertise in the aviation industry and who are able, collectively, to represent a balanced view of the issues important to general aviation, major air carriers, air cargo carriers, regional air carriers, business aviation, airports, aircraft manufacturers, the financial community, aviation industry workers, and airline passengers. At least one member appointed under this subparagraph shall have detailed knowledge of the congressional budgetary process.

(B) Two members appointed by the Speaker of the House of Representatives.

(C) Two members appointed by the minority leader of the House of Representatives.

(D) Two members appointed by the majority leader of the Senate.

(E) Two members appointed by the minority leader of the Senate.

(3) TASK FORCES.—The Commision shall establish an aviation funding task force and an aviation safety task force to carry out the responsibilities of the Commission under this subsection.

(4) FIRST MEETING.—The Commission may conduct its first meeting as soon as a majority of the members of the Commission are appointed.

(5) HEARINGS AND CONSULTATION.—

(A) HEARINGS.—The Commission shall take such testimony and solicit and receive such comments from the public and other interested parties as it considers appropriate, shall conduct 2 public hearings after affording adequate notice to the public thereof, and may conduct such additional hearings as may be necessary.

(B) CONSULTATION.— The Commission shall consult on a regular and frequent basis with the Secretary, the Secretary of the Treasury, the Committee on Commerce, Science, and Transportation and the Committee on Finance of the Senate, and the Committee on Transportation and Infrastructure and the Committee on Ways and Means of the House of Representatives.

(C) FACA NOT TO APPLY.—The Commission shall not be considered an advisory committee for purposes of the Federal Advisory Committee Act (5 U.S.C. App.).

(6) DUTIES OF AVIATION FUNDING TASK FORCE.—

(A) REPORT TO SECRETARY.—

(i) IN GENERAL.—The aviation funding task force established pursuant to paragraph (3) shall submit a report setting forth it comprehensive analysis of the Administration's budgetary requirements through fiscal year 2002, based upon the independent assessment under subsection (a), that analyzes alternative financing and funding means for meeting the needs of the aviation system through the year 2002. The task force shall submit a preliminary report of that analysis to the Secretary not later than 6 months after the independent assessment is completed under subsection (a). The Secretary shall provide comments on the preliminary report to the task force within 30 days after receiving the report. The task force shall issue a final report port of such comprehensive analysis within 30 days after receiving the Secretary's comments on its preliminary report.

(ii) CONTENTS.—The report submitted by the aviation funding task force under clause (i)—

(I) shall consider the independent assessmentunder subsection (a);

(II) shall consider estimated cost savings, if any, resulting from the procurement and personnel reforms included in this Act or in sections 347 and 348 of Public Law 104-50, and additional financial initiatives;

(III) shall include specific recommendations to Congress on how the Administration can reduce costs, raise additional revenue for the support of agency operations, and accelerate modernization efforts; and

(IV) shall include a draft bill containing the changes in law necessary to implement its recommendations.

(B) RECOMMENDATIONS.—The aviation funding task force shall make such recommendations under subparagraph (A)(ii)(III) as the task force deems appropriate. Those recommendations may include—

(i) proposals for off-budget treatment of the Airport and Airway Trust Fund;

(ii) alternative financing and funding proposals, including linked financing proposals;

(iii) modifications to existing levels of Airport and Airways Trust Fund receipts and taxes for each type of tax;

(iv) establishment of a cost-based user fee system based on, but not limited to, criteria under subparagraph (F) and methods to ensure that costs are borne by users on a fair and equitable basis;

(v) methods to ensure that funds collected from the aviation community are able to meet the needs of the agency;

(vi) methods to ensure that funds collected from the aviation community and passengers are used to support the aviation system;

(vii) means of meeting the airport infrastructure needs for large, medium, and small airports; and

(viii) any other matter the task force deems appropriate to address the funding and needs of the Administration and the aviation system.

(C) ADDITIONAL RECOMMENDATIONS.—The aviation funding task force report may also make recommendations concerning—

(i) means of improving productivity by expanding and accelerating the use of automation and other technology;

(ii) means of contracting out services consistent with this Act, other applicable law, and safety and national defense needs;

(iii) methods to accelerate air traffic control modernization and improvements in aviation safety and safety services;

(iv) the elimination of unneeded programs; and

(v) a limited innovative program based on funding mechanisms such as loan guarantees, financial partnerships with for-profit private sector entities, government-sponsored enterprises, and revolving loan funds, as a means of funding specific facilities and equipment projects, and to provide limited additional funding alternatives for airport capacity development.

(D) IMPACT ASSESSMENT FOR RECOMMENDATIONS.—For each recommendation contained in the aviation funding task force's report, the report shall include a full analysis and assessment of the impact implementation of the recommendation would have on

(i) safety;

(ii) administrative costs;

(iii) the congressional budget process;

(iv) the economics of the industry (including the proportionate share of all users);

(v) the ability of the Administration to utilize the sums collected; and

(vi) the funding needs of the Administration.

(E) TRUST FUND TAX RECOMMENDATIONS.—If the task force's report includes a recommendation that the existing Airport and Airways Trust Fund tax structure be modified, the report shall—

(i) state the specific rates for each group affected by the proposed modifications;

(ii) consider the impact such modifications shall have on specific users and the public (including passengers); and

(iii) state the basis for the recommendations.

(F) FEE SYSTEM RECOMMENDATIONS.—If the task force's report includes a recommendation that a fee system be established, including an air traffic control performance-based user fee system, the report shall consider—

(i) the impact such a recommendation would have on passengers, air fares (including low-fare, high frequency service), service, and competition;

(ii) existing contributions provided by individual air carriers toward funding the Administration and the air traffic control system through contributions to the Airport and Airways Trust Fund;

(iii) continuing the promotion of fair and competitive practices;

(iv) the unique circumstances associated with interisland air carrier service in Hawaii and rural air service in Alaska;

(v) the impact such a recommendation would have on service to small communities;

(vi) the impact such a recommendation would have on services provided by regional air carriers;

(vii) alternative methodologies for calculating fees so as to achieve a fair and reasonable distribution of costs of service among users;

(viii) the usefulness of phased-in approaches to implementing such a financing system;

(ix) means of assuring the provision of general fund contributions, as appropriate, toward the support of the Administration; and

(x) the provision of incentives to encourage greater efficiency in the provision of air traffic services by the Administration and greater efficiency in the use of air traffic services by aircraft operators.

(7) DUTIES OF AVIATION SAFETY TASK FORCE.—

(A) REPORT TO ADMINISTRATOR.—Not later than 1 year after the date of the enactment of this Act, the aviation safety task force established pursuant to paragraph (3) shall submit to the Administrator a report setting forth a comprehensive analysis of aviation safety in the United States and emerging trends in the safety of particular sectors of the aviation industry.

(B) CONTENTS.—The report to be submitted under subparagraph (A) shall include an assessment of—

(i) the adequacy of staffing and training resources for safety personnel of the Administration, including safety inspectors;

(ii) the Administration's processes for ensuring the public safety from fraudulent parts in civil aviation and the extent to which use of suspected unapproved parts requires additional oversight or enforcement action; and

(iii) the ability of the Administration to anticipate changes in the aviation industry and to develop policies and actions to ensure the highest level of aviation safety in the 21st century.

(8) ACCESS TO DOCUMENTS AND STAFF.—The Administration may give the Commission appropriate access to relevant documents and personnel of the Administration, and the Administrator shall make available, consistent with the authority to withhold commercial and other proprietary information under section 552 of title 5, United States Code (commonly known as the "Freedom of Information Act"), cost

data associated with the acquisition and operation of air traffic service systems. Any member of the Commission who receives commercial or other proprietary data from the Administrator shall be subject to the provisions of section 1905 of title 18, United States Code, pertaining to unauthorized disclosure of such information.

(9) TRAVEL AND PER DIEM.—Each member of the Commission shall be paid actual travel expenses, and per diem in lieu of subsistence expenses when away from his or her usual place of residence, in accordance with section 5703 of title 5, United States Code.

(10) DETAIL OF PERSONNEL FROM THE ADMINISTRATION.—The Administrator shall make available to the Commission such staff, information, and administrative services and assistance as may reasonably be required to enable the Commission to carry out its responsibilities under this subsection.

(11) AUTHORIZATION OF APPROPRIATIONS.—There is authorized to be appropriated such sums as may be necessary to carry out the provisions of this subsection.

(c) REPORTS TO CONGRESS.

(1) REPORT BY THE SECRETARY BASED ON FINAL REPORT OF AVIATION FUNDING TASK FORCE.—

(A) CONSIDERATION OF TASK FORCE'S PRELIMINARY REPORT.—Not later than 30 days after receiving the preliminary report of the aviation funding task force, the Secretary, in consultation with the Secretary of the Treasury, shall furnish comments on the report to the task force.

(B) REPORT TO CONGRESS.—Not later than 30 days after receiving the final report of the aviation funding task force, and in no event more than 1 year after the date of the enactment of this Act, the Secretary, after consulting the Secretary of the Treasury, shall transmit a report to the Committee on Commerce, Science, and Transportationand the Committee on Finance of the Senate, and the Committee on Transportation and Infrastructure and the Committee on Ways and Means of the House of Representatives. Such report shall be based upon the final report of the task force and shall contain the Secretary's recommendations for funding the needs of the aviation system through the year 2002.

(C) CONTENTS.—The Secretary shall include in the report to Congress under subparagraph (B)—

(i) a copy of the final report of the task force; and

(ii) a draft bill containing the changes in law necessary to implement the Secretary's recommendations.

(D) PUBLICATION.—The Secretary shall cause a copy of the report to be printed in the Federal Register upon its transmittal to Congress under subparagraph (B).

(2) REPORT BY THE ADMINISTRATION BASED ON FINAL REPORT OF AVIATION SAFETY TASK FORCE.—Not later than 30 days after receiving the report of the aviation safety task force, the Administrator shall transmit the report to Congress, together with the Administrator's recommendations for improving aviation safety in the United States.

(d) GAO AUDIT OF COST ALLOCATION.—The Comptroller General shall conduct an assessment of the manner in which costs for air traffic control services are allocated between the Administration and the Department of Defense. The Comptroller General shall report the results of the assessment, together with any recommendations the Comptroller General may have for reallocation of costs and for opportunities to increase the efficiency of air traffic control services provided by the Administration and by the Department of Defense, to the Commission, the Administrator, the Secretary of Defense, the Committee on Transportation and Infrastructure of the House of Representatives, and the Committee on Commerce, Science, and Transportation of the Senate not later than 180 days after the date of the enactment of this Act.

(e) GAO ASSESSMENT.—Not later than 180 days after the date of the enactment of this Act, the Comptroller General shall transmit to the Commission and Congress an independent assessment of airport development needs.

· · ·

TITLE III—AVIATION SECURITY

· · ·

Sec. 302. [49 U.S.C. 44935 note]
Certification of Screening Companies.

The Administrator of the Federal Aviation Administration is directed to certify companies providing security screening and to improve the training and testing of security screeners through development of uniform performance standards for providing security screening services.

. . .

Sec. 307. [49 U.S.C. 44901 note] Passenger Profiling.

The Administrator of the Federal Aviation Administration, the Secretary of Transportation, the intelligence community, and the law enforcement community should continue to assist air carriers in developing computer-assisted passenger profiling programs and other appropriate passenger profiling programs which should be used in conjunction with other security measures and technologies.

Sec. 308. [49 U.S.C. 44901 note] Authority to Use Certain Funds for Airport Security Programs and Activities.

(a) IN GENERAL.—Notwithstanding any other provision of law, funds referred to in subsection (b) may be used for the improvement of facilities and the purchase and deployment of equipment to enhance and ensure the safety and security of passengers and other persons involved in air travel.

APPENDIX F

COMPILATION OF SELECTED AVIATION LAWS

These laws include information on enforcement action by the Secretary of Transportation civil penalties, carrying weapons, conveying false information or threats, aircraft piracy, and interference with flight crew (air rage).

SUBPART IV—ENFORCEMENT AND PENALTIES

Chapter 461—Investigations and Proceedings

Sec.
46101. Complaints and investigations
46102. Proceedings
46103. Service of notice, process, and actions
46104. Evidence
46105. Regulations and orders
46106. Enforcement by the Secretary of Transportation and Administrator of the Federal Aviation Administration
46107. Enforcement by the Attorney General
46108. Enforcement of certificate requirements by interested persons
46109. Joinder and intervention
46110. Judicial review.

Sec. 46101. Complaints and investigations

(a) GENERAL.—(1) A person may file a complaint in writing with the Secretary of Transportation (or the Administrator of the Federal Aviation

Administration with respect to aviation safety duties and powers designated to be carried out by the Administrator) about a person violating this part or a requirement prescribed under this part. Except as provided in subsection (b) of this section, the Secretary or Administrator shall investigate the complaint if a reasonable ground appears to the Secretary or Administrator for the investigation.

(2) On the initiative of the Secretary of Transportation or the Administrator, as appropriate, the Secretary or Administrator may conduct an investigation, if a reasonable ground appears to the Secretary or Administrator for the investigation, about—

(A) a person violating this part or a requirement prescribed under this part; or

(B) any question that may arise under this part.

(3) The Secretary of Transportation or Administrator may dismiss a complaint without a hearing when the Secretary or Administrator is of the opinion that the complaint does not state facts that warrant an investigation or action.

(4) After notice and an opportunity for a hearing and subject to section 40105(b) of this title, the Secretary of Transportation or Administrator shall issue an order to compel compliance with this part if the Secretary or Administrator finds in an investigation under this subsection that a person is violating this part.

(b) COMPAINTS AGAINST MEMBERS OF ARMED FORCES.—The Secretary of Transportation or Administrator shall refer a complaint against a member of the armed forces of the United States performing official duties to the Secretary of the department concerned for action. Not later than 90 days after receiving the complaint, the Secretary of that department shall inform the Secretary of Transportation or Administrator of the action taken on the complaint, including any corrective or disciplinary action taken.

Sec. 46102. Proceedings

(a) CONDUCTING PROCEEDINGS.—Subject to subchapter 11 of chapter 5 of title 5, the Secretary of Transportation (or the Administrator of the Federal Aviation Administration with respect to aviation safety duties and powers designated to be carried out by the Administrator) may conduct proceedings in a way conducive to justice and the proper dispatch of business.

(b) APPEARANCE.—A person may appear and be heard before the Secretary and the Administrator in person or by an attorney. The Secretary may appear and participate as an interested party in a proceeding the Administrator conducts under section 40113(a) of this title.

(c) RECORDING AND PUBLIC ACCESS.—Official action taken by the Secretary and Administrator under this part shall be recorded. Proceedings before the Secretary and Administrator shall be open to the public on the request of an interested party unless the Secretary or Administrator decides that secrecy is required because of national defense.

(d) CONFLICTS OF INTEREST.—The Secretary, the Administrator, or an officer or employee of the Administration may not participate in a proceeding referred to in subsection (a) of this section in which the individual has a pecuniary interest.

§ 46103. Service of notice, process, and actions

(a) DESIGNATING AGENTS.—(1) Each air carrier and foreign air carrier shall designate an agent on whom service of notice and process in a proceeding before, and an action of, the Secretary of Transportation (or the Administrator of the Federal Aviation Administration with respect to aviation safety duties and powers designated to be carried out by the Administrator) may be made.

(2) The designation—

(A) shall be in writing and filed with the Secretary or Administrator; and

(B) may be changed in the same way as originally made.

(b) SERVICE.—(1) Service may be made—

(A) by personal service;

(B) on a designated agent; or

(C) by certified or registered mail to the person to be served or the designated agent of the person.

(2) The date of service made by certified or registered mail is the date of mailing.

(c) SERVING AGENTS.—Service on an agent designated under this section shall be made at the office or usual place of residence of the agent. If an air carrier or foreign air carrier does not have a designated agent, service may be made by posting the notice, process, or action in the office of the Secretary or Administrator.

Sec. 46104. Evidence

(a) GENERAL.—In conducting a hearing or investigation under this part, the Secretary of Transportation (or the Administrator of the Federal Aviation Administration with respect to aviation safety duties and powers designated to be carried out by the Administrator) may—

(1) subpoena witnesses and records related to a matter involved in the hearing or investigation from any place in the United States to the designated place of the hearing or investigation;

(2) administer oaths;

(3) examine witnesses; and

(4) receive evidence at a place in the United States the Secretary or Administrator designates.

(b) COMPLIANCE WITH SUBPOENAS.—If a person disobeys a subpoena, the Secretary, the Administrator, or a party to a proceeding before the Secretary or Administrator may petition a court of the United States to enforce the subpoena. A judicial proceeding to enforce a subpoena under this section may be brought in the jurisdiction in which the proceeding or investigation is conducted. The court may punish a failure to obey an order of the court to comply with the subpoena as a contempt of court.

(c) DESPOSITIONS.—(1) In a proceeding or investigation, the Secretary or Administrator may order a person to give testimony by deposition and to produce records. If a person fails to be deposed or to produce records, the order may be enforced in the same way a subpoena may be enforced under subsection (b) of this section.

(2) A deposition may be taken before an individual designated by the Secretary or Administrator and having the power to administer oaths.

(3) Before taking a deposition, the party or the attorney of the party proposing to take the deposition must give reasonable notice in writing to the opposing party or the attorney of record of that party. The notice shall state the name of the witness and the time and place of taking the deposition.

(4) The testimony of a person deposed under this subsection shall be under oath. The person taking the deposition shall prepare, or cause to be prepared, a transcript of the testimony taken. The transcript shall be sub-

scribed by the deponent. Each deposition shall be filed promptly with the Secretary or Administrator.

(5) If the laws of a foreign country allow, the testimony of a witness in that country may be taken by deposition—

(A) by a consular officer or an individual commissioned by the Secretary or Administrator or agreed on by the parties by written stipulation filed with the Secretary or Administrator; or

(B) under letters rogatory issued by a court of competent jurisdiction at the request of the Secretary or Administrator.

(d) WITNESS FEES AND MILEAGE AND CERTAIN FOREIGN COUNTRY EXPENSES.—A witness summoned before the Secretary or Administrator or whose deposition is taken under this section and the individual taking the deposition are each entitled to the same fee and mileage that the witness and individual would have been paid for those services in a court of the United States. Under regulations of the Secretary or Administrator, the Secretary or Administrator shall pay the necessary expenses incident to executing, in another country, a commission or letter rogatory issued at the initiative of the Secretary or Administrator.

(e) DESIGNATING EMPLOYEES TO CONDUCT HEARINGS.—When designated by the Secretary or Administrator, an employee appointed under section 3105 of title 5 may conduct a hearing, subpoena witnesses, administer oaths, examine witnesses, and receive evidence at a place in the United States the Secretary or Administrator designates. On request of a party, the Secretary or Administrator shall hear or receive argument.

Sec. 46105. Regulations and orders

(a) EFFECTIVENESS OF ORDERS.—Except as provided in this part, a regulation prescribed or order issued by the Secretary of Transportation (or the Administrator of the Federal Aviation Administration with respect to aviation safety duties and powers designated to be carried out by the Administrator) takes effect within a reasonable time prescribed by the Secretary or Administrator. The regulation or order remains in effect under its own terms or until superseded. Except as provided in this part, the Secretary or Administrator may amend, modify, or suspend an order in the way, and by giving the notice, the Secretary or Administrator decides.

(b) CONTENTS AND SERVICE OF ORDERS.—An order of the Secretary or Administrator shall include the findings of fact on which the order is based and shall be served on the parties to the proceeding and the persons affected by the order.

(c) EMERGENCIES.—When the Administrator is of the opinion that an emergency exists related to safety in air commerce and requires immediate action, the Administrator, on the initiative of the Administrator or on complaint, may prescribe regulations and issue orders immediately to meet the emergency, with or without notice and without regard to this part and subchapter II of chapter 5 of title 5. The Administrator shall begin a proceeding immediately about an emergency under this subsection and give preference, when practicable, to the proceeding.

Sec. 46106. Enforcement by the Secretary of Transportation and Administrator of the Federal Aviation Administration

The Secretary of Transportation (or the Administrator of the Federal Aviation Administration with respect to aviation safety duties and powers designated to be carried out by the Administrator) may bring a civil action against a person in a district court of the United States to enforce this part or a requirement or regulation prescribed, or an order or any term of a certificate or permit issued, under this part. The action may be brought in the judicial district in which the person does business or the violation occurred.

Sec. 46107. Enforcement by the Attorney General

(a) CIVIL ACTIONS TO ENFORCE SECTION 40106(b).—The Attorney General may bring a civil action in a district court of the United States against a person to enforce section 40106(b) of this title. The action may be brought in the judicial district in which the person does business or the violation occurred.

(b) CIVIL ACTIONS TO ENFORCE THIS PART.—(1) On request of the Secretary of Transportation (or the Administrator of the Federal Aviation Administration with respect to aviation safety duties and powers designated to be carried out by the Administrator), the Attorney General may bring a civil action in an appropriate court—

(A) to enforce this part or a requirement or regulation prescribed, or an order or any term of a certificate or permit issued, under this part; and

(B) to prosecute a person violating this part or a requirement or regulation prescribed, or an order or any term of a certificate or permit issued, under this part.

(2) The costs and expenses of a civil action shall be paid out of the appropriations for the expenses of the courts of the United States.

(C) PARTICIPATION OF SECRETARY OR ADMINISTRATOR.—On request of the Attorney General, the Secretary or Administrator, as appropriate, may participate in a civil action under this part.

Sec. 46108. Enforcement of certificate requirements by interested persons

An interested person may bring a civil action in a district court of the United States against a person to enforce section 41101(a)(1) of this title. The action may be brought in the judicial district in which the defendant does business or the violation occurred.

Sec. 46109. Joinder and intervention

A person interested in or affected by a matter under consideration in a proceeding before the Secretary of Transportation or civil action to enforce this part or a requirement or regulation prescribed, or an order or any term of a certificate or permit issued, under this part may be joined as a party or permitted to intervene in the proceeding or civil action.

Sec. 46110. Judicial review

(a) FILING AND VENUE.—Except for an order related to a foreign air carrier subject to disapproval by the President under section 41307 or 41509(f) of this title, a person disclosing a substantial interest in an order issued by the Secretary of Transportation (or the Administrator of the Federal Aviation Administration with respect to aviation safety duties and powers designated to be carried out by the Administrator) under this part may apply for review of the order by filing a petition for review in the United States Court of Appeals for the District of Columbia Circuit or in the court of appeals of the United States for the circuit in which the person resides or has its principal place of business. The petition must be filed not later than 60 days after the order is issued. The court may allow the petition to be filed after the 60th day only if there are reasonable grounds for not filing by the 60th day.

(b) JUDICIAL PROCEDURES.—When a petition is filed under subsection (a) of this section, the clerk of the court immediately shall send a copy of the petition to the Secretary or Administrator, as appropriate. The Secretary or Administrator shall file with the court a record of any proceeding in which the order was issued, as provided in section 2112 of title 28.

(c) AUTHORITY OF COURT.—When the petition is sent to the Secretary or Administrator, the court has exclusive jurisdiction to affirm, amend, modify, or set aside any part of the order and may order the Secretary or Administrator to conduct further proceedings. After reasonable notice to the Secretary or Administrator, the court may grant interim relief by staying the order or taking other appropriate action when good cause for its action exists. Findings of fact by the Secretary or Administrator, if supported by substantial evidence, are conclusive.

(d) REQUIREMENT FOR PRIOR OBJECTION.—In reviewing an order under this section, the court may consider an objection to an order of the Secretary or Administrator only if the objection was made in the proceeding conducted by the Secretary or Administrator or if there was a reasonable ground for not making the objection in the proceeding.

(e) SUPERME COURT REVIEW.—A decision by a court under this section may be reviewed only by the Supreme Court under section 1254 of title 28.

Chapter 463—Penalties

Sec.

46306. Registration violations involving aircraft not providing air transportation
46307. Violation of national defense airspace
46308. Interference with air navigation
46309. Concession and price violations
46310. Reporting and recordkeeping violations
46311. Unlawful disclosure of information
46312. Transporting hazardous material
46313. Refusing to appear or produce records
46314. Entering aircraft or airport area in violation of security requirements
46315. Lighting violations involving transporting controlled substances by aircraft not providing air transportation
46316. General criminal penalty when specific penalty not provided

Sec. 46301. Civil penalties

(a) GENERAL PENALTY.—(1) A person is liable to the United States Government for a civil penalty of not more than $1,000 for violating

(A) chapter 401 (except sections 40103[a] and [d], 40105, 40116, and 40117), chapter 411, chapter 413 (except sections 41307 and 41310[b]–[f]), chapter 415 (except sections 41502, 41505, and 41507–41509), chapter 417 (except sections 41703, 41704, 41710, 41713, and 41714), chapter 419, subchapter II of chapter 421, chapter 441 (except section 44109), section 44502(b) or (c), chapter 447 (except sections 44717 and 44719–44723), chapter 449 (except sections 44902, 44903[d], 44904, 44907[a]–[d][1][A] and [d][1][C]–[f], and 44908), or section 46302, 46303, or 47107(b) (including any assurance made under such section) of this title;[1]

(B) a regulation prescribed or order issued under any provision to which clause (A) of this paragraph applies;

(C) any term of a certificate or permit issued under section 41102, 41103, or 41302 of this title; or

(D) a regulation of the United States Postal Service under this part.

---

1. This subparagraph contains an amendment made by section 5(77)(A)(ii) of Public Law 104-287 (110 Stat. 3396) to reflect the probable intent of Congress. The amendment technically could not be executed because of amendments made to this subparagraph by sections 502(c) and 1220(b) of Public Law 104-264 (110 Stat. 3263 and 3286).

(2) A person operating an aircraft for the transportation of passengers or property for compensation (except an airman serving as an airman) is liable to the Government for a civil penalty of not more than $10,000 for violating

(A) chapter 401 (except sections 40103[a] and [d], 40105, 40106[b], 40116, and 40117), section 44502 (b) or (c), chapter 447 (except sections 44717–44723), or chapter 449 (except sections 44902, 44903[d], 44904, and 44907–44909) of this title; or[2]

(B) a regulation prescribed or order issued under any provision to which clause (A) of this paragraph applies.

(3) A civil penalty of not more than $10,000 may be imposed for each violation under paragraph (1) of this subsection related to—

(A) the transportation of hazardous material; or

(B) the registration or recordation under chapter 441 of this title of an aircraft not used to provide air transportation.

(4) A separate violation occurs under this subsection for each day the violation (other than a violation of section 41715) continues or, if applicable, for each flight involving the violation (other than a violation of section 41715).

(5) PENALTY FOR DIVERSION OF AVIATION REVENUES.—The amount of a civil penalty assessed under this section for a violation of section 47107(b) of this title (or any assurance made under such section) or section 47133 of this title may be increased above the otherwise applicable maximum amount under this section to an amount not to exceed 3 times the amount of revenues that are used in violation of such section.

(6) Notwithstanding paragraph (1), the maximum civil penalty for violating section 41715 shall be $5,000 instead of $1,000.

(b) SMOKE ALARM DEVICE PENALTY.—(1) A passenger may not tamper with, disable, or destroy a smoke alarm device located in a lavatory on an aircraft providing air transportation or intrastate air transportation.

(2) An individual violating this subsection is liable to the Government for a civil penalty of not more than $2,000.

(c) PROCEDURAL REQUIREMENTS.—(1) The Secretary of Transportation may impose a civil penalty for the following violations only after notice and an opportunity for a hearing:

---

2. This subparagraph contains an amendment made by section 5(77)(B) of Public Law 104-287 (110 Stat. 3396) to reflect the probable intent of Congress. The amendment technically could not be executed because of the amendment made to this subparagraph by section 502(c) of Public Law 104-264 (110 Stat. 3263).

(A) a violation of subsection (b) of this section or chapter 411, chapter 413 (except sections 41307 and 41310[b]–[f]), chapter 415 (except sections 41502, 41505, and 41507–41509), chapter 417 (except sections 41703, 41704, 41710, 41713, and 41714), chapter 419, subchapter II of chapter 421, or section 44909 of this title.

(B) a violation of a regulation prescribed or order issued under any provision to which clause (A) of this paragraph applies.

(C) a violation of any term of a certificate or permit issued under section 41102, 41103, or 41302 of this title.

(D) a violation under subsection (a)(1) of this section related to the transportation of hazardous material.

(2) The Secretary shall give written notice of the finding of aviolation and the civil penalty under paragraph (1) of this subsection.

(d) ADMINISTRATIVE IMPOSITION OF PENALTIES.—(1) In this subsection—

(A) "flight engineer" means an individual who holds a flight engineer certificate issued under part 63 of title 14, Code of Federal Regulations.

(B) "mechanic" means an individual who holds a mechanic certificate issued under part 65 of title 14, Code of Federal Regulations.

(C) "Pilot" means an individual who holds a pilot certificate issued under part 61 of title 14, Code of Federal Regulations.

(D) "repairman" means an individual who holds a repairman certificate issued under part 65 of title 14, Code of Federal Regulations.

(2) The Administrator of the Federal Aviation Administration may impose a civil penalty for a violation of chapter 401 (except sections 40103[a] and [d], 40105, 40106[b], 40116, and 40117), chapter 441 (except section 44109), section 44502(b) or (c), chapter 447 (except section 44717 and 44719–44723), chapter 449 (except sections 44902, 44903(d), 44904, 44907[a]–[d][1][A] and [d][1][C]–[f]; 44908, and 44909), or section 46302, 46303, or 47107(b) (as further defined by the Secretary under section 47107[1] and including any assurance made under section 47107[b]) of this title or a regulation prescribed or order issued under any of those provisions. The Administrator shall give written notice of the finding of a violation and the penalty.[3]

---

3. This paragraph contains an amendment made by section 5(77)(E) of Public Law 104-287 (110 Stat. 3397) to reflect the probable intent of Congress. The amendment technically could not be executed because of amendments made to this paragraph by sections 502(c) and 1220(b) of Public Law 104-264 (110 Stat. 3263 and 3286).

(3) In a civil action to collect a civil penalty imposed by the Administrator under this subsection, the issues of liability and the amount of the penalty may not be reexamined.

(4) Notwithstanding paragraph (2) of this subsection, the district courts of the United States have exclusive jurisdiction of a civil action involving a penalty the Administrator initiates if—

(A) the amount in controversy is more than $50,000;

(B) the action is in rem or another action in rem based on the same violation has been brought;

(C) the action involves an aircraft subject to a lien that has been seized by the Government; or

(D) another action has been brought for an injunction based on the same violation.

(5)(A) The Administrator may issue an order imposing a penalty under this subsection against an individual acting as a pilot, flight engineer, mechanic, or repairman only after advising the individual of the charges or any reason the Administrator relied on for the proposed penalty and providing the individual an opportunity to answer the charges and be heard about why the order shall not be issued.

(B) An individual acting as a pilot, flight engineer, mechanic, or repairman may appeal an order imposing a penalty under this subsection to the National Transportation Safety Board. After notice and an opportunity for a hearing on the record, the Board shall affirm, modify, or reverse the order. The Board may modify a civil penalty imposed to a suspension or revocation of a certificate.

(C) When conducting a hearing under this paragraph, the Board is not bound by findings of fact of the Administrator but is bound by all validly adopted interpretations of laws and regulations the Administrator carries out and of written agency policy guidance available to the public related to sanctions to be imposed under this sec tion unless the Board finds an interpretation is arbitrary, capricious, or otherwise not according to law.

(D) When an individual files an appeal with the Board under this paragraph, the order of the Administrator is stayed.

(6) An individual substantially affected by an order of the Board under paragraph (5) of this subsection, or the Administrator when the Administrator decides that an order of the Board under paragraph (5) will have a

significant adverse impact on carrying out this part, may obtain judicial review of the order under section 46110 of this title. The Administrator shall be made a party to the judicial review proceedings. Findings of fact of the Board are conclusive if supported by substantial evidence.

(7)(A) The Administrator may impose a penalty on an individual (except an individual acting as a pilot, flight engineer, mechanic, or repairman) only after notice and an opportunity for a hearing on the record.

(B) In an appeal from a decision of an administrative law judge as the result of a hearing under subparagraph (A) of this paragraph, the Administrator shall consider only whether—

(i) each finding of fact is supported by a preponderance of reliable, probative, and substantial evidence;

(ii) each conclusion of law is made according to applicable law, precedent, and public policy; and

(iii) the judge committed a prejudicial error that supports the appeal.

(C) Except for good cause, a civil action involving a penalty under this paragraph may not be initiated later than 2 years after the violation occurs.

(D) In the case of a violation of section 47107(b) of this title or any assurance made under such section—

(i) a civil penalty shall not be assessed against an individual;

(ii) a civil penalty may be compromised as provided undersubsection (f); and

(iii) judicial review of any order assessing a civil penalty may be obtained only pursuant to section 46110 of this title.

(8) The maximum civil penalty the Administrator or Board may impose under this subsection is $50,000.

(9) This subsection applies only to a violation occurring after August 25, 1992.

(e) PENALTY CONSIDERATIONS.—In determining the amount of a civil penalty under subsection (a)(3) of this section related to transportation of hazardous material, the Secretary shall consider—

(1) the nature, circumstances, extent, and gravity of the violation;

(2) with respect to the violator, the degree of culpability, any history of prior violations, the ability to pay, and any effect on the ability to continue doing business; and

(3) other matters that justice requires.

(f) COMPROMISE AND SETOFF.—(1)(A) The Secretary may compromise the amount of a civil penalty imposed for violating—

(i) chapter 401 (except sections 40103[a] and [d], 40105, 40116, and 40117), chapter 441 (except section 44109), section 44502(b) or (c), chapter 447 (except sections 44717 and 44719–44723), or chapter 449 (except sections 44902, 44903[d], 44904, 44907[a]–[d][l][A] and [d][1][C]–[f], 44908, and 44909) of this title; or

(ii) a regulation prescribed or order issued under any provision to which clause (i) of this subparagraph applies.[4]

(B) The Postal Service may compromise the amount of a civil penalty imposed under subsection (a)(l)(D) of this section.

(2) The Government may deduct the amount of a civil penalty imposed or compromised under this subsection from amounts it owes the person liable for the penalty.

(g) JUDICIAL REVIEW.—An order of the Secretary imposing a civil penalty may be reviewed judicially only under section 46110 of this title.

(h) NONAPPLICATION.—(1) This section does not apply to the following when performing official duties:

(A) a member of the armed forces of the United States.

(B) a civilian employee of the Department of Defense subject to the Uniform Code of Military Justice.

(2) The appropriate military authority is responsible for taking necessary disciplinary action and submitting to the Secretary (or the Administrator with respect to aviation safety duties and powers designated to be carried out by the Administrator) a timely report on action taken.

Sec. 46302. False information

(a) CIVIL PENALTY.—A person that, knowing the information to be false, gives, or causes to be given, under circumstances in which the information reasonably may be believed, false information about an alleged attempt being made or to be made to do an act that would violate section 46502(a),

---

4. This subparagraph contains an amendment made by section 5(77)(F) of Public Law 104-287 (110 Stat. 3397) to reflect the probable intent of Congress. The amendment technically could not be executed because of amendments made to this subparagraph by sections 502(c) and 1220(b) of Public Law 104-264 (110 Stat. 3263 and 3286).

46504, 46505, or 46506 of this title, is liable to the United States Government for a civil penalty of not more than $10,000 for each violation.

(b) COMPROMISE AND SETOFF.—(1) The Secretary of Transportation may compromise the amount of a civil penalty imposed under subsection (a) of this section.

(2) The Government may deduct the amount of a civil penalty imposed or compromised under this section from amounts it owes the person liable for the penalty.

Sec. 46303. Carrying a weapon

(a) CIVIL PENALTY.—An individual who, when on, or attempting to board, an aircraft in, or intended for operation in, air transportation or intrastate air transportation, has on or about the individual or the property of the individual a concealed dangerous weapon that is or would be accessible to the individual in flight is liable to the United States Government for a civil penalty of not more than $10,000 for each violation.

(b) COMPROMISE AND SETOFF.—(1) The Secretary of Transportation may compromise the amount of a civil penalty imposed under subsection (a) of this section.

(2) The Government may deduct the amount of a civil penalty imposed or compromised under this section from amounts it owes the individual liable for the penalty.

(c) NONAPPLICATION.—This section does not apply to—

(1) a law enforcement officer of a State or political subdivision of a State, or an officer or employee of the Government, authorized to carry arms in an official capacity; or

(2) another individual the Administrator of the Federal Aviation Administration by regulation authorizes to carry arms in an official capacity.

Sec. 46304. Liens on aircraft

(a) AIRCRAFT SUBJECT TO LIENS.—When an aircraft is involved in a violation referred to in section 46301(a)(1)(A)–(C), (2), or (3) of this title and the violation is by the owner of, or individual commanding, the aircraft, the aircraft is subject to a lien for the civil penalty.

(b) SEIZURE.—An aircraft subject to a lien under this section may be seized summarily and placed in the custody of a person authorized to take custody of it under regulations of the Secretary of Transportation (or the Administrator of the Federal Aviation Administration with respect to aviation safety duties and powers designated to be carried out by the Administrator). A report on the seizure shall be submitted to the Attorney General. The Attorney General promptly shall bring a civil action in rem to enforce the lien or notify the Secretary or Administrator that the action will not be brought.

(c) RELEASE.—An aircraft seized under subsection (b) of this section shall be released from custody when—

(1) the civil penalty is paid;

(2) a compromise amount agreed on is paid;.

(3) the aircraft is seized under a civil action in rem to enforce the lien;

(4) the Attorney General gives notice that a civil action will not be brought under subsection (b) of this section; or

(5) a bond (in an amount and with a surety the Secretary or Administrator prescribes), conditioned on payment of the penalty or compromise, is deposited with the Secretary or Administrator.

Sec. 46305. Actions to recover civil penalties

A civil penalty under this chapter may be collected by bringing a civil action against the person subject to the penalty, a civil action in rem against an aircraft subject to a lien for a penalty, or both. The action shall conform as nearly as practicable to a civil action in admiralty, regardless of the place an aircraft in a civil action in rem is seized. However, a party may demand a jury trial of an issue of fact in an action involving a civil penalty under this chapter (except a penalty imposed by the Secretary of Transportation that formerly was imposed by the Civil Aeronautics Board) if the value of the matter in controversy is more than $20. Issues of fact tried by a jury may be reexamined only under common law rules.

Sec. 46306. Registration violations involving aircraft not providing air transportation

(a) APPLICATION.—This section applies only to aircraft not used to provide air transportation.

(b) GENERAL CRIMINAL PENALTY.—Except as provided by subsection (c) of this section, a person shall be fined under title 18, imprisoned for not more than 3 years, or both, if the person—

(1) knowingly and willfully forges or alters a certificate authorized to be issued under this part;

(2) knowingly sells, uses, attempts to use, or possesses with the intent to use, such a certificate;

(3) knowingly and willfully displays or causes to be displayed on an aircraft a mark that is false or misleading about the nationality or registration of the aircraft;

(4) obtains a certificate authorized to be issued under this part by knowingly and willfully falsifying or concealing a material fact, making a false, fictitious, or fraudulent statement, or making or using a false document knowing it contains a false, fictitious, or fraudulent statement or entry;

(5) owns an aircraft eligible for registration under section 44102 of this title and knowingly and willfully operates, attempts to operate, or allows another person to operate the aircraft when—

(A) the aircraft is not registered under section 44103 of this title or the certificate of registration is suspended or revoked; or

(B) the owner knows or has reason to know that the other person does not have proper authorization to operate or navigate the aircraft without registration for a period of time after transfer of ownership;

(6) knowingly and willfully operates or attempts to operate an aircraft eligible for registration under section 44102 of this title knowing that—

(A) aircraft is not registered under section 44103 of this title;

(B) the certificate of registration is suspended or revoked; or

(C) the person does not have proper authorization to operate or navigate the aircraft without registration for a period of time alter transfer of ownership;

(7) knowingly and willfully serves or attempts to serve in any capacity as an airman without an airman's certificate authorizing the individual to serve in that capacity;

(8) knowingly and willfully employs for service or uses in any capacity as an airman an individual who does not have an airman's certificate authorizing the individual to serve in that capacity; or

(9) operates an aircraft with a fuel tank or fuel system that has been installed or modified knowing that the tank, system, installation, or modification does not comply with regulations and requirements of the Administrator of the Federal Aviation Administration.

(C) CONTROLLED SUBSTANCE CRIMINAL PENALTY.—(1) In this subsection, "controlled substance" has the same meaning given that term in section 102 of the Comprehensive Drug Abuse Prevention and Control Act of 1970 (21 U.S.C. 802).

(2) A person violating subsection (b) of this section shall be fined under title 18, imprisoned for not more than 5 years, or both, if the violation is related to transporting a controlled substance by aircraft or aiding or facilitating a controlled substance violation and the transporting, aiding, or facilitating—

(A) is punishable by death or imprisonment of more than one year under a law of the United States or a State; or

(B) that is provided is related to an act punishable by death or imprisonment for more than one year under a law of the United States or a State related to a controlled substance (except a law related to simple possession of a controlled substance).

(3) A term of imprisonment imposed under paragraph (2) of this subsection shall be served in addition to, and not concurrently with, any other term of imprisonment imposed on the individual.

(d) SEIZURE AND FORFEITURE.—(1) The Administrator of Drug Enforcement or the Commissioner of Customs may seize and forfeit under the customs laws an aircraft whose use is related to a violation of subsection (b) of this section, or to aid or facilitate a violation, regardless of whether a person is charged with the violation.

(2) An aircraft's use is presumed to have been related to a violation of, or to aid or facilitate a violation of—

(A) subsection (b)(1) of this section if the aircraft certificate of registration has been forged or altered;

(B) subsection (b)(3) of this section if there is an external display of false or misleading registration numbers or country of registration;

(C) subsection (b)(4) of this section if

(i) the aircraft is registered to a false or fictitious person; or

(ii) the application form used to obtain the aircraft certificate of registration contains a material false statement;

(D) subsection (b)(5) of this section if the aircraft was operated when it was not registered under section 44103 of this title; or

(E) subsection (b)(9) of this section if the aircraft has a fuel tank or fuel system that was installed or altered—

(i) in violation of a regulation or requirement of the Administrator of the Federal Aviation Administration; or

(ii) if a certificate required to he issued for the installation or alteration is not carried on the aircraft.

(3) The Administrator of the Federal Aviation Administration, the Administrator of Drug Enforcement, and the Commissioner shall agree to a memorandum of understanding to establish procedures to carry out this subsection.

(e) RELATIONSHIP TO STATE LAWS.—This part does not prevent a State from establishing a criminal penalty, including providing for forfeiture and seizure of aircraft, for a person that—

(1) knowingly and willfully forges or alters an aircraft certificate of registration;

(2) knowingly sells, uses, attempts to use, or possesses with the intent to use, a fraudulent aircraft certificate of registration;

(3) knowingly and willfully displays or causes to be displayed on an aircraft a mark that is false or misleading about the nationality or registration of the aircraft; or

(4) obtains an aircraft certificate of registration from theAdministrator of the Federal Aviation Administration by—

(A) knowingly and willfully falsifying or concealing a material fact;

(B) making a false, fictitious, or fraudulent statement; or

(C) making or using a false document knowing it contains a false, fictitious, or fraudulent statement or entry.

Sec. 46307. Violation of national defense airspace

A person that knowingly or willfully violates section 40103(b)(3) of this title or a regulation prescribed or order issued under section 40103(b)(3) shall be fined under title 18, imprisoned for not more than one year, or both.

Sec. 46308. Interference with air navigation

A person shall be fined under title 18, imprisoned for not more than 5 years, or both, if the person—

(1) with intent to interfere with air navigation in the United States, exhibits in the United States a light or signal at a place or in a way likely to be mistaken for a true light or signal established under this part or for a true light or signal used at an air navigation facility;

(2) after a warning from the Administrator of the Federal Aviation Administration, continues to maintain a misleading light or signal; or

(3) knowingly interferes with the operation of a true light or signal.

Sec. 46309. Concession and price violations

(a) CRIMINAL PENALTY FOR OFFERING, GRANTING, GIVING, OR HELPING TO OBTAIN CONCESSIONS AND LOWER PRICES.—An air carrier, foreign air carrier, ticket agent, or officer, agent, or employee of an air carrier, foreign air earner, or ticket agent shall be fined under title 18 if the air carrier, foreign air carrier, ticket agent, officer, agent, or employee—

(1) knowingly and willfully offers, grants, or gives, or causes to be offered, granted, or given, a rebate or other concession in violation of this part; or

(2) by any means knowingly and willfully assists, or willingly allows, a person to obtain transportation or services subject to this part at less than the price lawfully in effect.

(b) CRIMINAL PENALTY FOR RECEIVING REBATES, PRIVILEGES, AND FACILITIES.—A person shall be fined under title 18 if the person by any means—

(1) knowingly and willfully solicits, accepts, or receives a rebate of a part of a price lawfully in effect for the foreign air transportation of property, or a service related to the foreign air transportation; or

(2) knowingly solicits, accepts, or receives a privilege or facility related to a matter the Secretary of Transportation requires be specified in a currently effective tariff applicable to the foreign air transportation of property.

Sec. 46310. Reporting and recordkeeping violations

(a) GENERAL CRIMINAL PENALTY.—An air carrier or an officer, agent, or employee of an air carrier shall be fined under title 18 for intentionally—
    (1) failing to make a report or keep a record under this part;
    (2) falsifying, mutilating, or altering a report or record under this part; or
    (3) filing a false report or record under this part.
(b) SAFETY REGULATION CRIMINAL PENALTY.—An air carrier or an officer, agent, or employee of an air carrier shall be fined under title 18, imprisoned for not more than 5 years, or both, for intentionally falsifying or concealing a material fact, or inducing reliance on a false statement of material fact, in a report or record under section 44701(a) or (b) or any of sections 44702–44716 of this title.

Sec. 46311. Unlawful disclosure of information

(a) CRIMINAL PENALTY.—The Secretary of Transportation, the Administrator of the Federal Aviation Administration with respect to aviation safety duties and powers designated to be carried out by the Administrator, or an officer or employee of the Secretary or Administrator shall be fined under title 18, imprisoned for not more than 2 years, or both, if the Secretary, Administrator, officer, or employee knowingly and willfully discloses information that—
    (1) the Secretary, Administrator, officer, or employee acquires when inspecting the records of an air carrier; or
    (2) is withheld from public disclosure under section 40115 of this title.
(b) NONAPPLICATION.—Subsection (a) of this section does not apply if—
    (1) the officer or employee is directed by the Secretary or Administrator to disclose information that the Secretary or Administrator had ordered withheld; or

(2) the Secretary, Administrator, officer, or employee is directed by a court of competent jurisdiction to disclose the information.

(c) WITHHOLDING INFORMATION FROM CONGRESS.—This section does not authorize the Secretary or Administrator to withhold information from a committee of Congress authorized to have the information.

Sec. 46312. Transporting hazardous material

A person shall be fined under title 18, imprisoned for not more than 5 years, or both, if the person, in violation of a regulation or requirement related to the transportation of hazardous material prescribed by the Secretary of Transportation under this part—

(1) willfully delivers, or causes to be delivered, property containing hazardous material to an air carrier or to an operator of a civil aircraft for transportation in air commerce; or

(2) recklessly causes the transportation in air commerce of the property.

Sec. 46313. Refusing to appear or produce records

A person not obeying a subpoena or requirement of the Secretary of Transportation (or the Administrator of the Federal Aviation Administration with respect to aviation safety duties and powers designated to be carried out by the Administrator) to appear and testify or produce records shall be fined under title 18, imprisoned for not more than one year, or both.

Sec. 46314. Entering aircraft or airport area in violation of security requirements

(a) PROHIBITION.—A person may not knowingly and willfully enter, in violation of security requirements prescribed under section 44901, 44903(b) or (c), or 44906 of this title, an aircraft or an airport area that serves an air carrier or foreign air carrier.

(b) CRIMINAL PENALTY.—(l) A person violating subsection (a) of this section shall be fined under title 18, imprisoned for not more than one year, or both.

(2) A person violating subsection (a) of this section with intent to commit, in the aircraft or airport area, a felony under a law of the United States or a State shall be fined under title 18, imprisoned for not more than 10 years, or both.

Sec. 46315. Lighting violations involving transporting controlled substances by aircraft not providing air transportation

(a) APPLICATION.—This section applies only to aircraft not used to provide air transportation.

(b) CRIMINAL PENALTY.—A person shall be fined under title 18, imprisoned for not more than 5 years, or both, if—

(1) the person knowingly and willfully operates an aircraft in violation of a regulation or requirement of the Administrator of the Federal Aviation Administration related to the display of navigation or anticollision lights;

(2) the person is knowingly transporting a controlled substance by air-craft or aiding or facilitating a controlled substance offense; and

(3) the transporting, aiding, or facilitating—

(A) is punishable by death or imprisonment for more than one year under a law of the United States or a State; or

(B) is provided in connection with an act punishable by death or imprisonment for more than one year under a law of the United States or a State related to a controlled substance (except a law related to simple possession of a controlled substance).

Sec. 46316. General criminal penalty when specific penalty not provided

(a) CRIMINAL PENALTY.—Except as provided by subsection (b) of this section, when another criminal penalty is not provided under this chapter, a person that knowingly and willfully violates this part, a regulation prescribed or order issued by the Secretary of Transportation (or the Administrator of the Federal Aviation Administration with respect to aviation safety duties and powers designated to be carried out by the Administrator) under this part, or any term of a certificate or permit issued under section 41102,

41103, or 41302 of this title shall be fined under title 18. A separate violation occurs for each day the violation continues.

(b) NONAPPLICATION.—Subsection (a) of this section does not apply to chapter 401 (except sections 40103[a] and [d], 40105, 40116, and 40117), chapter 441 (except section 44109), chapter 445, chapter 447 (except sections 44717–44723), and chapter 449 (except sections 44902, 44903[d], 44904, and 44907–44909) of this title.

Chapter 465—Special Aircraft Jurisdiction of the United States

Sec.

Sec. 46501. Definitions

In this chapter—

(1) "aircraft in flight" means an aircraft from the moment all external doors are closed following boarding—

(A) through the moment when one external door is opened to allow passengers to leave the aircraft; or

(B) until, if a forced landing, competent authorities take over responsibility for the aircraft and individuals and property on the aircraft.

(2) "special aircraft jurisdiction of the United States" includes any of the following aircraft in flight:

(A) a civil aircraft of the United States.

(B) an aircraft of the armed forces of the United States.

(C) another aircraft in the United States.

(D) another aircraft outside the United States—

(i) that has its next scheduled destination or last place of departure in the United States, if the aircraft next lands in the United States;

(ii) on which an individual commits an offense (as defined in the Convention for the Suppression of Unlawful Seizure of Aircraft) if the aircraft lands in the United States with the individual still on the aircraft; or

(iii) against which an individual commits an offense (as defined in subsection [d] or [e] of article 1, section I of the Convention for the Suppression of Unlawful Acts against the Safety of Civil Aviation) if the aircraft lands in the United States with the individual still on the aircraft.

(E) any other aircraft leased without crew to a lessee whose principal place of business is in the United States or, if the lessee does not have a principal place of business, whose permanent residence is in the United States.

(3) an individual commits an offense (as defined in the Convention for the Suppression of Unlawful Seizure of Aircraft) when the individual, when on an aircraft in flight—

(A) by any form of intimidation, unlawfully seizes, exercises control of, or attempts to seize or exercise control of, the aircraft; or

(B) is an accomplice of an individual referred to in subclause (A) of this clause.

Sec. 46502. Aircraft piracy

(a) IN SPECIAL AIRCRAFT JURISDICTION.—(1) In this subsection—

(A) "aircraft piracy" means seizing or exercising control of an aircraft in the special aircraft jurisdiction of the United States by force, violence, threat of force or violence, or any form of intimidation, and with wrongful intent.

(B) an attempt to commit aircraft piracy is in the special aircraft jurisdiction of the United States although the aircraft is not in flight at the time of the attempt if the aircraft would have been in the special aircraft jurisdiction of the United States had the aircraft piracy been completed.

(2) An individual committing or attempting or conspiring to commit aircraft piracy—

(A) shall be imprisoned for at least 20 years; or

(B) notwithstanding section 3559(b) of title 18, if the death of another individual results from the commission or attempt, shall be put to death or imprisoned for life.

(b) OUTSIDE SPECIAL AIRCRAFT JURISDICTION.—(1) An individual committing or conspiring to commit an offense (as defined in the Convention for the Suppression of Unlawful Seizure of Aircraft) on an aircraft in flight outside the special aircraft jurisdiction of the United States—

(A) shall be imprisoned for at least 20 years; or

(B) notwithstanding section 3559(b) of title 18, if the death of another individual results from the commission or attempt, shall be put to death or imprisoned for life.

(2) There is jurisdiction over the offense in paragraph (1) if—

(A) a national of the United States was aboard the aircraft;

(B) an offender is a national of the United States; or

(C) an offender is afterwards found in the United States.

(3) For purposes of this subsection, the term "national of the United States" has the meaning prescribed in section 101(a)(22) of the Immigration and Nationality Act (8 U.S.C. 1101(a)(22)).

[Sec. 46503 Repealed by section 60003 of P.L. 103-322]

Sec. 46504. Interference with flight crew members and attendants

An individual on an aircraft in the special aircraft jurisdiction of the United States who, by assaulting or intimidating a flight crew member or flight attendant of the aircraft, interferes with the performance of the duties of the member or attendant or lessens the ability of the member or attendant to perform those duties, shall be fined under title 18, imprisoned for not more than 20 years, or both. However, if a dangerous weapon is used in assaulting or intimidating the member or attendant, the individual shall be imprisoned for any term of years or for life.

Sec. 46505. Carrying a weapon or explosive on an aircraft

(a) DEFINITION.—In this section, "loaded firearm" means a starter gun or a weapon designed or converted to expel a projectile through an explosive, that has a cartridge, a detonator, or powder in the chamber, magazine, cylinder, or clip.

(b) GENERAL CRIMINAL PENALTY.—An individual shall be fined under title 18, imprisoned for not more than 10 years, or both, if the individual—

(1) when on, or attempting to get on, an aircraft in, or intended for operation in, air transportation or intrastate air transportation, has on or about the individual or the property of the individual a concealed dangerous weapon that is or would be accessible to the individual in flight;

(2) has placed, attempted to place, or attempted to have placed a loaded firearm on that aircraft in property not accessible to passengers in flight; or

(3) has on or about the individual, or has placed, attempted to place, or attempted to have placed on that aircraft, an explosive or incendiary device.

(c) CRIMINAL PENALTY INVOLVING DISREGARD FOR HUMAN LIFE.—An individual who willfully and without regard for the safety of human life, or with reckless disregard for the safety of human life, violates subsection (b) of this section, shall be fined under title 18; imprisoned for not more than 15 years, or both.

(d) NONAPPLICATION.—Subsection (b)(1) of this section does not apply to—

(1) a law enforcement officer of a State or political subdivision of a State, or an officer or employee of the United States Government, authorized to carry arms in an official capacity;

(2) another individual the Administrator of the Federal Aviation Administration by regulation authorizes to carry a dangerous weapon in air transportation or intrastate air transportation; or

(3) an individual transporting a weapon (except a loaded firearm) in baggage not accessible to a passenger in flight if the air carrier was informed of the presence of the weapon.

Sec. 46506. Application of certain criminal laws to acts on aircraft

An individual on an aircraft in the special aircraft jurisdiction of the United States who commits an act that—

(1) if committed in the special maritime and territorial jurisdiction of the United States (as defined in section 7 of title 18) would violate section 113, 114, 661, 662, 1111, 1112, 1113, or 2111 or chapter 109A of title 18, shall be fined under title 18, imprisoned under that section or chapter, or both; or

(2) if committed in the District of Columbia would violate section 9 of the Act of July 29, 1892 (D.C. Code §22-1112), shall be fined under title 18, imprisoned under section 9 of the Act, or both.

Sec. 46507. False information and threats

An individual shall be fined under title 18, imprisoned for not more than 5 years, or both, if the individual—

(1) knowing the information to be false, willfully and maliciously or with reckless disregard for the safety of human life, gives, or causes to be given, under circumstances in which the information reasonably may be believed false information about an alleged attempt being made or be made to do an act that would violate section 46502(a), 46504, 46505, or 46506 of this title; or

(2)(A) threatens to violate section 46502(a), 46504, 46505, or 46506 of this title, or causes a threat to violate any of those sections to be made; and

(B) has the apparent determination and will to carry out the threat.

APPENDIX G

ANSWERS TO COMMONLY ASKED AIRLINE SECURITY QUESTIONS

Q. Do I have to have a photo ID to fly?

A. The FAA does not prohibit an airline from transporting any passenger who does not present a photo ID. There are alternative procedures available that allow airlines to transport passengers without ID. However, some airlines choose not to use such procedures, which is their prerogative.

Q. Why didn't the airline ask for my ID?

A. The FAA does not require all passengers to present ID. The FAA requires that airlines apply additional security measures to passengers who are unable to produce ID upon request.

Q. Can an airline exceed minimum FAA requirements?

A. Yes. The FAA sets minimum requirements for airlines to follow. Should airlines wish to exceed these requirements, the FAA cannot prohibit them from doing so.

Q. Who is responsible for the people performing security screening at U.S. airports?

A. Preboard screeners are either direct airline employees or, in most cases, contracted by the airline to perform security-screening functions. The FAA requires airlines to screen all items entering the sterile area of the airport.

Q. Why did I alarm at one walk-through metal detector and not another?

A. The FAA calibrates each walk-through metal detector to the same minimum standards, using FAA-approved test items. However, walk-through metal detectors may respond differently depending upon the physical environment in which they are operated.

Q. Why can I carry the same item through one passenger-screening checkpoint and not through others?

A. Some airlines and airports have stricter interpretations of deadly and dangerous items. What one airline will allow, others may not.

Q. What items are prohibited beyond the passenger-screening checkpoint?

A. The FAA prohibits airlines from allowing dangerous or deadly items through the passenger-screening checkpoint. Because of the subjective description of dangerous items, it is the airline's responsibility to determine what it will allow. Most airlines will prohibit items such as scissors, trade tools, and items resembling firearms.

Q. Does the FAA allow airlines to fly prisoners on the same flight with other passengers?

A. Title 14, Code of Federal Regulations, Section 108.21 sets forth requirements for transporting prisoners, and allows airlines to transport prisoners on the same flight with other passengers.

INDEX